James Schuyler

the dark knight system

a repertoire with 1...Nc6

EVERYMAN CHESS

Gloucester Publishers plc   www.everymanchess.com

First published in 2013 by Gloucester Publishers Limited, Northburgh House,
10 Northburgh Street, London EC1V 0AT

British Library Cataloguing-in-Publication Data
A catalogue record for this book is available from the British Library.

ISBN: 978 1 85744 995 2

Distributed in North America by The Globe Pequot Press, P.O Box 480,
246 Goose Lane, Guilford, CT 06437-0480.

All other sales enquiries should be directed to Everyman Chess, Northburgh House,
10 Northburgh Street, London EC1V 0AT
tel: 020 7253 7887 fax: 020 7490 3708
email: info@everymanchess.com; website: www.everymanchess.com

Everyman Chess Series
Chief advisor: Byron Jacobs
Commissioning editor: John Emms
Assistant editor: Richard Palliser

Typeset and edited by First Rank Publishing, Brighton.
Cover design by Horatio Monteverde.

About the Author

James Schuyler is a FIDE Master. He was Nevada State Champion in 2007 and won the Virginia State Championship in both 2011 and 2012. He has been teaching chess for over 25 years.

Contents

Introduction

1...♞c6 and the Kevitz System

Why another repertoire book on 1...♞c6 - ? Didn't one come out just a few years ago? As it turns out, the subject matter here is completely different, as are the types of positions reached. 1...♞c6 isn't really an opening yet, but the starting point for many openings. This book generally concerns itself with Black's plans for using 1...♞c6 to force ...e7-e5, as played by Tony Miles, for instance. This idea is properly known as the Kevitz System. (Wisnewski's repertoire book on ...♞c6 was all about the Nimzowitsch and Chigorin Defences, in which Black plays 1...d5 or 2...d5.)

The Dark Knight System?

For reasons I will lay out, I will be recommending a fianchetto of the king's bishop if White resists the ...e7-e5 advance. These are in fact the most common positions, and they have a much different feel from a typical Kevitz System. Furthermore, I believe that the fianchetto is a substantial improvement over the commonly played moves, and therefore a new name is in order. Since it is a black knight venturing out from a dark square to initiate a strategy of dark-square control... need I go on?

Does the Dark Knight System work?

It works wonderfully, and in two ways. Firstly, it can throw White on his own devices as early as move one! When forced to improvise, even titled players can play shockingly weak moves or expend their time and energy in the opening. Secondly, the opening is fully sound and playable against all calibre of opposition. Black is fundamentally okay so there will be no need to abandon the repertoire just because your opponents are no longer surprised. Furthermore, this book is intended to leave you a step or two ahead of even very well-prepared opponents.

I would like to take the opportunity to say that, in general, the quality of play in Dark Knight variations has been low for both colours. In many common positions, as early as moves six, five, four, and three (!) the unquestionably best moves have been rarely or *never* played! To some extent this is understandable in an "unorthodox" opening, particularly for White, who has more important things to worry about. It is less understandable for Black, who can hardly be surprised by his own opening. However, from Black's standpoint, this is highly correctable – and what better opening to use than one in which there is a long history of incompetence by the opponent, even at the GM level? I suggest that Black's practical results (which are by no means bad) can be substantially improved.

Who plays it?

As far as I know, nobody plays the Dark Knight in exactly the fashion I will be recommending, but many strong players use large parts of the repertoire, and most of the bits and pieces have been tested in high-level encounters.

In spite of the relative obscurity of the Kevitz System, it should be noted that it was one of Miles's regular weapons against both 1 e4 and 1 d4, and IM Zvonimir Mestrovic plays it frequently – they each have hundreds of 1...♘c6 (with the idea of ...e7-e5) games to their credit.

It has also seen use by GMs Bogoljubow, Mikenas, Short, Hoi, Lazic, Velimirovic, Benjamin, Gausel, Svidler, Huang Thong Tu, Hort, A.Sokolov, Sulskis, Godena, Izeta Txabarri, Gulko, Klinger, Rogers, Olafsson, Tolnai, Art.Minasian, Ubilava, Sadler, Anand, Dizdarevic, Gonzales, Speelman, Mohr,

Bachmann, Zarnicki, Gelashvili, Leko, Johansen, Shkuro, Rohde, Karpatchev, Ermenkov, Bezgodov, and de facto GM Nikolaevsky – not to mention IMs Kjeldsen, Cvetkovic, Przewoznik, Vlassov, Danailov, Tarlev, Barle (frequently), Z.Nikolic, Vujadinovic, Wohl, Sommerbauer, Mascaro, Matikozian, O'Donnell, Eid, Ambrus, Kos, Bus, and presumably many others that I have missed.

So, as we can see, not only are strong players willing to play these positions (and against other strong players) they do so over and over, in some cases without any expectation of surprising their opponents. This says a lot about the hidden consensus as to the merits of the opening among those in the know.

Coverage

This is a repertoire book, but I am not adhering slavishly to the concept. Sidelines for Black are presented if they are useful or enlightening. One situation that sometimes comes up is that a main line, while objectively fine for Black, offers very few winning chances. In this case, I will try to offer an alternative which makes it more practical to play for a win, normally with substantial additional risk (otherwise it would have been chosen as the main line).

Transpositions to other openings are obviously frequent, but I will not abandon the reader just because we have reached a position that happens to be known by a different name. I will mention transpositions when available *and cover the transpositions that I recommend.*

That being said, it is not simple to fit a whole Black repertoire into one volume, and decisions needed to be made about what to devote space to. Except for here, I will not waste space expressing the wish that I had more space. However, if certain positions receive light treatment, this is generally the reason. When deciding what to focus on, I weighed both frequency and danger, only intentionally ignoring White moves that are both rare and weak. Besides, space aside, I see no point bogging down the reader with information he won't need.

Transpositions? Aargh!

Why would anyone want to learn independent Dark Knight and Kevitz positions when they are just going to have to learn regular (transpositional) openings on top of it? One part of the answer is that a player may greatly enjoy the non-transpositional positions, and these are reached frequently. Another important part is that White normally has to give up valuable options in order to enter the transposition. For instance, in the Pirc reached through the Dark Knight System, White can only play the Classical Variation which, though fairly popular, is just not very challenging for Black. Admittedly, Black's knight reaches the slightly unusual square c6, and does so unusually early, but I will

demonstrate that this is not a problem. With White's options limited and Black committed to this sideline, the study material is relatively small.

To continue, a player who plays 1 e4 e5 must typically learn the Ruy Lopez, Two Knights, Scotch, King's Gambit, Vienna, and other sidelines. Compared to this, the Scotch reached via the Dark Knight is a light workload, not particularly dangerous, and not a popular choice for White. Therefore, play the Dark Knight System still.

Oh, the humanity!

I am admittedly human and, furthermore, fallible, but I will refrain from continuously hedging in the text (e.g. "If my analysis holds up, it seems to me that perhaps Black may indeed have the better practical chances, though this idea is untried and further investigation is needed"). If there are particular doubts about conclusions, the normal solution is not to express them, but to rectify them.

Hopefully I am far less fallible with the help of chess engines, especially *Houdini* (whom I sometimes refer to affectionately as "Mr. H"). Everything presented is computer-checked, which offers the reader substantial protection when relying on the analysis. However, I have only used long computer-generated variations when absolutely necessary; i.e. there are no relevant human games to draw from, and the positions aren't settling down into something that can be understood and assessed. In other words, fairly often.

I am inevitably prone to error when I quote statistics, or when I say that a move is new. These statements are necessarily based on games I have access to. I will try to avoid saying, "according to my database" every time, since that should be taken as a given. And I apologize in advance to the true originators for such errors in attribution.

Untested? (*gasp*!)

In opening books, untested – or lightly tested – moves are typically treated like embarrassing relatives, introduced quickly for propriety's sake and then shuffled off to somewhere they won't bother anyone. Admittedly it is far *easier* to discuss and analyse moves that have been played repeatedly by GMs, but ultimately moves need to stand on their own merits, and we should not shy away from a little work in order to play better chess. Besides, isn't it *good* to catch our opponents unprepared?

As for enemy novelties, it is also sensible to be ready, especially if it is a computer novelty. After all, if "my" *Houdini* says a move is best, my opponent's will too, and I will soon be facing this move at the board.

Who?

"I" is me, James Martin Schuyler. "You" is you, the reader. "We" is not the royal we – it is me and you, the reader. "Our" opening is the Dark Knight System. I am nobody in particular. My qualification for writing this book is the fact that I wrote the excellent book you are now holding in your hands.

Assessments

Chess writers will often tell you that your understanding of a position is more important than the objective assessment. No doubt this is true, but this is not a good reason to be unconcerned with assessments. An objectively poor position will require a great deal of preparation and understanding in order to be worth playing. Also, what if your opponent happens to understand it too?! Wouldn't it be better to take the time to understand a sound position instead of a questionable one?

I will try to convey as much of my understanding as possible, but I am also extremely concerned with the objective quality of the position (to the extent that it is possible to determine it). I do not want to place us one or two inaccuracies away from an extremely difficult position, nor do I want our opponent to have the luxury of one or two inaccuracies and still retain chances for an advantage.

If you are not concerned with assessments, simply ignore them, or cross out the words and write in crayon, "Black is okay". I do not find this useful, but it is sufficient for many and true as far as it goes – if the position were not extremely playable, it would not be in the book.

Houdini is not the final arbiter of anything – especially since it is people who must play the positions – but he is a far stronger player than I am, and he is nothing if not objective, so when looking for what passes for the truth, his assessments carry considerable weight. When his opinions have not made sense to me, I have looked deeper. Typically, I have become convinced, but sometimes I am able to convince him – rarely do we continue to disagree.

Assessments in this book are intended to apply to narrow ranges. "Equal" corresponds to an advantage for one player of no more than 0.09 pawns. "Comfortably equal" is the more pleasant half of that range. "Tiny advantage", "tiny edge", or "slightly better" is an advantage of 0.10 to 0.17 pawns, while "nearly equal" would be a similar disadvantage. In most chess works, such positions are simply labelled as equal, but I believe that there is far too big a difference between +0.15 and -0.15 (two to three inaccuracies or even two to three tempi in many positions) to let it go without mention. An "edge" or "small advantage" is between 0.18 and 0.25 pawns. In other works, such positions are often called "approximately equal" or ±/=. I understand that the style of assessment I am using implies a degree of precision that is difficult to attain, but I would rather strive for precision and risk falling short than strive for vagueness in the hopes of evading criticism.

I have not found it necessary to include in the repertoire positions worse than a quarter pawn disadvantage, but they are not uncommon in the notes. I have not tried to be as precise in my descriptions of theoretically unimportant positions, but the unadorned words "advantage" and "better" mean approximately 0.26 to 0.39 pawns, while 0.4 to 0.6 is a "comfortable advantage" and more would be "clearly better" or some such, while more than one pawn would be "nearly winning".

Personal history (with 1...♞c6)

My love affair with 1...♞c6 goes back to the late '80s, and my trusty old *Batsford Chess Openings*. I had owned it for some time before I came across a single line by Bogoljubow concerning the amazing 1 d4 ♞c6!?. Should White "take the bait" and try to play a kind of mirrored Alekhine's, a wonderfully interesting position may be reached: 2 d5 ♞e5 3 f4 ♞g6 4 e4 e5 5 f5(??) ♕h4+ 6 ♔d2 ♕xe4(?) 7 fxg6 ♕xd5+ 8 ♔e1 ♕xd1+ 9 ♔xd1 hxg6.

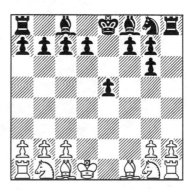

Although labelled as unclear, Black's compensation seemed tremendous to me, with three premium pawns and the half-open h-file for a small knight. My shoddy but practical analysis confirmed this: after 10 ♘c3?! c6 11 ♘f3 f6! 12 ♗d3?! ♘e7 13 ♗d2 d5 14 ♗e2 ♘f5

White will be lucky to survive, even should he find a defence to 15...e4 and 16...♘g3 17 ♖g1 ♗c5. This is, in fact, what many players tend to do as White. Importantly, after the correct 10 c4! I still preferred Black.

Two of Bogo's opponents were kind enough to allow 5...♕h4+!. Alas, after 26 years of 1...♘c6, I have yet to bring this variation to the board during a tournament game. (And now I never will. Even if White plays into it, I will be obligated to correct Black's sixth move. More on this in Chapter Three.) On the plus side, I have yet to encounter any real opening difficulties against any calibre of opposition.

Therefore, play the Dark Knight System!

Weak Colour Complex

There is no way to play chess well while adhering to a single idea, or even two or three ideas – the game is far too complicated – but I have noticed that, in the Dark Knight System, one concept assumes far greater than normal importance, and that is the notion of the weak colour complex. In many of the high-level games that Black wins, it is by taking advantage of White's weaknesses on the dark squares. I would assume that most readers are familiar with the idea of a weak colour complex, but since it is especially important in the DKS, I will prattle on about it anyway.

In some positions, a player is more likely to have problems because of weaknesses on a single colour. The conditions:

♟ Most of the player's pawns are on a single colour (at least in a certain area of the board). Naturally, the weak colour complex will occur on the opposite colour.

♟ The player is missing the bishop that he would need to guard the weak colour.

♟ The player's king is in the vicinity of the weak squares.

♟ The player's opponent still has the bishop that can infiltrate on the weak colour.

A player will usually experience problems if three of the conditions are met. Furthermore, if you notice two conditions in your opponent's position, it is worth seeing if you can aggravate his situation.

A few more observations:

♟ Obviously, if a player's opponent has no access to the "weak" squares, there is no weak colour complex, regardless of what other conditions are present.

♟ A knight is a handy piece for the invader to have, because it allows him to extend the attack to the other colour. (A knight sitting on a weak dark square attacks light squares).

♟ A space advantage is no protection against a weak colour complex – it can even be a vulnerability.

♟ Weak colour complexes are common in fianchetto openings – for the opponent of the player that fianchettos, that is. This is because of how each player is likely to set up their pawns, and also because the fianchettoed bishop (the one that is likely to be infiltrating the enemy weaknesses) has extra protection against being traded off for a knight.

The weak colour complex will not come up often in the theoretical section because it does not usually appear in a full-blown form until the middle-game, but the idea permeates the games section.

Section One

1 d4 ♞c6

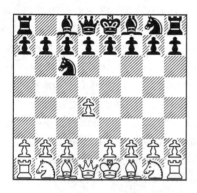

The Dark Knight first caught my attention as a defence to 1 d4. Although playing it against 1 e4 requires very little additional knowledge, Black may find it useful that his 1 d4 opponents are unlikely to know the ins and outs of the Scotch and the Pirc. Besides, since it is not so easy (for most of us) to meet 1 d4, it is especially nice to find an effective defence. It even neutralizes the London, Trompowsky, and other white "easy" systems.

Apart from 2 e4 which is covered via 1 e4 in Section Two, White has three main moves:

2 ♘f3 – Chapter One
2 c4 – Chapter Two
2 d5 – Chapter Three

Others:

a) 2 e3 e5 (or 2...d6 and 3...g6, to keep things interesting – White's pawn on e3 makes a poor impression in this King's Indian type of position) 3 ♘f3 sees White try to play a French with an extra move, but this move order gives Black a few good options. 3...e4 4 ♘fd2 f5 5 c4 ♘f6 6 ♘c3 ♝e7! transposes to line B2 in Chapter Seven. Also possible is 3...exd4 4 exd4 d5 (an Exchange French) to dry up the game. Instead, 3 c4 transposes to A2; whereas 3 d5 is schizophrenic nonsense: 3...♘ce7 4 c4 d6 5 ♘c3 f5 6 ♝d3 ♘f6 7 ♝c2 g6 gave Black an extremely comfortable version of a King's Indian in J.Paasikangas Tella-T.Lindqvist, Finnish Team Championship 1996 (see Game 1).

b) 2 ♘c3 e5 will soon transpose, after 3 d5 ♘ce7 4 e4 or 3 dxe5 ♘xe5 4 e4, into positions considered in Chapter Four (see 4 ♘c3 in lines A and B respectively).

c) 2 c3 e5 3 e4 – see 3 c3 at the beginning of Chapter Four.

d) 2 ♗g5?! looks like an attempt to outdo Black in the weird department, though it does prevent ...e7-e5 for now. Black must not shy away from the bizarre: 2...f6! (breaking the pin and challenging White to prove that the bishop is well placed on the rim) 3 ♗h4 d5! (this is not normal for us, but White has given us space and time and centre, so we do not wish to be disturbed by a belated d4-d5) 4 e3 (4 c4?! e5! 5 dxe5 ♗b4+ 6 ♘c3 d4 7 a3 ♗e7 8 ♘d5 fxe5 9 ♘xe7 ♘gxe7 is just good for Black) 4...♘h6! 5 ♘c3 (5 c4 e5 or 5 ♗d3 e5! 6 dxe5 ♘xe5 7 ♘c3 c6 8 ♘f3 ♘xd3+ 9 ♕xd3 ♘f5) 5...♘f5 6 ♗g3 and we have a few sound choices (6...e6, 6...g6), but the point of our play is to pursue the bishop, so let's go!

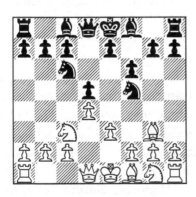

6...h5!? 7 ♗e2 g6 8 ♘f3 ♗e6 (time to take a break; 8...h4 9 ♗f4 g5 10 ♘xg5 fxg5 11 ♗h5+ ♔d7 12 ♗xg5 is pretty

dangerous) 9 ♗f4 ♗f7 10 h4 a6 11 0-0 ♕d7 and 12...0-0-0 is equal.

e) 2 f4!? is another radical way to prevent 2...e5. In the very limited practice, Black has done well with 2...d5 3 ♘f3 ♗g4 4 e3 f6!?; e.g. 5 c4 e5! 6 cxd5 ♕xd5 7 ♘c3 ♗b4 and White was already worse in C.Depasquale-A.Ker, New Zealand Championship 2001; while after 5 ♗b5 ♕d6 6 0-0 a6 7 ♗xc6 ♕xc6 8 c3 ♘h6 9 ♘bd2 0-0-0 10 ♕e1 ♗f5 11 ♕e2 e6 12 ♖e1 ♗e4 13 c4 ♗b4 14 cxd5 exd5 15 a3 ♗xf3 16 ♕xf3 ♗xd2 17 ♗xd2 f5, Black had continuously maintained his grip on e4 and went on to win with his good knight versus bad bishop in J.Vialatte-F.Giroux, Paris 2006 (see Game 2). Of course, White also has 3 e3 ♗f5 4 ♗d3 e6! 5 ♘f3 ♘f6 6 0-0, and although White has no advantage, he has reached a Stonewall position with which he is presumably comfortable.

Nothing wrong with any of that, but taking the opponent out of his comfort zone is one of the things this book is about, and for this purpose the brand-spanking-new, I-just-made-it-up, 2...f5!? fits the bill. No sane person would play the Stonewall against the Dutch – White gives up the e4-square without getting the e5-square in return – so only 3 d5 can be critical. But will the Stonewall player be happy in the resulting positions? He may not play 3 d5 at all, but here's what happens if he does: 3 d5 ♘b4! 4 a3 ♘a6 5 ♘c3 ♘f6 6 ♘f3 ♘c5! 7 e3 (or 7 b4 ♘ce4

8 ♗b2 a5 9 b5 e6 10 dxe6 ♗c5! 11 ♘xe4 ♘xe4 12 ♗d4 d6 13 e3 ♗xe6 14 ♗d3 ♕e7 with a bizarre position that slightly favours Black) 7...e6 8 dxe6 ♘xe6 (8...d5!?) 9 ♗d3 g6 10 0-0 d5 and while Mr. H calls it equal, I would be far more comfortable sitting behind the black pieces.

Seeing how the black army converges upon the e4-square, White may rethink his decision to evict the ♘b4, but leaving it there is not convenient either, since White must fortify the d5-pawn and he can no longer play ♗d3; e.g. 4 c4 ♘f6 5 ♘c3 g6 6 g3 ♗g7 7 ♗g2 0-0 8 ♘f3 e6 is equal.

Alternatively, White may try to address the weak e4-square by placing a black pawn there: 4 e4!? fxe4 5 a3 (otherwise 5...c6!) 5...♘a6 6 ♘c3 ♘f6 7 ♗e3 c6!? (7...g6 leads to more "normal" positions) 8 ♗xa6 bxa6 9 dxc6 d5 10 ♘ge2 e6.

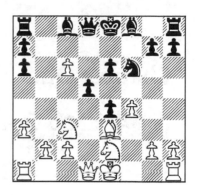

Mr. H likes White here, but what do you think? Without further ado, the not sane Stonewall Attack vs. Dark Knight Dutch, which I can't wait to see happen in real life: 1 d4 ♘c6 2 f4 f5! (I'm giving this move an upgrade as of now) 3 ♘f3 e6 4 e3 ♘f6 5 ♗d3 b6! 6 0-0 ♗b7 7 a3 (if White doesn't play this soon, ...♘b4 is going to be extremely annoying) 7...♘e7 (7...g6!?) 8 c4 ♘c8! with ...♗e7 ...0-0 ...♘d6 coming, and a wonderfully fun equal position.

Chapter One
1 d4 ♘c6 2 ♘f3

This is the most common reply, and a very logical one for a 1 d4 player. White stops Black's planned 2...e5, while trying to maintain a familiar position (unlike 2 d5).

2...d6

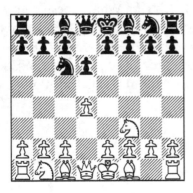

There may be nothing wrong with 2...d5, but with 2...d6 Black continues to fight for the e5-square. Also, after 2...d6 Black's ♘c6 will usually be presented with an excuse to move soon, freeing the c-pawn to join in the battle for the centre. While the knight is not exactly glued to the board in Chigorin-type positions (i.e. after 2...d5), it may not find a convenient opportunity to relocate for some time, leaving the c-pawn out of play.

White has:

> **A: 3 c4** *19*
> **B: 3 d5** *22*
> **C: 3 ♗f4** *26*
> **D: 3 g3** *30*
> **E: 3 ♗g5** *33*

Instead:

a) 3 e4 is covered via 1 e4 – see Chapter Five.

b) 3 ♘c3 ♘f6 4 e4 also reaches Chapter Five.

c) 3 e3 can be met by 3...g6.

d) 3 h3!? may be a trick to induce 3...e5 4 e4, which is now some sort of Philidor. 4...exd4 5 ♘xd4 g6!? is not really bad, but 3...♘f6 4 ♘c3 g6 5 e4 will transpose into lines we are more familiar with – see line C1 in Chapter Five again.

e) 3 c3 was used to good effect in B.Kurajica-Z.Mestrovic, Bosnian Team

Championship 2003, continuing 3...e5 4 e4 ♘f6 5 ♗d3 (5 ♗b5!?) 5...♗e7 6 ♘bd2 and White went on to win. Instead, 3...♘f6 4 e4! g6 transposes to 4 c3 g6 at the beginning of Chapter Five.

A: 3 c4 g6!

Until I started researching this book, I always played 3...e5?! here, but if White follows up correctly, 4 d5! will lead to unpleasant positions for Black (though this is not widely known). The text move is in keeping with the idea of provoking d4-d5 while leaving the a1-h8 diagonal open, a common theme in the Dark Knight.

4 d5!

White should play this now, while Black is mid-fianchetto, or it will be less effective.

4 ♘c3 ♗g7 5 e4 ♗g4 6 ♗e3 e5 7 d5 ♘d4 8 ♗e2 ♗xf3 9 ♗xf3 c5 is a comfortable variation of the Modern Defence in which Black has outscored White, though the game should be equal after 10 dxc6 bxc6 11 0-0 ♘e7 12 c5! 0-0. Another option is 9...♘e7!?, and

if 10 ♗xd4?! exd4 11 ♘e2 c5 12 dxc6?! ♗xc6 13 ♘xd4?! then 13...♕a5+ 14 ♔f1 ♕c5 regains the pawn with a clear advantage.

On 5 d5 Black could transpose to our main line with 5...♘b8, though 5...♘e5!? 6 ♘xe5 ♗xe5 7 e4 ♘f6! 8 ♗d3 0-0 9 ♘e2?! (9 0-0 c6! 10 h3! improves, when White retains an edge) 9...♘d7 is more fun. This was actually played in M.Tratar-M.Srebrnic, Slovenian Championship 2010, and A.Ipatov-R.Antoniewski, German League 2011. Black has equalized, reached a fascinating new position and, furthermore, went on to win both times (see Games 3 and 4).

4...♘b8 5 ♘c3 ♗g7 6 e4 ♘f6 7 ♗e2 0-0

This is now an obscure King's Indian variation that can arise via 1 d4 ♘f6 2 c4 g6 3 ♘c3 ♗g7 4 e4 d6 5 ♘f3 0-0 6 ♗e2 ♘c6!? (6...e5 is "normal") 7 d5 ♘b8. It is also...

Position One

White's position certainly is large and, indeed, he has the advantage, but

Black has counterplay on the dark squares. One important thing to realize is that both ...e7-e5 and ...c7-c5 are poor at this stage in the game (though they are frequently played). Both moves take squares away from Black that he will enjoy using, while neither move puts any pressure on White's centre, or anywhere else for that matter. If that's not clear enough, notice that ...e7-e5 or ...c7-c5 will place Black two tempi down in a main line King's Indian (Petrosian System) or Benoni. Meanwhile, ...c7-c6 or ...e7-e6 actually does pressure White's centre while reserving the c5- and e5-squares for Black's pieces. Even so, there's no rush, since White has no convenient pawn break. Because Black has good control over when and how much the board opens up, it makes sense for him to wait for a particularly good opportunity.

Since Black's play is on the dark squares, White has a space advantage, and the game is not open, the trade ...♗g4xf3 suggests itself – but in spite of the favourable factors, it is still no bargain to part with the bishop pair. In any case, Black is not the one in control of the trade, since White could have played h2-h3 at any point going back to move five. Indeed, GM Neverov and IM Bonin did choose 5 h3 when confronted with this situation. Personally, that would please me, as it costs White a tempo and saves me from a difficult decision. If you prefer ...♗g4, play it as soon as White plays ♗e2.

We will need to look carefully at:

A1: 8 h3 *20*
A2: 8 0-0 *21*

A1: 8 h3 ♘bd7

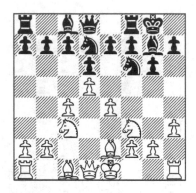

With h2-h3 included, it becomes possible to start considering ...e7-e5, though the immediate 8...e5 9 ♗g5 has scored 100% for White.

9 ♗e3

Logically, White takes measures against 9...♘c5.

9...♘c5!

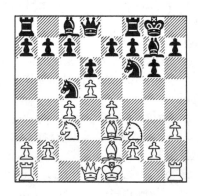

But we play it anyway! White's dark bishop is way too valuable to trade.

10 ♕c2

In Y.Balashov-G.Kuzmin, USSR Championship, Vilnius 1980, White played 10 e5 ♘fd7 (10...♘fe4!?) 11 exd6 exd6 12 ♗d4 ♘f6 and the game soon petered out to a draw (see Game 5).

10 ♗xc5?! dxc5 11 e5?! (11 0-0 e5!) is no good because of 11...♘d7 12 e6 fxe6 13 dxe6 ♘e5 14 ♕b3 ♘c6 15 0-0 ♗xe6 16 ♕xb7 ♘d4 with the better game for Black.

10...a5 11 0-0 ♘fd7!

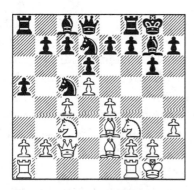

Black's main idea is to play 12...e5. This resembles Yates's plan in line D of this chapter. Black improves his pieces and clamps down on the dark squares before engaging in pawn play. White should also be concerned about the positional damage he could suffer after (for instance) 12 ♖ad1 ♗xc3!? 13 bxc3, though this is obviously a double-edged sword.

Now if 12 ♘d4 e5 13 ♘db5 f5 with good play, or 12 ♗d4 ♗xd4 13 ♘xd4 e5 14 dxe6 fxe6 15 ♖ad1 e5 16 ♘f3 b6 17 ♖fe1 ♗b7 18 ♗f1 ♔g7 19 ♖e3 ♘e6 with equality. Black may consider

...♖xf3 at some point. As in many similar cases, White hurts his own position by trading off Black's fianchettoed bishop.

A2: 8 0-0 a5

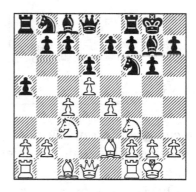

8...♗g4!? is a logical alternative.

9 ♘d4

9 ♘e1 is also played, when 9...♘a6 10 ♘d3 b6 11 ♗e3 ♘c5 or 11...♘d7 is similar to the main line. 9 h3 is seen as well, with a likely transposition to A1; e.g. after 9...♘fd7 10 ♗e3 ♘a6 and 11...♘ac5.

9...♘a6

9...e5?! is more common, but this move of Stefano Rosselli del Turco's is the most accurate. Piece play before pawn play in this variation!

10 ♗e3 ♘c5 11 f3 e5! 12 ♘b3 ♘fd7

The two-time Italian Champion's 12...b6 13 ♕d2 ♘e8?! 14 ♖ae1 f5 15 exf5 ♘xb3 16 axb3 gxf5 17 f4 was not very successful in S.Flohr-S.Rosselli del Turco, Zürich 1934.

13 ♕d2 b6

White may be slightly better because of his extra space, but he has no pawn play.

Meanwhile, we can advance ...f7-f5 at any time; we are also threatening 14...♘xb3 15 axb3 ♘c5, which will force White to play an awkward move to defend the b-pawn (or else give up his good bishop).

B: 3 d5

The time to play this was move two. Now White will have great difficulty finding an advantage.

3...♘e5

The most accurate reply, though there is a tendency for the positions to dry up

early. If Black must play for a win, 3...♘b8 is better, probably transposing to line A above.

4 ♘xe5

If White delays this capture, presumably with 4 e4, Black plays 4...♘f6 5 ♘c3 ♘xf3 6 ♕xf3 g6 and the fianchettoed bishop will enjoy its open diagonal, while White's queen will soon need to move again (but to no particular effect); as for example in R.Fischer-J.Schuyler, Richmond 2008 (see Game 6).

Sometimes in blitz White tries to avoid trading my "problem" knight by playing 4 ♘d4, but White's knight is no better off after 4...c5. If 5 dxc6 ♘xc6 6 e4, we are in a Sicilian with Black having slipped in an extra move while White's attention was diverted. Focus on the board, White!

4...dxe5 5 e4

This is nearly automatic, but not obligatory – in L.Altounian-J.Schuyler, Las Vegas 2008, White played 5 c4 e6 6 ♘c3 ♘f6 7 g3!? (see Game 7).

5...♘f6!

The move Black wants and needs to play is ...e7-e6, but after 5...e6?? Black is already lost! Then 6 ♗b5+! ♗d7 7 dxe6! ♗xb5 8 ♕h5! was brutal in J.Bonin-J.Schuyler, New York 1988 (see Game 8). I shouldn't feel too badly, I suppose – Mestrovic has made this blunder, and Miles made it twice!! (Since Miles was Miles, he actually lost neither game.)

White now has:

B1: 6 ♘c3 *23*
B2: 6 ♗b5+ *24*

6 ♗d3 is less common and less logical. H.Keskar-J.Schuyler, Norfolk 2008, continued 6...e6 7 c4 ♗c5 8 0-0 0-0 9 ♘c3 exd5 10 cxd5, when I set about blockading the d-pawn with 10...♘e8 11 ♗e3 ♗xe3 12 fxe3 ♗d7 13 ♕f3 c5 14 ♕g3 f6 15 ♖ad1 ♘d6 and Black is a bit better already. The game concluded 16 b3 b5 17 ♕h4 ♕a5 18 ♖c1 b4 19 ♘a4 ♖ac8 20 ♖f3 c4 21 ♗f1 cxb3 22 ♖xc8 ♖xc8 23 axb3 ♗xa4 24 bxa4 b3 25 ♕g4 b2 26 ♕e6+ ♔h8 27 ♖xf6 ♕d8 0-1.

Three years later, H.Keskar-J.Schuyler, Hampton 2011, went 7 dxe6 ♗xe6 with comfortable equality, albeit with a long struggle for a win (see Game 9).

B1: 6 ♘c3 e6!

This is still the move Black needs to play – and now he actually can, as my computer explained to me a few years ago. This is of great theoretical importance because following 6...a6 or 6...g6,

White is doing well with 7 f4!.

7 ♗b5+ ♗d7 8 dxe6 ♗xb5!

Previously, both Jonathan Speelman and Emmanuel Bricard have tried 8...fxe6, each securing a draw – though if you see the games, you may not be so eager to repeat their methods.

Instead, after 8...♗xb5, White has several paths to the endgame, but almost no chance of extracting anything from the position.

9 ♘xb5

White should capture neither the queen nor the f-pawn, though this is not simple for him to figure out.

a) 9 ♕xd8+ ♖xd8 10 ♘xb5 has been

played four times, but it is slightly weaker than the text. Then 9...fxe6! 11 ♘xc7+ ♔f7 12 ♘b5 ♖c8! (better than 12...♘xe4?!, as in I.Kreitner-H.Stenzel, Long Island 1997) 13 ♘c3 ♗b4 14 ♗d2 ♗xc3 15 ♗xc3 ♘xe4 16 ♗xe5 ♖xc2 is equal.

b) 9 exf7+ costs a move (as opposed to waiting for ...f7xe6) and improves Black's king position, so it is not a good idea. 9...♔xf7 10 ♘xb5 (or 10 ♕xd8+ ♖xd8 11 ♘xb5 ♘xe4 12 f3 a6 13 fxe5 axb5 and Black has slightly the better of the probable draw) 10...♕xd1+ 11 ♔xd1 ♘xe4 12 ♔e2 c6 13 ♘c3 ♘xc3 14 bxc3 is roughly equal again.

9...♕xd1+ 10 ♔xd1 0-0-0+ 11 ♔e2 a6 12 ♘c3 ♗b4 13 ♘d5 ♘xd5 14 exd5 ♖xd5 15 exf7

White has a nominal edge because of the isolated e-pawn, but the game is all but drawn. Still, let's be careful and avoid any mishaps by taking the a7-g1 diagonal immediately before White's bishop entrenches itself on e3: i.e. 15...♗c5 16 ♗e3 ♗xe3 17 ♔xe3 ♖f8 18 ♖ad1, and now let's centralize the king:

18...♖d6 19 ♔e4 ♖xf7 20 f3 ♔d7 – although White can't win, he can try to lose if he likes with 21 ♔xe5 ♖e7+ 22 ♔f4 ♖e2.

B2: 6 ♗b5+ ♗d7

6...♘d7?, as in E.Bukic-Z.Mestrovic, Belgrade 1978, is an experiment that should not be repeated. Had White seen 7 ♕h5! our hero would have found himself a pawn down for nothing.

7 ♕e2

7 ♕d3 is rarely played: 7...a6 8 ♗xd7 ♕xd7 9 0-0 (D.Haessel-J.Schuyler, Pawtucket 2008, continued 9 ♘c3 e6 10 ♗g5 ♗b4 11 0-0-0 0-0-0 12 f3 ♕e7 13 ♕c4 h6 with equality, though there was still some play, and I went on to win – see Game 10) 9...e6 10 c4 ♗e7 11 ♘c3 is obviously similar to the main line. White's queen has some extra options, but his d-pawn is pinned. These differences are important enough to change Black's best method of counterplay: 11...b5! 12 ♖d1 b4 13 ♘e2 0-0 14 ♗g5 a5 with a slight edge for White.

One important point of Black's queenside expansion is that it secures the c5-square for his bishop, ensuring that it won't get shut out of play (as it would if White were allowed to seize space on the queenside with a2-a3 and b2-b4). White's knight has also been taken out of contact with the important d5-square. Notice that if White ever plays d5xe6, and for some reason Black doesn't feel like recapturing with a piece, ...f7xe6 is positionally sound because the f-file is valuable and the e6-pawn controls critical squares.

Hold on! Couldn't 12...b4 have been prevented? Indeed, 12 a3 is possible for White and not a bad move, but 11...b5 was not played with only 12...b4 in mind. After 12 a3 0-0 13 ♖d1 exd5 14 cxd5 ♖fd8, Black's idea is to play 15...c5 and, if White doesn't capture, 16...♘e8 and 17...♘d6. White's edge is tiny.

7...a6

I'm not crazy about 7...g6!? with that silly pawn sitting on e5, but it does avoid spending a tempo on 7...a6, and Mestrovic is 2-0 with it, which suggests it is worth a try in a must-win game. Check out D.Rasic-Z.Mestrovic, Croatian Team Championship 2001, and J.Barle-Z.Mestrovic, Slovenian Championship 1997, in the games section (Games 11 and 12).

8 ♗xd7 ♕xd7 9 0-0

Somehow White has done well with 9 ♗g5, though it is not a move that should cause problems. In P.Staniszewski-H.Kaulfuss, Darmstadt 1996, Black

certainly had the right idea and was a bit better following 9...e6 10 ♗xf6 gxf6 11 dxe6 fxe6 (11...♕xe6 is also good) 12 0-0?! (12 ♕h5+ ♕f7) 12...0-0-0 13 ♕c4 ♖g8 14 ♘c3, even if he went on to lose after the passive 14...♖e8?! (here 14...♔b8 15 ♖fd1 ♗d6 16 b4 f5 was better).

For White, the most accurate continuation may be 10 ♘c3 ♗b4 11 0-0 ♗xc3 12 bxc3 exd5 13 ♗xf6 gxf6 14 ♖fd1 ♕b5 15 ♕f3 0-0-0, though he has nothing to show for it – instead he should have been accurate on move three!

Alternatively, the untried 9...h6!? is playable, although in this case 10 ♗xf6 exf6 11 0-0 f5 12 exf5 ♕xf5 13 ♘c3 ♗d6 14 ♘e4 0-0 15 c4 is a tiny edge for White.

9...e6 10 c4 ♗e7!

Allowing Black to castle short. Instead 10...♗c5?! 11 ♗g5 spells trouble.

11 ♘c3 0-0 12 ♖d1 exd5 13 cxd5

White's d5-pawn is currently an asset, and Black has two possible ways to neutralize it. First, he can attack it directly with ...c7-c6. This is definitely worth considering in some similar positions, but it doesn't work so well here; e.g. 13...c6?! 14 ♗g5! ♖fd8 15 ♗xf6 ♗xf6 16 dxc6 ♕xc6 and the eternal knight sets in with 17 ♘d5.

If Black tries to prepare this with ...h7-h6 (in fact not a bad move at all) it is unlikely he will be fully ready for 14...c6 anyway; e.g. 13...h6 14 a3 (14 ♗e3 ♘g4!) 14...c6 15 ♗e3 cxd5 16 ♘xd5 ♘xd5 17 ♖xd5 ♕e6 18 ♖ad1 and while Black's position is playable, it is very dull, and White has a small but clear advantage.

The second plan is very appropriate here, which is a timely ...♘e8 and ...♘d6. This idea is useful in many variations of the Dark Knight, but especially the ones starting with 3 d5. The point of the knight transfer is fourfold: the knight is safe, as White's own d-pawn shields it from attack; the knight is active – centralized and controlling the important e4-, f5-, c4-, and b7-squares; the knight blockades the strong d-pawn, so Black does not need to worry about an eventual d5-d6 by White; and finally, the knight has cleared itself from the f-file, so it is now possible (and usually desirable) for Black to play ...f7-f5. Coincidentally, the ...f7-f5 break also does (at least) four things: frees Black's rook(s), isolates White's d-pawn (or pressures White's e-pawn), clears the second rank for easy defence of the c7- and g7-pawns, and gains space.

Therefore, 13...♖ad8 14 ♗g5 ♘e8 15 ♗xe7 ♕xe7 16 ♖ac1 ♘d6 17 b3 f5 and with all Black has accomplished, perhaps White should resign? Unfortunately, chess is not quite that simple, but Black can now start fighting on equal terms.

C: 3 ♗f4

White plays the London System, which stops the ...e7-e5 break for now, but the bishop bites a granite pawn on d6.

3...♘f6!

To be honest, I've always played 3...♗g4?! here, intending to force through ...e7-e5 one way or another (4 c4 e5!; 4 e3 e5!; or 4 ♘bd2 ♘xd4! 5 ♘xd4 e5). However, in researching this book, I found that 4 d5! ♘b8 gives White a large advantage. Although this has only been played once in my database and never against me, I believe it is a bad idea to play moves one knows to be poor, however unlikely it might be to encounter the refutation. This kind of "hope chess" is bad for one's confidence and psychology – one is no longer in control of the game.

As for 3...♗g4?!, it is not actually surprising that this move is questionable – there are virtually no cases in the Dark Knight where the bishop goes to g4 early. With Black's pawns set up on dark squares, it is costly to trade the light-squared bishop for a knight, and the bishop rarely has anywhere decent to retreat to. Should you wish to ignore my advice and take your chances, I will point out that 4 d5! is White's only good move, and it goes so far against the grain for a typical London System player that you, too, may never encounter it.

4 e3

If 4 d5?!, then 4...e5! 5 dxc6 exf4 6 cxb7 ♗xb7 7 ♕d4 d5! 8 ♕xf4 ♘e4! 9 c3 ♗d6 10 ♕c1 0-0 11 e3 c5 and, with 12...d4! coming, White's tiny material advantage does not make up for all of his pathetic grovelling. Instead, 5 ♗g5 ♘e7 6 c4 (or 6 ♘c3 h6 7 ♗xf6 gxf6 8 e4 a6 9 ♗d3 f5) 6...♘e4! 7 ♗d2 (7 ♗h4?! c6!) 7...g6 is equal.

4...g6

4...♘h5 has done well in practice; for instance, 5 ♗g5 h6 6 ♗h4 g5 7 ♗g3 ♘xg3 8 hxg3 ♗g7 reaches a position Black is normally happy to have even with a tempo less. However, White once again has the annoying novelty 5 d5! ♘xf4 6 exf4 ♘b8 7 ♘c3 and Black's knight excursions have placed him too far behind in development, a situation he will have trouble fixing; e.g. 7...g6 8 ♕d4!.

5 ♗e2 ♗g7

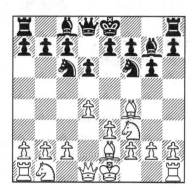

White has:

C1: 6 0-0 *27*
C2: 6 h3 *28*

C1: 6 0-0 0-0 7 h3

Black is finally ready to play 7...♘h5, so White prepares a retreat, but this is still a slow move. Instead:

a) 7 c3 ♘h5 8 ♗g5 h6 9 ♗h4 g5 10 ♘e1 ♘f6 11 ♗g3 ♘e4 12 ♘d2 ♘xg3 13 hxg3 e5 14 ♘d3 ♗e6 15 ♗f3 d5 is equal. Of course, White wasn't playing for an advantage anyway, but this isn't the position he wanted either.

b) 7 c4 e5! 8 ♗g5 (or 8 dxe5 ♘e4 9 h3 dxe5 10 ♗h2 ♗f5 with an edge) 8...h6 9 ♗h4 g5 10 ♗g3 exd4 11 ♘xd4 ♘xd4 12 exd4 ♘e4 13 ♘c3 ♖e8 and Black is a little better.

7...e5!

After this unplayed novelty, White is the one who must be careful to keep the balance. Furthermore, in doing so, he may not be able to maintain his typically comfortable London structure.

8 ♗h2

8 dxe5 gives up more of the centre for no gain. Black's point is 8...♘e4! and White's extra e-pawn is pinned to the b2-pawn. 9 ♕d5?! dxe5 10 ♕xe4 exf4 11 ♘c3 fxe3 just makes matters worse for White.

8...exd4!

A second annoyance for the London System player, who is hoping for ...e5-e4 at some point, after which White has excellent long-term prospects because of the h2-bishop, which makes it hard for Black to generate meaningful play on the kingside, whereas White has no difficulties making progress on the queenside, due in large part to that same piece. It is not hard to see why that bishop appeals to so many players! However, we will be sure to maintain control over it.

9 exd4

9 ♘xd4 may be slightly preferable (because the f3-square will be useful for the e2-bishop), but White players do not seem to consider such moves. In any case, 9...♖e8 is still the correct re-sponse, and Black is comfortably equal.

9...♖e8

Simple chess! Black has no problems at all. Moves worth considering in the near future are ...♗f5 (...♗e6), ...♘e4 (...♘d5), ...♗h6, ...♕d7, ...♖b8, ...b7-b5. If ♘bd2, then ...a7-a5 is a good idea, while if ♘c3, then ...a7-a6 and ...b7-b5 is effective.

C2: 6 h3 0-0 7 c3

This slows White's queenside play to a crawl, but it does avoid problems on the long diagonal.

7 c4?! is a bad idea. Black was al-ready better following 7...e5! 8 ♗h2

exd4 9 exd4 ♘e4! in K.Gunasekaran-K.Akshayraj, Dhaka 2005, and went on to win after 10 ♘c3? (but if 10 ♗f4! ♖e8 11 0-0 g5! 12 ♗e3 g4! 13 hxg4 ♘g3! 14 ♖e1 ♘xe2 15 ♖xe2 ♗xg4 with a big edge to Black) 10...g5! 11 0-0 ♘xf3+ 12 ♗xf3 ♘xd4 with a free pawn.
7...♘d7

I shall soon try the untried 7...a5!?. I do like the idea of avoiding the ...e7-e5 break for the time being, as it makes contact with the enemy where he is already fortified. Black's plan is 8 0-0 a4 9 ♘bd2 a3 10 b4 ♘d5 11 ♕c1 ♘xf4 12 exf4 – equal according to my computer, but this does not even vaguely resemble the position White was hoping to play. Notice how we have rid ourselves of the London bishop, while starting to soften the long diagonal for our own dark-squared bishop.

Naturally, White could stop the a-pawn with 8 a4, in which case we go to plan B: 8...♘d5 9 ♗h2 e5 10 0-0 exd4 (the mini-operation succeeds – White must give up the b4- or f4-square) 11 exd4 ♗h6! 12 ♖e1 ♖e8 13 ♘bd2 ♘f4 14

♗xf4 ♗xf4 15 ♕b3 d5 16 ♗d3 ♖xd1 17 ♖xd1 ♘e7 and although White is not worse, he is once again without his favourite bishop. I've played the London System quite a lot, so I know exactly how annoying these ideas can be.
8 0-0 e5 9 ♗h2 ♕e7

This is the main line – which shows that every once in a while a main line is actually good! Interestingly enough, *Houdini* prefers White, but extensive practice shows the opposite. Black normally continues with 10...f5, 11...♔h8, and then looks for a good opportunity to shut out White's London bishop with ...f5-f4!. Perhaps Mr. H is underestimating the problem of the h2-bishop. Sometimes Black prepares ...f5-f4 with ...e5-e4 and ...g6-g5 (or just ...g6-g5). Meanwhile, White shoves the a- and b-pawns. Sooner or later the c6-knight gets kicked and usually re-routes itself to the f7-square via d8. These ideas come to life in P.B.Pedersen-D.Bekker Jensen, Danish Team Championship 2008, and R.Valenti-V.Tkachiev, Corsica (rapid)

1997 (see Games 13 and 14); whereas V.Golod-E.Sutovsky, Netanya (rapid) 2009 (Game 15) shows Black, a strong GM, fail utterly to contain the London bishop.

D: 3 g3

A subtle (read: boring) move. Mestrovic has responded 3...e5!? here five times, drawing all comers from expert to GM. This is a good bet for Black theoretically, since the endgame after 4 dxe5 ♘xe5 5 ♘xe5 dxe5 6 ♕xd8 ♔xd8 gives only a tiny edge for White. Perhaps your opponent will turn away from this Mutually Assured Dullness, but I would as soon not give him the opportunity. Thus, the usual solution:

3...g6!?

When we must look at:

> **D1: 4 d5** *30*
> **D2: 4 ♗g2** *31*

D1: 4 d5

If White is going to kick the knight, he should do it now – though, accord-ing to my database, 4 d5 has never actually been played.

4...♘b8

I have selected this retreat over other options in many variations, and the more I think about it, the more I like it. Like General MacArthur, the knight shall return, likely settling on the newly soft c5-square. Incidentally, if ...♘b4 is played, it is with a similar idea: ...a7-a5, ...♘a6 and ...♘c5.

5 ♗g2 ♗g7 6 0-0 ♘f6

I also like 6...e5!? 7 dxe6 (7 e4 ♘d7 8 c4 ♘e7 is likely to transpose to D2; e.g. 9 ♘c3 0-0) 7...fxe6 8 e4 ♘h6! 9 c4 ♘f7.

7 c4 0-0 8 ♘c3

This line was topical in the 1920s (!) with Frederick Yates seen frequently behind the black pieces against the best players of his day, while Alekhine and Grünfeld championed White. Rich-ard Réti played both colours. Yates was able to defeat Réti, Kmoch, and Alekhine, the last of these games win-ning a brilliancy prize at Carlsbad 1923.

8...♘bd7

The most common move, 8...e5?!,

didn't work in the 1920s and still doesn't work in the 21st century. Even with the centre closed, Black will lose too many tempi with his knights in order to play ...f7-f5. Another common move, 8...c5?!, is equally illogical and unsuccessful.

The board resembles **Position One**, with White's fianchetto not particularly helpful to him. Black should develop and establish his pieces on the dark squares before initiating pawn play.

9 h3

Prophylaxis against ...♘g4 and ...♘ge5.

9...a5 10 ♗e3

Or 10 e4 ♘c5 11 ♕c2 and now, with the knight anchored on the c5-square, Black is ready for 11...e5 (12 dxe6 ♗xe6 =) 12...♘fd7 and 13...f5.

10...♘c5

Black intends 11...♘fe4 with near equality. 11 ♘d4 ♗d7 transposes to H.Kmoch-F.Yates, Hastings 1927/28, a beautiful demonstration by Black of how to build an attack (see Game 16).

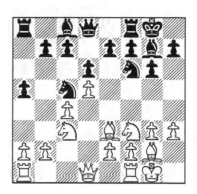

D2: 4 ♗g2 ♗g7 5 0-0

5 d5 is playable now and at any point, but it was most forcing on move four, when Black was obligated to play ...♘b8. Now Black also has 5...♘e5, 5...♘b4!?, and 5...♘a5(!) as in A.Galliamova-M.Krasenkow, Koszalin 1997 (see Game 17), though transposing to D1 with 5...♘b8 is obviously simplest.

5...♘f6 6 c4 0-0 7 ♘c3

By transposition we have reached the fianchetto variation of the King's Indian Defence. There is an obscure but logical sideline for Black that has been played successfully by strong players.

7...♘d7!?

This prepares both ...e7-e5 and ...f7-f5, and holds up White's c4-c5 break. The immediate 7...e5 is frequently played, but White has done very well with 8 d5 ♘e7 9 c5!.

8 e4

8 d5 ♘a5 (or 8...♘ce5 9 ♘xe5 ♘xe5 10 ♕b3 and now 10...c5, 10...a5 or 10...b6 is level) 9 ♕a4 c6 10 ♗g5 ♘c5 11 ♕b4 ♘a6 12 ♕a4 ♘c5 is a draw.

8...e5

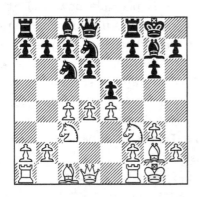

9 d5

These other moves are almost as common:

a) 9 ♗g5 ♗f6!? (9...f6) 10 ♗xf6 ♘xf6

11 h3 (11 d5 ♘b8!) 11...♖e8 12 a3 (12 d5 ♘b8!) was A.Kotov-A.Lein, USSR Team Championship 1962; then 12...exd4 12 ♘xd4 a6 is a tiny edge for White.

b) 9 ♗e3?! exd4 10 ♘xd4 ♘de5 11 ♘xc6 bxc6 12 ♕a4 c5 and Black is better; e.g. 13 ♘d5 c6 14 ♘c3 ♖b8! 15 ♖ad1 (15 b3 ♘d3!) 15...♖b4 16 ♕c2 ♘xc4 with a big advantage.

9...♘e7 10 ♘e1 f5 11 ♘d3 h6 12 f4

This is not a very good move, but it's what White has been playing for. Black must try to prove that White's position is overextended.

12...exf4 13 ♘xf4

13 ♗xf4 ♘b6! 14 ♕b3 fxe4 15 ♘xe4 ♘f5 is equal.

13...♘e5 14 ♕b3 fxe4 15 ♘xe4

15 ♗xe4 g5 16 ♘e6 ♖xf1+ 17 ♔xf1 ♗xe6 18 dxe6 c6 gives Black the advantage, since if 19 ♕xb7?! ♘xc4 20 ♗xc6? ♖b8 21 ♕a6 ♕f8+ 22 ♔g2 ♗d4, White's exposed king loses him the game.

15...g5 16 ♘h5 ♖xf1+ 17 ♗xf1 ♗h8

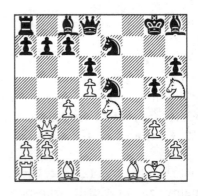

Things are still complicated, but Black is slightly better due to White's looser position.

E: 3 ♗g5?!

Preventing ...e7-e5 for now, this move has given Black plenty of practical problems, but objectively it is poor to allow Black to play ...h7-h6 and ...g7-g5 for free with White's knight already committed to f3.

3...h6 4 ♗h4

4 ♗f4 g5 5 ♗g3 comes to the same thing; 5 ♗d2 g4 wins the d-pawn; while after 5 ♗c1 White may die of shame. As a matter of fact, my engine recommends both 5 ♗c1 *and* 4 ♗c1, which certainly makes clear what it thinks of this whole 3 ♗g5 fiasco.

4...g5 5 ♗g3 g4!

Dare I say it? This logical move is another strong, unplayed novelty which fully turns the tables. White has deliberately provoked these moves, only to find that his knight has nowhere to go. He will also find his ♗g3 awkwardly placed.

6 ♘g1!

Limiting the damage. Others are clearly worse.

a) 6 d5 gxf3 7 dxc6 bxc6 8 exf3 ♖b8! with some advantage to Black in a complicated position.

b) 6 ♘h4?! e6! threatens 7...♗e7, trapping the knight, which explains the following contortions: 7 h3 h5 8 e4 ♗e7 9 d5 ♗xh4 10 ♗xh4 ♕xh4 11 dxc6 g3 12 f3 bxc6 and Black pockets a pawn.

6...♗g7 7 e3 h5 8 h3 h4 9 ♗h2 ♘h6 10 hxg4 ♘xg4 11 ♘c3 e5

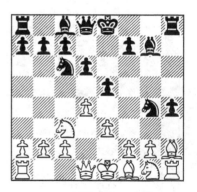

Black has an edge in this bizarre position.

Chapter Two
1 d4 ♞c6 2 c4

To my mind, this is already a lax move. White puts up no resistance to Black's logical follow-up. Presumably some players are hoping for a Chigorin (after 2...d5).

2...e5

3 d5

Instead:

a) The lame 3 e3 offers Black a few methods: 3...exd4 4 exd4 d5 5 ♘f3 ♘f6 is an equal Exchange French position. 3...d5!? is a kind of Chigorin/Albin which has been played repeatedly by many GMs – with poor results, however.

Personally, I like 3...♗b4+ 4 ♘c3 ♗xc3 5 bxc3 d6, playing a kind of Nimzo-Indian with ...e7-e5 in one go. After 6 ♗d3 f5! or 6 ♘f3 e4 7 ♘d2 f5, the game can also be thought of as a reversed Grand Prix Attack (cf 1 e4 c5 2 ♘c3 ♘c6 3 f4 e6 4 ♘f3 d5 5 ♗b5). Of course, 4 ♗d2 is also possible: 4...exd4 5 ♗xb4 (5 exd4? ♕e7+! wins the d-pawn) 5...♘xb4 6 exd4 ♘f6 (not 6...♕e7+ 7 ♗e2 ♕e4?! 8 ♔f1! and Black's queen is worse than White's king) 7 ♘f3 d5 is at least equal – the exchange of bishops will help Black in the coming isolated queen pawn position. If instead 7 a3 ♘c6 8 d5?!, then 8...♕e7+! 9 ♗e2 ♘e5 and Black is better, as White must figure out some way to develop and guard the c4-pawn.

b) 3 dxe5 ♘xe5 (3...d6!?) cannot be dangerous either. Black's position resembles a Budapest Gambit, but without any of the inconvenience normally associated with recovering the e-pawn; e.g. 4 e3 ♘f6 5 ♘c3 ♗b4 6 ♗d2 0-0 7 ♗e2 c6!? was fine and worked out well for Black in R.Aghasaryan-A.Chibukh-chian, Kajaran 2011 (see Game 18). And 4 e4?! is an especially bad idea: after 4...♗c5 White is already worse and must be very careful; e.g. 5 ♗e2 ♕h4! or 5 ♘f3 ♘g4 6 ♘d4 d5!? 7 cxd5 ♕f6 8 ♗e3 ♘xe3 9 fxe3 ♕h4+ and White will be needing both his chess resources and his sense of humour as he plays 10 ♔d2.

c) 3 ♘f3 transposes to 1 c4 ♘c6 2 ♘f3 e5 3 d4, covered at the beginning of Chapter Seven.

3...♗b4+!

3...♘ce7 is played 90% of the time, and with excellent results, but if White really understands what's going on, Black will be forced to play positions I cannot recommend; e.g. 4 ♘f3! ♘g6 5 h4! ♗b4+ 6 ♘bd2 h5 7 g3 ♘f6 8 ♘g5!? and Black doesn't have much to look forward to – White has all the squares and will soon have the bishop pair unless Black makes a pathetic retreat. Black also needs to worry (after 5 ♘c3 ♘f6) about all of the "dynamic" tries mentioned in Richard Palliser's 2005 book on the Tango, some of which pose questions to which Black has yet to find answers. (Whenever Black reaches the Tango via the Dark Knight, White is already committed with a pawn on e4, which takes away all "dynamic" tries, leaving "classical" tries, which Palliser rightly considers to be pleasant for Black.)

Attempts to transpose to a King's Indian with 4 ♘f3 d6 do not bring happiness either, because (to make a long story short) White gets to break on the queenside early with 6 c5 or 7 c5.

Instead, with 3...♗b4+, Black develops his bishop before it gets obstructed by ...♘e7 or ...d7-d6, incidentally solving his space issues and defusing White's h2-h4-h5 ideas. What could be more logical?

White blocks with:

A: 4 ♗d2 36
B: 4 ♘d2 40

4 ♘c3?! is legal and it doesn't lose material. So much for its positive points. 4...♘ce7 5 ♕c2 (otherwise 5...♗xc3+) 5...a5 6 a3 ♗xc3+ 7 ♕xc3 d6 8 e4 f5 gives Black a comfortable position typical of this chapter. Our development is simple and we can consider clamping down on the queenside with ...a5-a4 when we feel we can spare the time. 9 ♕g3 ♘g6 10 exf5 ♗xf5 11 h4 ♕e7 12 ♘e2 ♘f6 13 h5 ♘f8 14 ♘c3 ♘8d7 15 ♕g4 ♗c2! might make White feel like a tough guy, but it does not lead to an advantage.

A: 4 ♗d2 ♗xd2+

5 ♕xd2

Alternatively, 5 ♘xd2 ♘ce7 6 d6!? (or 6 e4 d6 7 ♗d3 ♘f6! – in this particular position it is too costly to play 7...f5?!, activating both White's ♗d3 and his ridiculous ♘d2; instead, Black plans ...0-0, ...♘g6, ...♕e7, ...♘h5, and/or ...a7-a5, ...b7-b6, ...♗d7) 6...cxd6 7 ♘e4 ♕a5+ 8 ♕d2 ♕xd2 9 ♔xd2 ♘f5 10 g4 ♘h4 11 ♘xd6+ ♔e7 12 c5 b6 13 b4 ♘f6 14 ♘f3 ♘xf3+ 15 exf3 ♘e8 is equal.

5...♘ce7

A1: 6 d6!? *36*
A2: 6 ♘c3 *38*

Here 6 ♕g5 ♘g6 7 ♕xd8 ♔xd8 8 ♘c3 d6 is just equal, though not without play.

A1: 6 d6!?

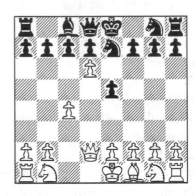

6...cxd6

A.Hoffman-A.Fernandez, Mar del Plata 1996, went 6...♘c6?! 7 ♘c3 cxd6 8 ♘b5 ♘f6 9 ♘xd6+, and gives a good example of what Black must avoid (see Game 19).

7 ♕xd6

7 ♘c3 ♘f6 (or 7...d5 8 ♘xd5 ♘xd5 9 ♕xd5 ♕e7!) 8 ♘f3 d5 9 cxd5 (or 9 ♘xe5 d6 10 ♘f3 ♗e6) 9...d6 10 e4 0-0 is no problem for Black.

7...♘f6! 8 ♘c3

8 ♕xe5 frees Black's d-pawn and does nothing to address White's development – he is still four (!) moves away from castling kingside and the queen-side is not a safe place: 8...0-0 9 ♘c3 d5! 10 cxd5 (10 e3 ♗e6 11 ♘f3 ♘g6 12 ♕d4 dxc4 13 ♕xd8 ♖axd8 is equal; or 10 ♘f3 ♘c6 11 ♕f4 ♕a5 12 cxd5 ♘xd5 13 ♕d2 ♘xc3! 14 ♕xc3 ♘b4 15 ♘d4 ♖d8 with considerable pressure; or 10

0-0-0 ♗d7! 11 ♘f3 ♖c8 12 cxd5? ♖e8 13 ♕d4 ♘exd5 14 ♔b1 ♘xc3+ 15 bxc3 ♘e4, winning) 10...♘exd5 11 ♘xd5 ♘xd5 12 a3 (this sad move is necessary to prevent 12...♕a5+; castling just loses after 12 0-0-0?? ♗e6, with 13...♖c8+ 14 ♔b1 ♘c3+ coming) 12...♖e8 13 ♕d4 (after thirteen moves, White's kingside is hilarious – the most plausible explanation is that he rolled very bad dice in his Chaturanga game) 13...b5! 14 ♘f3 ♗b7 15 e3 ♕c7 16 ♗e2 ♖ad8 gives Black plenty for the pawn.

8...0-0

Which brings us to:

Position Two

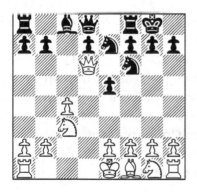

This position has never occurred, but it is the obvious way to disturb Black's easy play after 3...♗b4+, so I think it will be contested many times in the future. Furthermore, Black's methods of counterplay are tricky and therefore require special attention.

The first time I saw this position was on an analysis board about 25 years ago, when my teacher was trying to ex-

plain to me why people didn't play 3...♗b4+. It seemed obvious at the time that Black's position was bad – after all, the d-pawn is hopelessly backward. How can Black possibly evict White's queen and achieve the ...d7-d5 advance?

Often we can't, but there are other options and, depending on how White continues, it is actually possible to "play around" White's queen and leave the d7-pawn alone for the foreseeable future. After all, it is securely guarded and Black's pieces do have other ways to develop. This idea is demonstrated by the variation 9 e4 ♘c6 10 ♘f3 ♕a5! 11 0-0-0 (11 ♗d3 ♖e8 12 ♗c2 b6 13 a3 ♕c5 or 12 0-0 ♖e6 13 ♕a3 ♕xa3 14 bxa3 and White can stop bragging about his superior structure) 11...a6 12 ♔b1 ♖e8 13 a3 b5 14 cxb5 axb5 15 ♗xb5 ♗a6.

Black's whole army is activated and the d-pawn is neither an obstruction to Black nor a target for White's counterplay. Black's compensation is more than sufficient. Notice the ...a7-a6, ...b7-b5 idea, which develops Black's bishop, weakens White's control over d5, and opens lines against White's king. It is powerful enough that it can sometimes be used even when White has not castled queenside (and ...b7-b5 can occasionally be played without ...a7-a6).

Was White's play too co-operative? Presumably 9 e4 is the culprit, providing a target for Black's ...♘f6 and ...♛a5. It also leaves a hole on the d4-square which could turn into a long-term problem, although it did stop ...♘f5, a useful move for Black. Therefore 9 e3 ♖e8 10 ♘f3 ♘f5 11 ♕d2 d6! (11...b5!? is a great try, but 12 ♘xb5 ♗b7 13 ♗e2 ♘e4 14 ♕c2 ♕a5+ 15 ♘c3 ♘xc3 16 bxc3 ♘d6 17 ♖xd7 ♖ab8 is a little better for White) 12 ♗e2 (12 ♖d1 ♕b6 13 ♗e2 ♗e6 14 0-0 h6 or 14...♖ad8!?; or 12 e4 ♘e7 13 0-0-0 ♕b6 14 ♕xd6 ♕xf2 15 ♘xe5 and 15...♘f5, 15...♗g4!?, 15...♗e6!?, or 15...♘c6!? with equal chances in all cases) 12...b6 13 e4 ♘e7 14 0-0 ♗b7 15 ♕d3.

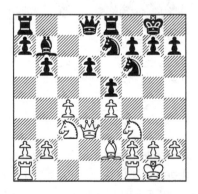

By playing for ...d6-d5 (with the queenside fianchetto) Black has managed to provoke e3-e4 again, which is

once again a target, and again leaves the dark squares weak. On the other hand, if Black doesn't find a plan, he may find himself statically worse with his backward d-pawn, despite White's "bad" bishop. It is Black's idle ♘e7 that will save the day by repositioning to target those soft dark squares: 15...♘g6 16 g3 ♘f8! 17 ♖ad1 ♘e6! 18 ♕xd6 ♘d4 (or 18...♕xd6 19 ♖xd6 ♘c5) 19 ♕xd8 ♘xe2+ 20 ♘xe2 ♖axd8, which is at least equal for Black.

Can White save a tempo by keeping his e-pawn flexible? Not unless he wants an e-pawn shoved up his king's file: 9 ♘f3 ♖e8 (or the wild 9...e4 10 ♘d4 e3 11 fxe3 b5! 12 ♘dxb5 a6 13 ♘c7 ♖a7 14 ♘7d5 ♘exd5 15 cxd5 ♖b7 with excellent play) 10 ♖d1 ♘f5 11 ♕a3 (11 ♕d2 e4 12 ♕c2 d5! with advantage) 11...e4 12 ♘d4 ♘xd4 13 ♖xd4 e3 and although Black's d-pawn remains, White now has a matching one on the lovely e2-square, and has at least as much to worry about.

A2: 6 ♘c3 d6

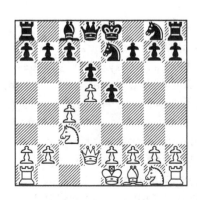

7 e4

7 ♘f3 f5 8 g3 was V.Rao-J.Schuyler, New York 1986 (see below).

7...f5

7...♘f6 is surely playable, hoping for a better opportunity to play ...f7-f5, but I prefer this active move in spite of a few downsides; i.e. weakening the e6-square, and opening the game for White's lousy bishop. Black's rook will soon be enjoying the f-file, and the ♘e7 will gain access to d4 via the f5-square.

After 7...f5, there is only one game in my database, H.Titz-C.Barlocco, Dresden 2004:

8 exf5 ♗xf5 9 ♗d3 ♘f6 10 ♘ge2!

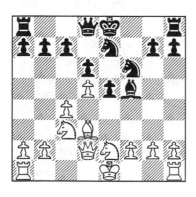

This knight covers the soft f4-square. Instead, ♘f3 is vulnerable to ...♗g4 and will be loose if White finds it necessary to play g2-g3.

10...0-0 11 0-0 ♗xd3 12 ♕xd3 ♘h5

This typical move usually provokes White into playing g2-g3, a long-term weakness.

13 g3 ♕d7 14 f3 a6 15 ♖ad1 ♖ae8 16 ♘e4 h6

An important move: ♘g5-e6 must be prevented.

17 c5 ♘f6 18 ♘2c3

There is nothing wrong with this, but knights that control e4 are not permitted to control d4 as well!

18...♘f5! 19 b4 ♘xe4 20 ♘xe4 g5

This is intended to discourage White from playing f3-f4, which would undermine Black's knight as it arrives on d4.

21 ♔g2 ♘d4

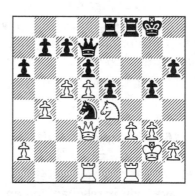

The position has been equal since move six, but somehow Black contrived to win in 75 moves (see Game 20).

It is now my great displeasure to

show V.Rao-J.Schuyler, New York 1986. I had not yet started to use 1...♘c6 regularly, but it seemed like the perfect choice against the straight-laced, booked-up senior master. We pick up after 1 d4 ♘c6 2 c4 e5 3 d5 ♗b4+ 4 ♗d2 ♗xd2+ 5 ♕xd2 ♘ce7 6 ♘c3 d6 7 ♘f3 f5.

8 g3!? ♘f6 9 e4 h6

Generally a useful move, preventing ♘g5 and making ...g7-g5 possible. Here Black prepares to play 10...fxe4.

10 exf5 ♗xf5 11 ♗g2 0-0 12 0-0

I was justifiably happy with my position. *Houdini* prefers Black and suggests ...♕d7, ...♗h7, ...♖f7, ...♖af8. However, I was a 15-year-old expert, therefore...

12...g5?!? 13 h4 g4 14 ♘h2 ♔h7 15 f3 gxf3 16 ♖xf3 ♗g6?! 17 ♖af1 ♘eg8 18 g4 ♕e7 19 h5 ♗e8 20 ♕d3+ ♔g7 21 ♘e4?!

I have been barely hanging on, but there is a light at the end of the tunnel since I will be in good shape if I can reach an endgame. Also, it seems that White's attack is not simple to play.

21...♖f7 22 ♘g3 ♗d7 23 ♕e3 b6 24 g5?!

hxg5 25 ♕xg5+ ♔h8 26 ♘f5 ♗xf5 27 ♖xf5 ♖af8 28 h6 ♕e8

29 ♕g6??

White, short on time and frustrated about being unable to break through, commits a horrible blunder, allowing his queen and rook to be forked. Instead, after 29 ♖xf6!? ♘xf6 30 ♖xf6 ♕e7 31 ♖xf7 ♕xg5 32 ♖xf8+ ♔h7 a crazy endgame arises – presumably White has some advantage.

29...♘h7???

From completely winning to completely losing in one move, as we approach the time control. In my haste I both overlooked the fork and the fact that 29 ♕g6 attacks f7. White's position would have disintegrated completely after 29...♘e7. If you think I'm over this after just 26 years, you would be wrong. I resigned shortly.

B: 4 ♘d2

Considering the pawn structure and the closed position, it will be fine for us to trade off our dark-squared bishop for a knight.

Besides, White's knight would have controlled the important e4-square, a job for which White's dark-squared bishop is uniquely unsuited. I beat future-GM Jesse Kraai (then a senior master) in this variation, though the game doesn't survive. Apparently I am not one of those awesome people who remember every game they have ever played.

4...♘ce7

5 a3

Just about everyone plays this, but White has more challenging moves:

a) 5 ♘f3 and now Black can't play 5...d6?? 6 ♕a4+, so 5...♗xd2+ is nearly forced: 6 ♗xd2 (don't worry about 6 ♕xd2 d6 7 ♕g5 ♘g6 8 ♕xd8+ ♔xd8 9 e4 h6! 10 ♗d3 ♘8e7 11 0-0 f5 with equal chances) 6...d6 7 e4 f5 8 exf5 ♘f6 9 ♗e2 0-0 10 0-0 ♘xf5! with interest in ...e5-e4, or ...a7-a5, ...♘d7, ...♘c5, (...b7-b6), while ...h7-h6 is generally very useful as well. *Houdini* claims that all roads lead to equality, but the fact that he likes 11 ♗c1 a whole bunch seems like a bad omen for White.

b) 5 ♕a4!? was played in B.Avrukh-I.Ben Menachem, Israeli Team Championship 1999 – an annoying move because it pins the d-pawn, complicating the defence of e5 (if Black has to play ...♘g6 in order to guard the pawn, it defeats the purpose of 3...♗b4+). The game continuation 5...c5 6 a3 (6 ♘f3!?) 6...♗xd2+ 7 ♗xd2 ♘f6 8 ♘f3 e4 (8...0-0!?; 8...♘e4!?) 9 ♘h4 0-0 10 d6 was pleasant for White.

Although Black has ways to try to make 5...c5 work, I prefer 5...a5 6 a3 (after 6 ♘f3 e4 7 a3 ♗xd2+ 8 ♘xd2 f5 9 g3 ♘f6 10 ♘b3 0-0 11 ♗h3 d6 12 ♘d4 ♗d7 13 ♕c2 a4 14 0-0 ♕e8 White's bishops barely register as an asset; 15...b5!? is likely to follow) 6...♗xd2+ 7 ♗xd2 ♘f6 8 ♘f3 ♘e4! 9 ♗e3 0-0 10 ♕c2 (10 ♘xe5 ♘f5 11 ♗f4 d6 12 ♘f3 g5 13 ♗c1 ♕f6 14 h3 h5 or 14...♘h4 gives Black considerable pressure for the pawn) 10...♘f6 11 ♘xe5 d6 12 ♘f3 (or 12 ♘d3 ♖e8 13 ♗d2 ♗f5 14 e3 c6 15 dxc6 ♘xc6 and 16...d5) 12...c6! 13 dxc6 ♗f5 14 ♕a4 bxc6 with full compensation; e.g. 15 ♖d1 ♖e8 16 ♗d4 ♘e4 17 e3 c5 18 Bc3 Nxc3 19 bxc3 Ng6 20 Be2 Rb8 21 0-0 Nf4 or 21...Be4!?, or 15 Bd4 Ne4 16 g4!? Bg6 17 h4 h6 with just a big mess.

For the cowardly it is not strictly necessary to sacrifice a pawn: 8...e4 (instead of 8...Ne4!) 9 Nd4 0-0 is playable, though White has a small advantage after 10 Qc2 (or 10 e3 d6 11 Be2 Bg4 12 f3, or 10 g3 c5 11 Nb5 Nf5 12 e3 b6 intending 13...a6, 14...Bxb5 and 15...Nd6) 10...d6 11 g3 c6 12 dxc6 Nxc6 13 Nxc6 bxc6 14 Bg2 d5 15 cxd5 cxd5 16 Bc3.

c) 5 Qc2!? f5 6 Nf3 Bxd2 7 Nxd2 d6 8 e4 Nf6 9 Bd3 was tried in S.Ariste Castano-J.Salgado Gonzalez, Saragossa 1998, at which point Black panicked and played 9...f4?, a decision which led to difficulties since he lacked counterplay against White's big queenside (10 c5! is best). Instead, 9...0-0! 10 exf5 Qe8 is absolutely fine for Black; e.g. 11 f3 Qh5 12 g4?! Qh4+ 13 Kd1 h5 14 g5 Qxg5 15 Ne4 Qxf5 16 Ng5 e4!, or 11 h3 Qh5 12 g4?! Nxg4 13 Be2 Bxf5 14 Qd1 Qh4 15 Bxg4 Bxg4 16 Qxg4 Qxf2+ 17 Kd1 Nf5 18 Ne4 Qd4+ and the suffering of White's king is far greater than our small material investment.

5...Bxd2+ 6 Bxd2

6 Qxd2 d6 7 Qg5 is pointless because of 7...h6! 8 Qxg7?! Ng6 9 Nf3 (White should probably prefer 9 h4! Nf6 10 h5 Rh7 11 Qxh7 Nxh7 12 hxg6 fxg6 13 Rxh6 Nf8 14 Nf3, when 14...c6

or 14...Qd7 gives Black slightly the better chances) 9...Nf6 10 Ng5 Qe7 11 g4 Nxg4 12 Ne4 Bf5 13 Ng3 Bd7 14 Bh3 0-0-0 15 Bxg4 and now in D.Justo-P.German, Buenos Aires 1995, Black spoiled some fine work with 15...Bxg4?! 16 Ne4 Bf5 17 Nf6 which was approximately equal, whereas 15...Rdg8! 16 Bxd7+ Kxd7 17 Nf5 Rxg7 18 Nxe7 Nxe7 would have left him with chances to convert his advantage.

6...d6 7 e4 f5 8 exf5

Since the main line offers White nothing, it makes sense that in M.Gurevich-D.Zoler, Antwerp 1998, White looked for and found something else – 8 Qh5+!? – and was immediately rewarded by 8...Kf8?!, after which Black's static king provided a nice target for Gurevich's kingside storm (see Game 21). Instead, 8...g6 9 Qh4 fxe4 10 f3 exf3 11 Nxf3 Nf5 12 Qxd8 Kxd8 13 Bd3 Nf6 leaves White with enough for the pawn, but no more than that; e.g. 14 0-0 Rf8 15 Rae1 Ke7 (15...Ke8!?, 15...a5!?) and now Mr. H sees nothing better than 16 Ba5 Kd7 17 Bd2 Ke7, repeating position.

8...Bxf5 9 Ne2 Nf6 10 Ng3

Either 10...Bg6, as in E.Arlandi-M.Lanzani, San Marino 1998 (see Game 22), or 10...0-0, as in G.Grigore-P.Brochet, Creon 1999 (see Game 23), is good enough for equality, though in the latter game Black contrived to lose.

Chapter Three
1 d4 ♘c6 2 d5

White takes the bull by the horns – a surprisingly uncommon reaction. It is worth noting that this is how Miles played against his own specialty when he faced Zvonimir Mestrovic.

2...♘e5

White normally chooses between:

A: 3 e4 *43*
B: 3 f4 *46*

Others:

a) After 3 ♘f3 Black may wish to try 3...♘xf3 4 exf3 e5 (or 4...e6 or 4...g6), but I don't care for it – White has de-velopment, space, and open lines in exchange for his anti-positional cap-ture. Simply 3...d6 transposes to 1 d4 ♘c6 2 ♘f3 d6 3 d5 ♘e5 in Chapter One.

b) 3 ♗f4 ♘g6 4 ♗g3 – does the bishop dominate the knight, or does the knight dominate the bishop? In the blitz game E.Bacrot-C.Bauer, Ajaccio 2007, it looked like the latter after 4...♘f6 5 ♘c3 e5 6 e4?! ♗b4 7 ♗d3 d6 8 f3 ♘h5 9 ♗f2 c6! 10 dxc6 bxc6 11 g3 ♗a5 12 f4?! ♘f6 13 f5 ♘e7 14 ♘ge2 ♘g4, when Black has a huge advantage (though he went on to lose). Bauer's method of meeting 3 ♗f4 should be copied exactly. 6 dxe6 is an improve-ment for White, but Black has nothing to fear after 6...fxe6 and 7...♗b4.

c) 3 ♘c3 e6 will soon transpose to other lines in this chapter; e.g. 4 dxe6 fxe6 5 e4 (see line A) or 4 f4 ♘g6 5 dxe6 fxe6 6 e4 (see 6 ♘c3!? in line B).

A: 3 e4 e6

Mestrovic played 3...d6!? 4 f4 ♘d7 5 ♘c3 c6 and went on to draw with GM

Drasko (Game 24). Black has also scored well with 3...♘g6?!, which can transpose into lines considered below, but his position is highly suspect after 4 h4!.

4 dxe6!

4 f4?! is seen here most often and seemed fine the first 55 times it was used, but on the 56th, the German master Lutz Diebl played 4...exd5! and drew with GM Gyimesi in the Bundesliga. Bravo! If White takes the knight, Black draws by perpetual: 5 fxe5 ♕h4+ 6 ♔e2 ♕h5+ 7 ♔d2 ♕h6+ 8 ♔c3 ♕c6+ 9 ♔d3 ♕a6+ etc.

If 6 g3?, as Gyimesi actually played, then 6...♕xe4+ 7 ♕e2 ♕xh1 8 ♘f3 b6 9 ♘c3 and now, rather than Diebl's premature 9...♗a6?, the preliminary 9...c6! maintains Black's nearly winning advantage (10...♗a6 is still coming to extricate the queen).

Meanwhile, White doesn't need to go in for Gyimesi's contortions (Gyimnastics?) to avoid a forced draw; he can play 5 exd5 or 5 ♕xd5, although he cannot hope for an opening advantage after such concessions. The best re-

sponse is 5 ♘c3! ♘g6 6 ♕xd5 ♘f6 7 ♕d3 ♗c5 8 ♗e3 ♕e7 9 0-0-0 0-0 10 ♘f3 with a small advantage for White.

Diebls's 4...exd5 was tested again in V.Erdos-R.Rapport, Hungarian Team Championship 2012, to produce another entertaining draw (see Game 25).

If it is Black who is keen to avoid the draw, he needs to forego 4...exd5 and play 4...♘g6, transposing to positions considered in line B below.

4...fxe6

This recapture is certainly dynamic, although the somewhat exposed position of Black's king requires careful treatment.

Many players prefer 4...dxe6 5 ♕xd8+ ♔xd8, but Black's results have been poor – pretty much draws and losses. Nonetheless, Short made it look easy to defend in S.Gordon-N.Short, British Championship 2011, so his method could certainly be tried (see Game 26); and M.Gurevich-M.Rohde, Philadelphia (blitz) 1989, shows that it is possible for Black to win if White overextends (see Game 27).

5 ♘c3

This flexible move makes it hard for Black to activate his f8-bishop, since 5...♗c5?? loses to 6 ♕h5+ and 5...♗b4? is met by 6 ♕d4!, targeting Black's loose bits on b4, e5, and g7.

Alternatively:

a) 5 f4 ♘g6 is line B below. 5...♘f7!? and 5...♘c6!? are fine too, but no better than the text.

b) 5 ♘f3 ♘xf3 6 ♕xf3 ♕f6 is already equal according to Kalinin, but 7 ♕g3 will gain some advantage – White's queen is active while Black's is mainly awkward. Therefore, just 5...♘f7 which is similar to the main line (and transposes after 6 ♘c3 b6).

c) 5 ♗f4 is untried but should lead White to a normal plus; e.g. 5...♘g6 (5...♘f7!?) 6 ♗g3 ♗c5 7 ♘c3 a6 8 ♘f3 ♘h6 9 ♕d2 0-0 10 0-0-0 d6 11 h4 b5.

d) 5 ♗e3?! ♘f6 6 ♘c3 ♗b4 7 ♗d4?! ♘c6 8 a3 ♗a5 9 e5 ♘xd4 10 ♕xd4 ♘d5 is a pleasant position for Black.

5...b6!

The fastest way for Black to mobilize. The fianchettoed bishop is active and occupies a diagonal which may soon be lengthened by White's e4-e5. 5...♘c6!?, as recommended by *Rybka 3*, is also possible – after all, the knight retreats sooner or later, and c6 is not a bad square.

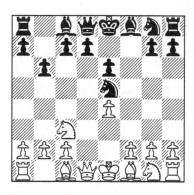

6 ♘f3

V.Burmakin-J.Ulko, Moscow 1995, continued 6 ♗f4 ♘g6?! 7 ♗g3 ♗b7 8 h4 h5?!, and after the simple 9 ♘f3 White would have been much better. Instead, 6...♘f7 7 ♘f3 ♗b4! 8 ♗d3 ♗xc3 9 bxc3 ♗b7 10 0-0 ♘f6 11 ♖e1 0-0 12 e5 ♘d5 13 ♗d2 c5 14 ♕e2 c4! 15 ♗xc4 ♖c8 16 ♗b3 ♕c7 is only a bit better for White.

6...♘f7!

It is a bad idea to activate White's queen with 6...♘xf3+, as tried by B.Savchenko.

7 ♗c4?!

Instead:

a) 7 ♗f4 transposes to 6 ♗f4 ♘f7 7 ♘f3 above.

b) 7 ♗d3 is stronger – at this stage White is more likely to play e5 than Black is. After 7...♗b7 8 0-0 ♘f6 9 ♕e2

♗b4 10 ♖e1 ♘g4! 11 h3 ♘ge5 12 ♘xe5 ♘xe5 13 ♕h5+ ♘f7 14 ♗f4 ♗xc3 15 bxc3 g6 16 ♕g4 ♕e7 White has a small advantage, though he has long-term concerns about his pawn structure. Black still has a useful choice as to where he should castle. 17...♕c5 is usually a good move.

7...♗b7 8 ♕e2 a6

This useful little move prevents ♘b5 and ♗a6, while preparing ...b6-b5-b4.

9 ♗b3 ♗b4

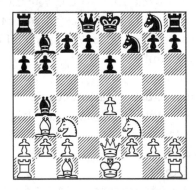

Here 9...♘f6?! was played in C.Crouch-A.Karpatchev, Cappelle la Grande, 1993, starting complications which objectively favour White. The straight-

forward 9...♗b4 can also lead to complications – e.g. 10 0-0 ♘f6 11 ♖d1 ♕e7 12 e5 ♗xc3 13 bxc3 ♘e4 14 ♖d4 ♘xc3 15 ♕d3 ♘d5 – but here Black is fine.

B: 3 f4 ♘g6

4 e4

Other moves:

a) 4 h4 is an interesting attempt to take advantage of Black's inflexible knight. In the expert section of the 1985 New York Open, I fell for White's trap and played 4...e5? 5 h5! ♘xf4!? 6 e3, though I went on to win an ugly miniature with 6...♕g5! 7 ♕f3 ♘xd5 8 ♕xd5 ♕g3+ 9 ♔d1 d6 10 ♗b5+ ♔d8 11 ♕xf7 ♘f6 12 ♘f3?? ♕xg2 13 ♖f1 ♗g4 14 ♗e2 ♕xf1+! 15 ♗xf1 ♗xf3+ 16 ♗e2 ♗d5 (trapping White's queen) 0-1. Hilarious!

Instead, 4...e6! 5 h5 ♘6e7 6 c4!? (6 dxe6 fxe6 7 e4 d5 transposes to 6 h4 d5 7 h5 ♘6e7 in the notes to Position Three below) 6...♘f6 7 ♘c3 ♘f5 8 ♕d3 (if 8 dxe6 fxe6 9 g4, then 9...♘xg4!? 10 e4 ♘fe3 or 10...♘fh6 is possible, but relatively simplest is 9...♘g3 10 ♖h3

♘xf1 11 g5 ♘xh5 12 ♖xh5 ♘g3 13 ♖h3 ♘f5 14 e4 ♘d6 15 ♘f3 ♘xc4 16 ♘h4 ♖g8 17 ♕h5+ g6 18 ♕xh7 ♖g7 19 ♕h6 ♖g8 with a draw) 8...♗c5! 9 e4 ♘g4 is fine for Black, according to Mr. H, though there are some crazy variations to consider:

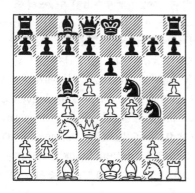

a1) 10 exf5 ♘f2 11 ♕g3 ♘xh1 12 ♕xg7 ♕h4+ 13 ♔d2 (or 13 ♔d1 ♕g4+! 14 ♕xg4 ♘f2+) 13...♖f8 14 ♘ge2 ♘f2 15 ♘b5 ♗b6 16 d6 ♕xh5 17 fxe6 ♘e4+ 18 ♔c2 ♘xd6 is in Black's favour.

a2) 10 dxe6 ♘f2 11 ♕d5 (not 11 exf7+? ♔f8 12 ♕d5 ♘xh1) 11...d6 12 ♕xf5 ♗xe6 13 ♕xc5 dxc5 14 ♔xf2 ♗xc4 with an unbalanced but roughly equal position.

a3) 10 ♘d1 ♘fh6 11 dxe6 f5! 12 ♗e2 ♕e7! with excellent play for the pawn.

b) 4 f5 overextends: 4...♘e5 5 ♗f4 d6 6 e4 g6! (in practice, Black has played 6...♘f6?! or 6...e6? but it is best to challenge White's space immediately) 7 ♘f3 ♗g7 8 ♗b5+ ♗d7 9 ♗xe5 ♗xe5 10 ♗xd7+ ♕xd7 11 ♘xe5 dxe5 12 0-0 ♘f6 with equality; e.g. 13 ♕d3 c6 14 c4 cxd5 15 cxd5 ♖c8 16 ♘c3 0-0.

c) 4 ♘f3 is legal and was in fact the move order for Onischuk-Shkuro mentioned below (see note 'e' to Position Three). 4...e6 5 dxe6 fxe6 6 e4 transposes to the main line, while 5 c4 ♗c5 will not bring White any happiness.

4...e5

4...e6 may transpose after 5 fxe6, or it may turn into a kind of mirrored Alekhine, which usually works badly for White because of the weak a7-g1 diagonal; e.g. 5 c4?! exd5 6 cxd5 ♗c5 or 5 ♘f3 exd5 6 exd5?! ♗c5. However, 5 ♘c3! exd5 6 ♕xd5! ♘f6 7 ♕d3 ♗c5 8 ♗e3 ♕e7 9 0-0-0 0-0 10 ♘f3 is better for White (though Black is still okay).

5 dxe6!

White's only good move.

a) 5 f5? could lead to the position mentioned in the introduction to this book after 5...♕h4+ 6 ♔d2 ♕xe4 7 fxg6 ♕xd5+ 8 ♔e1 ♕xd1+ 9 ♔xd1 hxg6, assessed as unclear by Bogoljubow. The endgame is favourable to Black, but that is a moot point because 6...♘f6! is even stronger – as one of my students, Matthew Shih, was kind enough to point out to me last year.

a1) 7 fxg6? ♘xe4+ 8 ♔e2 ♕f2+ 9 ♔d3 ♘c5+ 10 ♔c3 ♘a4+ 11 ♔b3 ♕b6+ 12 ♔c4 ♕a6+! 13 ♔b3 ♘c5+ 14 ♔c3 ♘e4+ 15 ♔b3 ♕b6+ 16 ♔c4 ♕b4+ 17 ♔d3 ♘f2+ wins White's queen.

a2) 7 ♘c3 ♗b4 8 fxg6 ♘xe4+ 9 ♔e2 ♕f2+ 10 ♔d3 f5 (10...♗xc3 11 ♔xe4! ♗a5 12 c3 hxg6 13 ♔d3 d6 14 ♔c4 ♗f5 15 ♕e2 ♕b6 may be better, but it's far more complicated, as Black will still be down material for some time) 11 ♘xe4 ♕d4+ 12 ♔e2 ♕xe4+ 13 ♗e3 f4 14 ♕d3 ♕xe3+ also leaves Black much better.

a3) 7 ♕f3 ♘xe4+ 8 ♔e2 ♘f4+ 9 ♗xf4 ♕xf4 10 ♕xf4 exf4 11 ♔f3 ♘f6 12 ♘c3 ♗b4 13 ♘ge2 (13 ♖e1+ ♔f8 14 ♗c4 b5! 15 ♗xb5 ♗b7) 13...d6 14 ♔xf4 h5! is relatively best, but still very good for Black.

b) 5 ♘f3? is apparently tempting (it has been played several times), but after 5...exf4 6 ♘c3 ♗c5 7 ♗d3 ♕e7! 8 ♕e2 d6 9 ♘a4 (9 ♗d2?! a6! is even worse) 9...♗b6 10 ♗d2 ♘f6 White has far too little for the pawn.

c) 5 ♕f3 exf4 6 ♘c3 (6 ♗xf4 ♘xf4 7 ♕xf4 ♕f6 8 ♕xf6 ♘xf6 leaves Black with a superior pawn structure and White with an acute shortage of dark-squared bishops) 6...♗c5 7 ♗xf4 ♘xf4 8 ♕xf4 ♕f6 9 ♕g3 d6 10 ♗b5+ ♔f8 11 ♘f3 ♕g6 and Black can look forward to a long and pleasant endgame.

d) 5 ♘e2 (or 5 ♘h3) 5...exf4 6 ♘xf4 ♗d6! already puts the enemy kingside under pressure: 7 ♘xg6?! hxg6 8 ♕f3 ♕h4+ 9 ♔d1 ♘f6 10 ♗d3 ♗e5 is obviously not satisfactory for White, but 7 ♕f3 ♘f6 8 ♘c3 0-0 9 ♗d3 leaves Black with several good ideas, the simplest being 9...♗e5 (9...c6!? 9...♘e5!?) 10 0-0 d6 11 h3 c5, when Black's activity and strong e5-point give him the advantage.

5...fxe6

The endgame after 5...dxe6 6 ♕xd8+ ♔xd8 is playable in theory, but with Black's slightly misplaced g6-knight, it is less appealing than the similar ending in line A (without 3 f4 ♘g6). In practice, Black's results are quite poor.

Instead, 5...fxe6 brings us to:

Position Three

Not to put too fine a point on it, but the players who have reached this position with the black pieces need collectively to have their heads examined. White's main asset is his powerful pawn duo on e4 and f4. Black's main asset is his central pawn majority. One need notice only one of these two things in order to come up with the correct plan (or at least the correct sixth move) for Black. In fact, I'm not even going to insult my readers by saying it out loud, so if you still don't know, see Wood-Penrose below and then read *Pawn Power in Chess* by Hans Kmoch.

Instead of taking the opportunity to strike in the centre, Black has generally been seduced by 6...♗c5, occupying the a7-g1 diagonal, presumably to stop White from castling. Naturally this is less important than the central battle and, what's worse, it doesn't even work. If White finds the bishop troublesome, he can trade it off with a timely ♘a4 or ♕e2 and ♗e3. To add insult to injury, White is usually better off castled long anyway. Sometimes 7...♗c5 is a good idea (or 7...♗b4+ 8 c3 ♗c5), but if there is a knight on c3, it is much better to put pressure on White's centre with 7...♗b4, which prepares ...♘f6-e4.

Black's e4-knight can be a very annoying piece. As we see in the following analysis, White's light squares are usually too weak (because he has had to play g2-g3) to allow him to eliminate the knight comfortably with ♗d3 and

♗xe4, even if this wins a pawn.

Let's get to the analysis.

6 ♘f3

Other moves:

a) 6 ♗d3 is less popular and less successful. Then Black has done fine with 6...♗c5, but 6...d5! is more accurate, as in B.Wood-J.Penrose, Southend 1957(!),

which continued 7 e5 ♘h6 8 ♗e3?!, and now not the game's 8...♘f5?! 9 ♗xf5 exf5 10 ♘f3 ♗e7?! (10...c5!) 11 c4 which is good for White, but instead 8...♘h4! 9 ♕e2 c5! and Black is better.

No better is 7 ♘c3 ♗b4 8 ♗d2 ♘h6 9 ♘f3 0-0 10 g3, when Black gently plays 10...e5!! and lets White try to work out the details with his king in the centre. The correct solution is 11 ♘xd5 ♗xd2+ 12 ♕xd2 c6 13 ♘e3 exf4 14 ♗c4+ ♔h8 15 ♕xd8 ♖xd8 16 gxf4 ♘xf4 17 ♖g1 b5 with equality. According to *Houdini*, 11 f5 dxe4 12 ♘xe4 ♗xd2 13 ♕xd2 ♗xf5 14 0-0-0 ♕e7 is also equal, but to me it looks a lot like White is down a pawn for nothing. Fortunately, it's not really our problem.

b) 6 ♗e3 is seldom played – although it prevents ...♗c5, White's important dark-squared bishop is vulnerable:

6...d5 (of course) 7 g3 (7 ♘c3 ♗b4 8 ♕d3 ♗xc3 9 ♕xc3 ♘f6 10 0-0-0 0-0 11 exd5 exd5 12 ♘f3 ♗g4 is equal) 7...c5! 8 ♘d2 ♕b6 9 ♖b1 (sad, but there's really nothing better: 9 f5 exf5 10 exd5 ♘f6 11 ♕e2 ♗e7 12 ♘c4 ♕a6 13 d6 b5! or 13 ♗xc5 0-0 14 d6 ♗d8 15 d7 ♗xd7 16 ♗xf8 ♘xf8 gives Black more than enough for a small exchange; while 9 ♗d3 ♗e7 10 ♘gf3 ♘h6 11 ♕e2 ♘g4 12 exd5 exd5 13 ♗g1 0-0 14 0-0-0 ♗d6 15 h3 ♘f6 is fine for Black) 9...♗d7 10 ♘gf3 ♘f6 11 e5 ♘g4 12 ♗g1 ♕c7 13 c4! d4 14 ♗d3 ♗c6 15 h3 ♘h6 16 ♗f2 ♗e7 17 0-0 0-0 18 b4 b6 19 ♘e4. White's play makes an excellent impression, but here Black has 19...♘xf4! 20 gxf4 ♖xf4 21 ♕e2 ♘f5 22 ♖b3 ♖f8, which reverses the initiative at the cost of a small material investment. *Houdini* calls it equal, but if I had the choice, I'd sit behind the black pieces.

c) 6 g3 d5 7 ♘f3 transposes to 6 ♘f3 d5 7 g3 below.

d) 6 h4!? has never been played, but it's a venomous move. The tactical justification is 6...♘xh4? 7 ♕g4! ♗e7 (7...♘g6 8 ♖xh7) 8 ♕xg7 with a large advantage for White. Correct is the anti-shocker 6...d5 even though 7 h5 ♘6e7 blocks the f8-bishop. After 8 ♘f3 ♘c6 9 ♘c3 ♗b4 10 ♗d2 ♘f6 11 e5 ♗xc3 12 ♗xc3 ♘e4 13 ♗d3 ♘xc3 14 bxc3 Black gets out of Dodge with 14...♕e7 15 ♘g5 ♗d7 16 ♗xh7 0-0-0, when White has space and a pawn, but is badly overextended with nowhere for his king. I will utter a naughty word: unclear.

e) The rare 6 ♘c3!? is logical, fighting for the d5-square, but Black forces ...d7-d5 anyway with 6...♗b4! 7 ♘e2 (other moves, such as 7 ♘f3 and 7 ♗d3, transpose elsewhere) 7...d5 8 ♕d3 c6 9 ♗d2 ♘f6 (after 9...dxe4 10 ♕xd8 ♔xd8 11 a3 ♗a5 White is a little better in the endgame) 10 e5 ♘g4 11 h3 ♘h6 12 0-0-0 0-0 13 g4 b5 14 ♔b1 ♗c5 15 ♗g2 a5 and although White had a head start in the race, it is difficult for him to advance further. Then 16 ♘d4!? ♕b6 17 ♘xc6 ♗b7 18 ♘xd5 exd5 19 ♘xa5 ♘xf4 20 ♗xf4 ♕xa5 21 ♗xd5+ ♔h8 22 ♗xh6 gxh6 is certainly complicated, but not unfavourable to Black.

The text move, 6 ♘f3, is by far the most common – apparently with good reason since White has won the last five games in a row from this position, most notably A.Onischuk-I.Shkuro, Ukrainian Team Championship 2009, which is a perfect example of what Black must avoid (see Game 28). Clearly we need some new and improved ideas.

6...d5!

This move is part of my original analysis that dates back to 1986, and inspired the above variations. In twenty-five opportunities, Black has somehow failed to try this, so we analyse in a vacuum. For most players, the following lines need hardly be memorized, but offer an excellent opportunity to get acquainted with the wide variety of plans for both sides.

7 ♘c3

a) The first thing I realized 26 years ago was that 7 f5?! is not a problem: 7...dxe4 8 ♕xd8+ ♔xd8 9 ♘g5 exf5 10 ♘f7+ ♔e8 11 ♘xh8 ♘xh8 12 ♘c3 c6 13 ♗c4 (13 g4!?) 13...♘f6 14 ♗e3 ♗d6 is a bit better for Black. As it turns out, 7...exf5 is also okay: 8 exd5 ♘f6 9 ♘c3 ♗b4 10 ♕e2+ ♔f7! 11 ♘g5+ ♔g8 12 ♗d2 ♗xc3 13 ♗xc3 ♘xd5 14 ♗d2 h6 15 ♘f3 ♔h7 16 0-0-0 ♖e8 and it is White who has the hard job of proving full

compensation.

Notice that Black isn't actually threatening 7...dxe4, so White has an array of options:

b) 7 e5 may not be best, but it is certainly critical.

White plans ♘g5 and ♘xh7, an argument he will try to enhance with h4-h5, ♗d3, or ♕h5. This plan is indeed dangerous, especially if Black is castled on that side of the board. However, Black does not skip his turns, and as long as White is pursuing this plan he is neither developing quickly nor attending to his own king. For instance, 7...♘h6! 8 g3 (or 8 ♗e3 ♘g4 9 ♕d2 ♘xe3 10 ♕xe3 ♕e7! 11 ♘c3 ♕b4) 8...c5 9 ♘g5 ♗e7 10 ♘xh7 (after 10 ♗b5+ ♔f8 White has to worry about both 11...c4 and 11...♘xe5) 10...♘f5 11 ♕h5 ♔f7, when Black has good compensation after White's failed attack; e.g. 12 ♘c3 ♔g8 13 ♘f6+ ♗xf6 14 ♕xg6 ♗e7 15 ♗g2 c4 16 0-0 ♖h6 17 ♕g4 ♕b6+ 18 ♔h1 ♗d7 and White is having trouble with development, the centre, and his king, which doesn't leave much to be happy about. There is also 8 h4!? ♗c5 9 h5 (or 9 ♗d3 ♘g4 when, according to *Houdini*, White has nothing better than 10 ♘d4 ♘h6 11 ♘f3, with a repetition) 9...♘e7 10 ♘g5 ♘hf5 11 ♕d3 h6 12 g4 ♘d4 13 c3 ♘dc6 14 ♘f3 a5! with equal chances. Black intends ...b7-b6, ...♗a6 (...♗b7), ...♕d7 (or ...d5-d4, ...♕d5), and will have the choice of which side to castle. White may enjoy his space, but may also find himself overextended.

Hold on: what's so great about 7...♘h6 - ?

I used to have problems in this position in blitz games because I didn't know the proper arrangement for the pieces – especially whether to play 7...♗c5 or 7...c5, and also whether to play ...♘h6 or ...♘8e7. As it turns out, it is not yet clear whether it is the bishop or the pawn that belongs on c5, so it makes sense to wait on that decision, but the knight is just about always best on the h6-square. All of ...♘g4, ...♘f5, and ...♘f7 are useful options from there, and it can hold up White's g- and f-pawns. Just as important, developing

the knight to h6 avoids a traffic jam on the e7-square, which may be needed for Black's other knight, not to mention the bishop and queen. (You may now resume your normal programming.)

c) The immediate 7 h4!? is also possible, but Black is already fine after 7...♗b4+! 8 c3 (not 8 ♗d2? dxe4!) 8...♗c5 9 h5 ♘6e7; e.g. 10 b4 ♗b6 11 c4!? dxc4 12 ♕xd8+ ♔xd8 13 ♗b2 (not 13 ♘g5? ♗d4!) 13...exf3 14 ♗xg7 ♘f5 15 ♗xh8 f2+ 16 ♔d2 ♘g3 17 c5 ♘xh1 18 cxb6 axb6 19 ♘c3 ♘e7, which is certainly no worse for Black.

d) 7 ♗d3 allows us to surprise White with 7...dxe4! 8 ♗xe4 ♕xd1+ 9 ♔xd1 ♘f6 10 ♗xg6 hxg6.

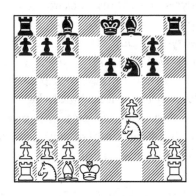

Although our pawns are vile, our bishop pair and overall activity are quite enough, particularly since the enemy king is a bit loose; e.g. 11 ♘bd2 ♗d6 12 ♘c4 b5 13 ♘ce5 ♗b7 14 ♔e2 ♗xe5 15 fxe5 ♘d7 and Black is more comfortable because of White's bad bishop; or 11 ♗e3?! ♗d6 12 ♘c3 ♘g4 13 ♔e2 0-0! 14 g3?! (14 ♗c1!) 14...b6! and suddenly White is in big trouble; or

11 ♘c3 ♗d7 12 ♘e5 (12 ♔e2 ♗d6! 13 ♘e5 ♗xe5 14 fxe5 ♘g4 nets a pawn) 12...0-0-0!! 13 ♘f7 ♗c6+ 14 ♘xd8 ♔xd8 15 h4 ♗xg2 16 ♖h2 ♗f3+ 17 ♔e1 ♗c5 and how is White going to untangle himself without shedding any material?

e) 7 c4!? does force 7...dxe4, but weakens White's position as well: 8 ♕xd8 ♔xd8 9 ♘g5 ♔e8 10 ♘xe4 ♘f6 11 ♗d3 b6 12 ♘bc3 ♗b7 13 0-0 ♖d8 and Black is comfortably equal.

f) 7 g3

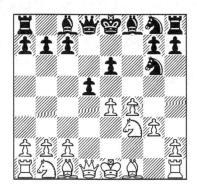

7...♗c5 (7...♗b4+ 8 c3 ♗c5 9 ♕e2 ♕e7 10 ♘bd2 ♘h6 11 ♘g5 0-0 12 h4 ♖e8 is okay, too) 8 ♕e2 (8 ♘c3 ♘f6! 9 e5 ♘g4 10 ♘d4 0-0 11 ♕xg4 ♗xd4 12 ♗d2 c5! 13 0-0-0 ♕b6 with equal chances) 8...♘f6 9 e5 ♘e4 10 ♗e3 ♗xe3 11 ♕xe3 ♘e7! 12 ♗d3 ♗d7 13 ♘bd2 ♘xd2 14 ♘xd2 (14 ♕xd2 c5) 14...0-0 15 0-0 ♘f5 and with 16...♕e7 (or 16...b6) and 17...c5 coming, Black has sufficient counterplay.

g) 7 exd5?! exd5 8 ♗d3 makes no sense – it surrenders the centre and activates Black's problem piece, the c8-

bishop. Unsurprisingly Black has many ways to play: 8...♗g4 9 0-0 ♗c5+ 10 ♔h1 ♘8e7 11 h3 ♗xf3 12 ♕xf3 0-0 seems simplest, or Black can enter an equal endgame with 8...♗b4+ and 9...♕e7+.

7...♗b4

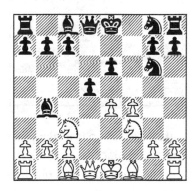

8 g3

White usually finds it necessary to play this sooner or later. Otherwise:

a) 8 ♗d3 ♗xc3 9 bxc3 dxe4 10 ♗xe4 ♕xd1+ 11 ♔xd1 ♘f6 12 ♗d3 0-0 13 ♖e1 ♘g4 14 ♗xg6 hxg6 15 h3 ♘f6 16 ♘e5 ♘h5 17 ♘xg6 ♘f6 18 ♘e7+ ♔f7 19 ♘xc8 ♘xf4! with equal chances.

b) 8 e5 ♘8e7 (8...c5 isn't bad either) 9 g3 0-0 10 ♗d3 c5 and Black's good centre and rapid deployment ensure that he will not be rolled up on the kingside and that his chances are not worse.

c) 8 ♕d3!? ♗xc3+! 9 ♕xc3 ♘f6 10 e5 ♘e4 11 ♕a3 ♕e7 12 ♕xe7 ♘xe7 13 ♗d3 b6 14 ♗xe4 dxe4 15 ♘g5 h6 16 ♘xe4 ♗b7 17 ♘c3 ♘f5 18 0-0 0-0-0 and Black has the d-file, while White's c1-bishop is a huge problem, a situation which fully compensates for the pawn.

8...♘f6! 9 ♗d2 0-0 10 e5 ♗xc3 11 ♗xc3 ♘e4 12 ♗d3 b6!

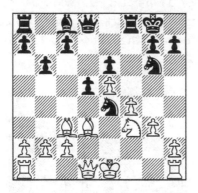

White's c3-bishop is a silly piece – at the moment Black is far better off keeping the e4-knight and blocking the other bishop.

a) 13 ♗xe4 dxe4 14 ♘g5 is pointless because of 14...h6! 15 ♘xe4?! ♗b7 16 ♕e2 ♕d5 17 ♘f2 ♘xf4! 18 gxf4 ♖xf4 19 ♖f1 (not 19 ♖d1?! ♖xf2!) 19...♖af8 20 ♗d2 (still not 20 ♖d1?! ♕xa2! 21 ♖d7 ♕a4 22 ♖xc7 ♗g2 and White is toast) 20...♖f3 21 a4 ♖8f5 22 0-0-0 ♖xe5 23 ♕xf3 ♕xf3 24 ♘d3 ♕d5 25 ♘xe5 ♕xe5 26 ♗c3 ♕e3+ 27 ♔b1 ♗d5 28 h4 g5 with some advantage to Black.

b) 13 ♕e2 ♗b7 14 0-0-0 ♕e8 15 ♗xe4 dxe4 16 ♘g5 e3 17 ♖he1 h6 18 ♘f3 ♘e7 19 ♕xe3 ♘d5 with enough play for the pawn; e.g. 20 ♕d3 a5 21 ♘d2 ♘b4! or 21 ♘d4 a4 22 a3 c5 23 ♘e2 b5.

c) 13 0-0 ♘e7 14 ♕e2 ♗b7 (14...♘c5? 15 ♗xh7+ is too strong) 15 ♖ad1 ♕e8 is equal.

Section Two
1 e4 ♞c6

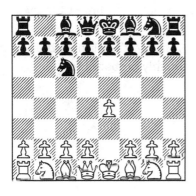

One might argue that it makes more sense to play the Dark Knight against 1 e4 than 1 d4, because the dangerous move 2 d5 is no longer available. On the other hand, White, as a 1 e4 player, is more likely to be familiar with the possible transpositions to the Scotch and the Pirc. Personally, I find the second argument to be more compelling than the first (for a decade I played 1 d4 Nc6 with *no* plan for defending the Scotch), but the reader can make up his own mind, or better yet just play 1...♞c6 against everything!

2 d4 (including The Scotch) – Chapter Four
2 ♞f3 (the Dark Knight Pirc) – Chapter Five
2 ♞c3 – Chapter Six

Other moves:

a) 2 ♗c4 commits the bishop way too early: 2...♞f6 3 ♞c3 e6! 4 d3 ♗b4 5 ♗d2 d5 6 exd5 exd5 7 ♗b5 0-0 8 ♞ge2 ♞e5! 9 a3 ♗d6 10 ♗g5 c6! was P.Cruz-A.Kogan, Lisbon 2000. Black has a big advantage, largely due to having shut White's light-squared bishop out of play.

b) 2 f4 is not as bad as it looks. 2...d5! 3 exd5 ♛xd5 4 ♞c3 leads to a bizarre kind of Scandinavian. Fortunately, 4...♛e6+! is more awkward for White than it is for Black; e.g. 5 ♗e2 ♞d4! or 5 ♛e2 ♞b4! or 5 ♞ge2 ♞d4! 6 d3 ♞f6 7 ♞e4 ♞f5 8 c3 g6 (8...♞xe4 9 ♛a4+) with some advantage to Black in all cases, according to *Houdini*.

3 e5 is a good Nimzowitsch Defence

for Black since White's pawn does not belong on f4 (at least until ...f7-f6 is played). In R.Barkman-S.Lejlic, Karlskrona 1997, Black used this to good effect: 3...♘h6 4 d4 ♗g4 5 ♗e2 ♗xe2 6 ♘xe2 ♘f5 7 c3 e6 8 ♕d3 h5 (8...♕h4+!) 9 ♘d2?! ♕h4+ with advantage due to White's light-square problems – White decided to pitch a pawn with 10 ♘g3 ♕xf4 11 ♘xf5 ♕xf5 12 ♕xf5 exf5, but he had no compensation.

Alternatively, Black can throw a clog in White's machinery with 3...g5!? 4 d4 gxf4 5 ♗xf4 ♗f5 6 c3 ♕d7 7 ♘f3 h5 8 ♗e2 0-0-0 9 ♘h4 ♗g4 10 ♘d2 ♗h6 as in H.Gohlke-S.Wiezer, Gorlitz 1985,

with a small advantage according to *New In Chess*. Actually, I don't believe Black is better, but the position is interesting and Black has the makings of a kingside attack. Wisnewski's recommendation is 3...d4!? – one idea is to clear the d5-square for Black's queen, but I am not keen on relinquishing control over e4.

For those who are interested, 2...e5 3 ♘f3 f5!? is the Adelaide Counter-Gambit, a wild and fascinating defence to the King's Gambit, but truly outside the scope of this book. Besides, there is also 3 ♘c3, with wildness that White is presumably prepared for.

Chapter Four
1 e4 ♞c6 2 d4 e5

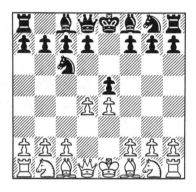

Now White has:

A: 3 d5 *57*
B: 3 dxe5 *73*
C: 3 ♘f3 *79* – The Scotch

On 3 c3, Black can transpose to a Ponziani with 3...♘f6 4 ♘f3; but 3...d5 4 dxe5 dxe4 5 ♕xd8 ♘xd8 is simpler and equal, while for a more interesting endgame Black can play 4...♗e6!? 5 exd5 ♕xd5 6 ♕xd5 ♗xd5 with full compensation; e.g. 7 f4 f6 8 exf6 ♘xf6 9 c4 ♗e6 10 ♘f3 0-0-0 11 ♘c3 ♘b4 with a large advantage to Black.

A: 3 d5 ♘ce7

White normally chooses between:

A1: 4 ♘f3 *58*
A2: 4 c4?! *62*

Others:

a) 4 f4? is a fairly common mistake at amateur level. The apparently hard-to-spot 4...♘g6! transposes to 1 d4 ♘c6 2 d5 ♘e5 3 f4 ♘g6 4 e4 e5 with the difference that White's only good move, 5 dxe6 *en passant*, is not permitted by the rules. How unfortunate! White does not have my sympathy though, since

4...exf4?! 5 ♗xf4 ♘g6 is also lousy.

b) Miles had a wonderful answer to 4 ♗e3 in 4...f5!?, with which he drew with Beliavsky and beat Campora (see Games 29 and 30). The point is to take advantage of the newly moved bishop, which is vulnerable to both ...f5-f4 and 5 exf5 ♘xf5. If Black does not play 4...f5, White may be able to stop the f8-dark bishop from developing comfortably, e.g. 4...♘g6 5 a3!?, though 5...b6 is satisfactory for Black.

c) 4 ♘c3 ♘g6 5 ♗e3 ♘f6 (5...♗b4!?) 6 a3 is very lightly tested. Then 6...b6 7 ♘f3 ♗c5 is fine, when 8 ♗xc5 bxc5 9 d6?! 0-0 and 10...♗b7 is at least equal.

d) 4 d6 has been played a few times and Black usually just takes, which is fine – but I prefer 4...♘g6, accelerating development after 5 dxc7 ♕xc7; e.g. 6 ♘c3 ♗b4 7 ♘e2 (after 7 ♗d2?! ♗xc3! 8 ♗xc3 ♘f6 9 ♗d3 0-0 10 ♘e2 ♖d8 and 11...d5, Black is better) 7...♘f6 8 a3 ♗c5 9 b4 ♗b6 and Black is fine, since 10 ♘b5?! runs into 10...♗xf2+ 11 ♔xf2 ♕b6+.

A1: 4 ♘f3 ♘g6

4...d6 is recommended by De Firmian in *MCO14* as a way to keep the play obscure. In my opinion, the reverse is true: 4...d6 will transpose to Pirc or King's Indian-type positions, whereas 4...♘g6 maintains a unique "Kevitzian" flavour. Furthermore, 4...d6?! 5 c4! ♘f6 6 ♘c3 g6 runs into 7 c5! which is indeed a certain kind of King's Indian – the bad kind.

After the text White has two important moves:

A11: 5 h4! *59*
A12: 5 ♗e3 *61*

After other moves, Black is already a statistical favourite, reaching positions similar to line A2.

a) 5 ♘c3 ♘f6 6 ♗g5?! (this is wrong, as usual; it was not too late for 6 h4! h5, though this is rarely played here) 6...h6! (Black can wait, but putting the question immediately places the most pressure on White to follow through with this ill-conceived exchange) 7 ♗xf6 ♕xf6 8 g3 ♗c5 9 ♗h3 a6 and Black is already a bit better due to his powerful dark-squared bishop – and if White doesn't prepare the exchange of light-squared bishops Black has a comfortable advantage.

b) 5 ♗d3 ♗c5 6 0-0 ♘f6 7 ♘c3 c6?! 8 ♘a4 ♗e7 was Y.Dembo-R.Goldin, Petah Tiqwa 1996, which Black went on to win – even so he should have preserved the bishop on the diagonal with 7...a6 or 7...a5.

A11: 5 h4!

This is the way to start posing problems for Black and his knight on g6.

5...h5

Black is forced to weaken his kingside or accept an extremely cramped position. But let's not forget that White has also weakened his kingside.

6 ♗g5

Alternatively:

a) 6 ♘c3 ♘f6 7 ♘g5!? (7 ♗g5 transposes to the main line) 7...♗b4! 8 ♗e2 d6 9 ♕d3 ♗d7 10 a3, and instead of 10...♗xc3+ as in M.Kravtsiv-K.Tarlev, Evpatoria 2007 (see Game 31), I prefer 10...♗c5, retaining the bishop for now; e.g. 11 g3 0-0 12 0-0 ♘g4 with a tiny edge to White. Black intends ...♕e7 and ...f7-f6 to evict the knight, and probably ...a7-a6 and ...b7-b5.

Riskier is 7...♗c5!? 8 d6! cxd6 9 ♗c4 0-0 10 0-0 b5! 11 ♘xb5 ♗a6 12 a4 ♖c8 13 ♗e2 d5 14 exd5 ♘xh4 15 ♗xh5 e4 – Black has solved the problem of his weak pawns by sacrificing them all and now has reasonable play for the pawn minus, but White had many other tries.

b) 6 g3 ♗c5 7 ♗g5 f6!? (7...♘f6 8 ♗h3 d6 9 ♗xc8 ♕xc8 10 ♗xf6 gxf6 is simpler – Black will play ...f6-f5 at his convenience, with near equality) 8 ♗d2 d6 9 ♘c3 ♗d7 10 ♗e2 ♘6e7 was a little better for White in H.Meissner-A.Miles, European Cup, Slough 1997, though Miles methodically ground out the win in an instructive ending (see Game 32).

c) 6 ♗e2 ♘f6 7 ♘c3 a6 8 ♗g5 ♗c5 9 0-0 d6 is already equal since Black has quickly established his bishop in the ideal position. Black will normally follow with 10...♕d7, breaking the pin and intending ...♘g4 or ...♕g4.

6...♘f6 7 ♘c3

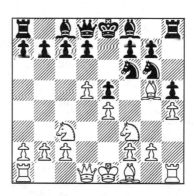

7...♗b4

7...♗c5 is a possible alternative. Then 8 ♘a4?! ♗b4+ 9 c3 ♗e7 10 ♗xf6 ♗xf6 11 d6 was A.Ivanov-J.Benjamin, US Championship, Parsippany 1996, which Ivanov won, but Black's inaccuracies are yet to come. Indeed, after 11...cxd6 12 g3!? d5?! 13 ♕xd5 d6? 14 ♗b5+ ♔f8 White was much better, but Benjamin could have played 12...b6 13 c4 (13 ♕xd6?! ♗b7 14 ♕d3 ♗c6 15 b3 d5 is great for Black) 13...♗b7 14 ♘c3 ♗e7, followed by ...♘f8-e6 – Black's extra pawn may not be much of an asset, but he is not suffering for having it.

However, the correct response to 7...♗c5, namely 8 ♘d2!, puts Black under some pressure.

8 ♘d2!

Instead:

a) 8 a3 ♗xc3+ 9 bxc3 c6 10 c4 d6 11 ♘d2 ♕a5 was L.Christiansen-J.Benjamin, US Championship 2000 (see Game 33). Black had nothing to complain about and went on to win.

b) 8 ♗e2 allows us to preserve the bishop with 8...d6 9 0-0 ♗d7 10 a3 ♗c5 11 ♕d3 a6 12 g3 ♗h3 13 ♖fd1 and break the annoying pin by 13...♕c8 (or 13...♕b8!?), when we're just about equal. (This queen manoeuvre should be kept in mind throughout this section.) 14...♘g4 is likely, targeting the f2-square.

The text move is more challenging.

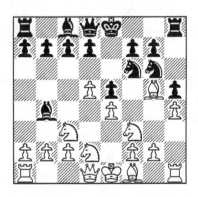

8...d6!

In E.Mortensen-C.Hoi, Ostrava 1992, Black played 8...c6 9 ♗e2 (9 g3!?) 9...♗xc3 10 bxc3 cxd5 11 ♗xh5 (11 exd5!?) 11...♘f4 12 ♗f3 ♘e6 13 ♗xf6 ♕xf6 14 exd5 ♘c5 15 g3 (15 h5!?) 15...d6 with only a tiny disadvantage, but White missed some good chances along the way.

After the text, we're in uncharted territory again, which is just how we like it. Right?! Right.

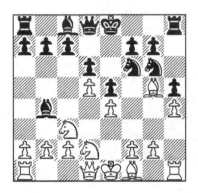

a) 9 ♗b5+ is certainly not a big deal after 9...♗d7 10 ♗xd7+ ♕xd7. Sure, we liked that bishop, but White has solved our space problem and helped us break the annoying pin on our f6-knight. Then 11 ♗xf6 gxf6 12 ♕f3 ♕g4 (12...♗xc3 13 ♕xc3 f5 14 g3 0-0-0 is okay, too) 13 ♕xg4 (or 13 ♕xf6 ♗xc3 14 bxc3 ♘f4! 15 ♘f3 ♕xg2 16 ♘g5 ♖f8 17 0-0-0 ♕xf2 18 ♘h7 ♘e2+ 19 ♔d2 ♕xf6 20 ♘xf6+ ♔e7 21 ♘xh5 ♖h8 22 ♔xe2 ♖xh5 23 ♖dg1 with a draw, presumably, though only Black can pretend to play for a win) 13...hxg4 14 g3 ♗xc3 15 bxc3 ♘e7 16 c4 f5 is level.

b) 9 ♗e2 ♘f4! (as in many similar positions, White does not want to take this knight, especially since his bishop is strong on the g5-square) 10 ♗b5+ ♔f8 (this time 10...♗d7 doesn't work well – White will gain the very useful g2-g3 with tempo) 11 0-0 ♗g4 12 f3 (or 12 ♕e1 ♗d7! – the situation has changed again already; the bishop exchange now brings equality: 13 ♗xd7 ♕xd7 and Black will follow with 14...♕g4 if possible, otherwise 14...c6, or similarly 13 ♗d3!? c6) 12...c6! 13 ♗a4 ♗xc3 14 bxc3 ♗d7 15 dxc6 ♗xc6 16 ♗xc6 ♕b6+ 17 ♔h1 ♕xc6 18 ♗xf4 exf4 19 ♘b3 d5 20 e5 ♘d7 21 ♖e1 ♖e8 22 ♕d4 ♖h6 is roughly equal.

There are many other ways the game could go, and White does have chances for an advantage, but the preceding lines give a good indication of Black's resources.

A12: 5 ♗e3

White doesn't actually play this very often, but Black's attacking ideas in this variation are too important and widely applicable to relegate to a footnote. Study carefully. Don't worry, it's fun and easy.

5...♘f6 6 ♗d3

Not 6 ♘bd2 c6! 7 c4?! (this is no good, but the alternative is to give up the centre) 7...♘g4! 8 ♗g5? ♕b6 9 ♕e2?! ♗c5 and White needs CPR.

6...♘g4! 7 ♗d2

Or 7 ♗g5 ♗e7 8 ♗d2 ♗c5, transposing.

7...♗c5 8 0-0 a5 9 h3 ♘f6

White has gotten h2-h3 for free, but free is still way too expensive – he must be extremely careful because of his weakened kingside:

a) 10 ♕e1 d6 11 ♗xa5?! ♗xh3! 12 gxh3 ♕d7 13 ♔h2 ♘f4 14 ♘g1 ♘g4+! 15 ♔h1 (not 15 hxg4?? ♕xg4 and ...♕g2 mate) 15...♘xf2+ 16 ♖xf2 ♗xf2 17 ♕xf2 ♖xa5 18 ♕f3 0-0 19 ♘c3 f5 20 exf5 ♘xd3 21 ♕xd3 ♖xf5 and Black is better because of White's weak king and awkward knights.

b) 10 a4 0-0 11 ♘a3 d6 12 ♕e1 (or 12 ♘c4 c6! 13 dxc6 d5! 14 exd5?! e4!) 12...♘h5 13 ♗e3 ♘gf4! 14 ♗xc5 ♕f6!! 15 ♗e3 ♗xh3 16 ♗xf4 ♘xf4 17 ♘h2 ♗xg2 18 ♕e3 ♗xf1 and even though White survives, Black maintains some material and positional pluses.

Note that in many similar positions White voluntarily spends a tempo on h2-h3(?) – a move which contributes greatly to his downfall. Note, too, that Black's attack with ...♘h5, ...♘gf4, ...♕f6 is so strong that he can sacrifice a full piece to accelerate it. One free tempo and the game would have been over.

A2: 4 c4?!

This weak move is almost as common as 4 ♘f3. It wastes a tempo in a critical position, obstructs the f1-bishop, and leaves a big hole on the d4-square. In exchange, White has fortified d5, but the price is too high – he has already squandered his first move advantage, and if he plays at all indifferently he will soon stand worse. White imagines he will eventually be playing c4-c5, but this is difficult to achieve.

4...♘g6

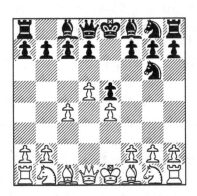

4...♘f6 is similar, when 5 ♘c3 ♘g6 transposes to a position often reached through the Tango. However, 6 h4! is a dangerous move here, and Black has both objective and practical problems. The text move order makes it difficult for White to play an early h2-h4 and so avoids this troublesome line.

White has:

> **A21: 5 ♘c3** *62*
> **A22: 5 ♗e3** *64*
> **A23: 5 ♘f3** *67*
> **A24: 5 ♗d3** *68*
> **A25: 5 g3** *70*
> **A26: 5 a3** *71*

By the way, I hate all these nested letters and numbers which make the book look like the awful, tedious outlines we had to write in seventh grade Social Studies. It makes my eyes glaze over just looking at it, and probably yours, too, so just read about 5 ♘c3 and 5 ♗e3 and then skip to line B. The rest doesn't much happen and it's pretty obvious anyway. Maybe someday, when you need to look something up, you'll thank me that the material is *so* well organized. I take cash and cheques.

A21: 5 ♘c3 ♗c5!

If 5...♘f6 then 6 h4! and Black is back on less solid ground.

6 ♘f3 ♘f6 7 ♗e2

By now 7 h4? is not possible because it does not address the threat of 7...♘g4!.

For 7 ♗d3, see A24, note 'b' to White's seventh move.

7...0-0

Black will be playing ...d7-d6 and usually ...a7-a5 soon, but this move order is the most accurate since 7...d6?! is met by 8 b4 (8...♗xb4?? 9 ♕a4+).

7...a5 is sometimes played, but White is actually quite far from being able to play ♘a4 because the e4-pawn would hang. Holding off on ...a7-a5 makes sense because·

1. Black may change his mind and play ...a7-a6.

2. Sometimes Black can prevent ♘a4 with ...♗d7 instead.

3. It is possible to allow the bishop to be traded off under some circumstances – I have recently noticed that tempi sometimes matter in chess.

8 0-0 d6

8...a5 9 ♘e1 d6 (which could just as easily have been 8...d6 9 ♘e1 a5) 10 ♘d3 ♗d4! was W.Weisser-L.Trumpp, German League 2003, in which White quickly reached a difficult position and got abused tactically (see Game 34).

9 ♕c2

In B.Perrusset-I.Moullier, Paris 2005,

White tried 9 a3 a5 10 ♗d2 ♕e7 11 ♖b1 ♗d7 12 b4?! axb4 13 axb4 ♗d4!, but she was worse after the queenside had opened and it was Black who was successful in the end (see Game 35).

9...♗d7

This stops ♘a4 for now.

Instead, D.Baramidze-E.Griezne, Baunatal 1999, continued 9...a6 10 a3 ♕e7 11 b4 ♗a7 12 ♘d1, when Black got to demonstrate the typical manoeuvre 12...♘h5 13 ♘e3 ♘gf4 which he used to good effect (see Game 36).

10 a3 a5

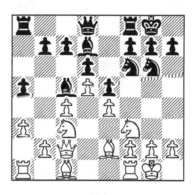

Black is slightly better.

If 11 ♖b1, we will certainly fix White's queenside pawns with 11...a4.

If 11 b3, we have available the slow plan 11...♕e7, 12...h6, 13...♘h5, 14...♘gf4, 15...♕f6, etc, which I provide because it's often necessary in similar positions – but here we just blast out 11...♘h5! 12 ♘xe5 (12 g3 is safer, but it does create a weakness, and Black is better after the simple 12...♘f6, menacing ...♗h3 and/or ...♘g4) 12...♘xe5 13 ♗xh5 ♕h4 14 ♗e2 f5 15 g3 ♕h3 16

♗f4 ♖ae8 (or 16...g5!? 17 ♗xe5 dxe5 18 exf5 ♖a6 with more than enough for the pawn) 17 b4 (not 17 ♗xe5? ♖xe5 18 ♗f3 f4 19 ♗g2 ♕h5 20 b4 ♗h3 21 bxc5 ♗xg2, winning) 17...axb4 18 axb4 ♗xb4 with clearly the better game for Black.

A22: 5 ♗e3 ♘f6

6 ♘c3

Other moves:

a) 6 ♗d3 b6! (6...♘h4!? 7 ♔f1 b6 8 g3 ♘g6 9 ♔g2 ♗c5 is similar, but White is certainly not suffering from his inability to castle) 7 ♘c3 ♗c5 (in V.Vilkov-A.Provotorov, Kaluga 1996, the only time this position has been reached, Black played the highly inconsistent 7...♗b4?! and went on to lose) 8 ♘f3 0-0 9 0-0 and there are many roads for both players, but they all lead to equal positions – the imminent and positionally favourable bishop trade balances White's space advantage; e.g. 9...a5 10 ♕d2 ♕e7 11 ♖fe1 d6 12 ♗xc5 bxc5 13 g3 a4 and the game is still balanced.

b) 6 f3 ♗b4+ (6...b6 is still interesting, but after 7 ♘c3 ♗c5 8 ♗xc5 bxc5 9 d6! White has balanced the chances) 7 ♘d2 ♕e7 (7...b6!?). Miles scored 4-0 from this position, beating GM Kaidanov and IMs Shirazi and Langeweg; e.g. 8 g3 0-0 9 ♗h3 c6 (or 9...a5 or 9...♗c5) and Black is better, going on to win in G.Kaidanov-A.Miles, Palma de Mallorca 1989 (see Game 37).

c) 6 ♗g5?! is ridiculous here and in all positions where Black can play ...h7-h6. The bishop is way too valuable to trade, and even when it's possible to retreat, ...h7-h6 is always a useful move for Black. So 6...h6! 7 ♗xf6 ♕xf6 and White has even more dark-square problems than usual. Black's queen is also very happy on the f6-square.

6...♗b4 7 f3

Against 7 ♕c2 or 7 ♗d3 Black plays exactly the same way.

7...♗xc3+

Black's results are excellent (+21 -12 =8) with this move, so there is little need to worry about alternatives. Sometimes Black plays 7...♕e7 with the idea of trading the dark-squared bishops, but this is time-consuming compared to the text, and hasn't worked well in real life.

Quoting Joel Benjamin: "This is important: *do not* hang your bishop with 7...d6 8 ♕a4+." (Actually, according to my database, 7...d6?? has been played three times and White has yet to play 8 ♕a4+, even in the game where White was a GM. I won't name the GM. Can this possibly be right?! Can you explain yourself, Pablo?)

8 bxc3 d6 9 ♕d2!?

In fact, just about anything is better than the lemon 9 c5?! that White squeezes out most of the time, which leads to:

Position Four

Apparently it is just too tempting to liquidate the weak c-pawn, but the lines that open are all going to be seized by Black; and while White's weakness on c4 is no more, he has an even bigger problem on c3, which is directly in the line of fire, sitting on Black's half-open c-file. The games all go the same way: 9...0-0 10 ♗d3 ♘d7! 11 cxd6 cxd6 12 ♘e2 ♕a5! (or 12...♕c7) 13 0-0 ♘c5, and ...♗d7/...♖ac8/...♘a4, or ...b7-b6/...♗a6/...♖ac8 on the queenside, and after White is pacified there, ...f7-f5 on the kingside. S.Brudno-J.Benjamin, Boston 2001, is a classic example (see Game 38), whereas in R.Mitchell-J.Schuyler, Bloomington 1991 (Game 39) Black focuses entirely

on the queenside, a strategy which is far less effective, as we will see.

Can things really be that simple for Black? Not quite, but if White wants to get any play, he pretty much needs to go crazy like a Grandmaster (in I.Jelen-E.Dizdarevic, Ljubljana 1992 – see Game 40 – White went crazy like an IM, which did not work), as in E.Rozentalis-M.Lazic, Genoa 2004, which went 9 c5 0-0 10 cxd6 cxd6 11 ♗d3

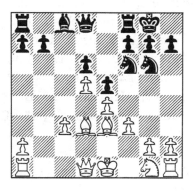

11...♕c7 12 ♘e2 ♘d7 13 h4!? ♘c5 14 h5 ♘e7 15 g4! and while White may not have been better, he certainly was scary, and he did go on to win after 15...♘xd3?! 16 ♕xd3 b5 17 ♘g3 a5 18 ♔f2 ♗a6 19 ♕d2 f6 20 ♘f5 ♖f7 21 ♖hg1 ♖c8 22 ♖ac1 ♔f8 23 ♕b2 ♘xf5 24 gxf5 ♕c4 25 ♕d2 h6 26 ♗b6 ♕a4 27 ♔g3 ♖b7 28 ♗e3 ♖bc7?? 29 ♗xh6 b4 30 ♔h4 bxc3 31 ♗xg7+ ♔e8 32 ♕g2 1-0.

Notice that White's pawn storm had less to do with blowing Black open than controlling the f5-square, preparing it for his knight. The square is especially important since, had Black been able to break with ...f7-f5, White's strategy would have failed. Notice, too, that Black was never losing – in fact, he was never significantly worse – until 28...♖bc7??. Instead 28...♖f7! (preparing the escape 29...♔e7 if necessary) would have pre-empted White's sacrificial attack and held the balance. White's ideal position wasn't so dangerous after all!

Let's go back to move 11, set up the proper defence without fear, and try to play a little more quickly and actively on the queenside: 11...♕a5! (or 11...♘d7 first) 12 ♘e2 ♘d7 13 h4 ♘e7 14 h5 h6 15 g4 f6 16 ♕d2 ♘c5 17 ♗c2 b6 18 ♘g3 (18 c4! ♕a6 is equal) 18...♗a6 19 ♘f5 ♘xf5 20 gxf5 ♖f7 21 ♖g1 ♔f8, followed by 22...♖c8 with pressure on the c3-pawn.

We now return to our regular programming.

9...b6

Palliser concludes that there is no point delaying castling, but I am finding that 9...0-0 10 h4! (intending 10...♘h5 11 ♗f2 or 11 ♘e2) is very

dangerous for Black, who must be extremely resourceful in a dizzying array of variations in order to avoid disaster. (See for yourself – I won't bore you with the details. Frankly, I wouldn't even know where to start.) After the text move, Black can bail out to the queenside if things get too hairy too quickly – a surprising but valuable option!

10 h4

Not forced, obviously, but if this is what White is about, he is likely to get right to it.

If 10 ♗d3 (or 10 ♘e2, for that matter), Black could castle, having lost nothing – but I would prefer to stay flexible with 10...♘d7; for example, 10 ♘e2 ♘d7 11 h4 h6 12 h5 ♘gf8! (in Z.Koczka-Zsu.Simon, Hungarian Team Championship 2003, 12...♘e7? was 1-0 in 30 moves) and 13...♘h7 will be like the main variation. If 10 ♗d3 ♘d7 11 ♘e2, Black can still delay ...0-0 in favour of 11...♘c5!. Can White keep waiting before committing to either castling or h2-h4 - ?

10...h6

This stops White's pawn from going to h6, which would leave Black with a big cramp and weaknesses on the dark squares.

11 g3

Someone will try 11 h5 ♘f8! (I just love this move – the knight heads for the open c5-square, whereas a knight on e7 would be going nowhere for a long time) 12 g4 ♘6h7! (preventing 13 g5 and preparing an eventual ...♘g5!, while ...♕h4+ is also sometimes useful) 13 ♗d3 ♘d7 (Black is at least equal in spite of White's space – his knights are happy pieces, unlike White's sad bishops) 14 ♔f2 ♘c5 15 ♔g2 a5 16 ♘e2 ♘g5 etc. It is even safe to castle kingside now.

11...♘d7

This transposes to A.Karpov-D.Chevallier, France 1993 (see Game 41). According to Palliser, this game was very influential and popularized the variation with ♗e3 for White. If so, the game's true theoretical significance was greatly overestimated – Black was fine well into the middlegame, and even better at one point. His only real problem was that he was playing Karpov!

12 ♘h3 ♘c5 13 ♘f2

So far we have followed the famous game, and Black could certainly continue more or less like Chevallier (who tried 13...♕d7 here), but I would rather play actively with 13...f5!?; e.g. 14 exf5 ♗xf5 15 ♗xc5 bxc5 16 ♗d3 0-0 17 0-0 ♕d7.

We no longer have to worry about a positional squeeze by White, real or imagined. White's knight will soon be established on the e4-square, but it has no forward movement and does not control important squares. One likely plan for us is ...♘e7-c8-b6 to close the b-file and pressure White's weakness on c4. We can also consider ...♖ab8-b6 and ...♖fb8. Black is clearly no worse and I believe White has to be careful that he is not punished for his overextended pawns.

A23: 5 ♘f3 ♘f6 6 ♘c3 ♗b4

This is a difficult decision, especially

since we will need to know the positions after 6...♗c5 anyway because of the different move orders White can use (see line A21 for this). Although Black's bishop is very strong on the a7-g1 diagonal, the doubled c-pawns are also a big problem for White, and one that cannot possibly be fixed. Not only are they targets in the late middlegame and endgame, they immobilize White's queenside, making it difficult for him to generate meaningful play on that side of the board. Furthermore, White is forced to play an awkward move like 7 ♗d3 or 7 ♕c2 to defend his e-pawn. Because it is possible to inflict the positional damage and still attack, I prefer to double the pawns if possible, though this is largely a matter of taste.

7 ♗d3

7 ♗d2?! keeps the pawns from being doubled, but it is bad nonetheless: 7...♗xc3 8 ♗xc3 ♘xe4 9 ♗xe5 ♘xe5 10 ♘xe5 ♕f6 11 ♘d3 0-0 12 ♗e2 d6 13 0-0 ♗f5 and Black has a significant advantage in activity.

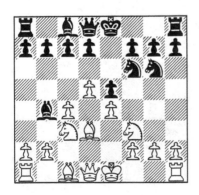

7...♗xc3+ 8 bxc3 d6 9 0-0 0-0 10 h3?!

This is not good, but it is always played, if it hasn't been played already. Even *Houdini* likes it! Black's attacking ideas should be familiar by now:
10...♘h5

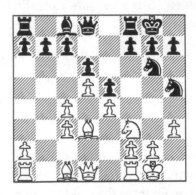

Black intends ...♘hf4 and ...♘h4, or ...♘gf4 and[1] ...♕f6. On the queenside, it will probably be necessary to play ...b7-b6 soon, while a2-a4 should be met by ...a7-a5 to eliminate counterplay. In theory White should be okay, but in reality Black has won every game. W.M.Buehl-J.Benjamin, Reno 1999 (see Game 42) is typical.

A24: 5 ♗d3 ♗c5

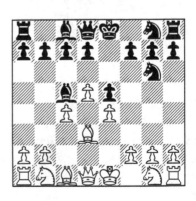

6 ♘c3

With 6 ♘e2!? ♘f6 7 0-0 White gets his knight to e2 without spending a tempo on h2-h3 (as compared to the main line), but he will still find that he has not found a route to an advantage: 7...0-0 (7...d6?! 8 b4!) 8 ♘bc3 a6 9 ♘g3 d6 10 ♘f5 ♘f4! 11 ♗e3 (not 11 ♗xf4?! exf4 12 ♕f3?! g6! 13 ♘h6+ ♚g7 14 ♕xf4 ♘h5 15 ♕d2 ♕h4! 16 b4 ♕f4! 17 ♕xf4 ♘xf4 winning, because the ♘h6 is still trapped) 11...♘d7! 12 ♗c2 g6 with equal play.

6...♘f6

7 h3

Given an exclamation mark by some sources, which to me seems a little extreme – the move is more like an arguably necessary evil.

a) Admittedly 7 h3 is far superior to 7 ♘ge2?? ♘g4 8 0-0? ♕h4, winning.

b) 7 ♘f3 isn't so great either. 7...0-0 8 0-0 a5 (8...a6 is also reasonable, but the text move is sound and Black is 5-0 with it) 9 a3 d6 10 ♖b1 ♘h5 with a dangerous initiative in practice. In A.Hahn-J.Bonin, New York (rapid) 2003, White

managed to block Black's favourite bishop with 11 b4 axb4 12 axb4 ♗b6 13 ♘a4 ♗a7 14 ♗c2 ♘hf4 15 c5, but Black's attack was still strong, and he won a topsy-turvy battle (see Game 43).

c) 7 ♗e3 b6! transposes to A22 above (the first note). 7...♗xe3 isn't the worst move ever, but it loses the f4-square for Black's knights, which love to settle there and checkmate White.

7...0-0 8 ♘ge2

8...a6

Not the only good move. 8...a5 is also worth considering – it slows down White's b2-b4, though it does leave Black's queenside less flexible and weakens the b5-square.

K.Ellmauer-D.Huber, Schwarzach 2001, went 8...d6 (8...a5 is a better move order) 9 0-0 a5 10 ♚h1?! (10 ♘g3) 10...♘h5 11 g4?? ♕h4?! (11...♘hf4!) 12 ♚g2 ♗xg4 13 hxg4 ♕xg4+ 14 ♘g3? (14 ♚h2) 14...♘gf4+ 15 ♗xf4 ♘xf4+ 16 ♚g1 ♕xg3+ 0-1. Short and sweet.

I.Jelen-Z.Mestrovic, Slovenian Team Championship 1996, saw 8...♘h5!? 9 g3?! (9 ♘a4!), which is incorrectly assessed by De Firmian as better for White – a case of annotating by result. The game continued preposterously with 9...♕f6?! 10 ♖h2 d6?! (10...♕d8! is equal) 11 ♘a4 ♗b4+?? 12 ♘ec3! and Black's h5-knight is toast.

Going back to move nine, it is true that White has more space, but his position is very loose. Simply 9...a6! followed by ...d7-d6 and ...c7-c6, and what moves does White imagine that he is going to be playing? For example, 9...a6 10 0-0 d6 11 ♔h2 ♘f6 12 ♖b1 c6 13 b4 ♕d7 14 ♘g1 ♗d4 15 ♘ce2 ♗a7 and White's position is slowly degrading.

9 0-0 d6 10 ♘g3!

Otherwise, the nasty 10...♘h5! is coming; e.g. 10 ♖b1 ♘h5! 11 b4 ♗a7 12 ♔h1 ♘hf4 and ...♕h4 or ...♘h4 with threats against g2, h3, and f2. (9...♘h5?! was no good because of 10 ♘a4! ♗a7 11 d6! with a small edge and a large disruption of Black's plans.)

The position after 10 ♘g3 has never been reached, but we have many reasonable and sensible moves such as 10...♗d7, 10...♖e8, or 10...h6 (with equal-

ity), and ...c7-c6 may be on the cards.

One interesting idea is ...♘f4. One thing we absolutely do not need to worry about is ♗xf4 exf4 – White's good bishop is too valuable to squander in such a fashion, and our pawn on f4 is strong, not weak. We will very much enjoy the use of the e5-square for our knight, bishop, rook, or queen. Even if ...g7-g5 is necessary to defend f4, Black's kingside will remain safe.

Another idea is ...♗d4 and ...c7-c5, anchoring the bishop. In this closed position, we will not mind if our bishop gets traded off, especially since we will wind up with a protected passed pawn on the d4-square (if the bishop is taken, either recapture can be considered, though ...e5xd4 is the typical answer). Naturally, White will not be eager to play d5xc6 (*en passant*) because of the loss of space and centre. 10...♗d4 is not the most accurate, but 10...h6 11 ♘a4 can definitely be met by 11...♗d4 and 12...c5.

A25: 5 g3

Taking the f4-square away from Black's knight is sensible, but this move is slow, and the white bishop is not going to be active on g2.

5...♘f6

6 ♗g2

If 6 ♘c3, we have that choice again – to take the strong diagonal or to double White's c-pawns. I prefer to have a queenside target, particularly since White has taken measures against our kingside play. Also, White's fianchetto leaves the c4-pawn without protection. So 6...♗b4 7 ♗g2 ♗xc3 8 bxc3 d6 9 ♘e2 (or 9 h4 h6 with a comfortably equal position very similar to A.Karpov-D.Chevallier in A22 – if 10 h5?! then 10...♘f8! with advantage) 9...0-0 and Black has won every game. White's plan to play f2-f4 is far too weakening – after ...e5xf4 g3xf4, White has problems on c4, e4, f4, g4, and h4. While Black is waiting for f2-f4, he can play ...b7-b6, ...♘d7, ...♘c5, ...f7-f5 and perhaps ...a7-a5 and ...♗a6. E.Schiendorfer-D.Recuero Guerra, Herceg Novi 2006, is a typical disaster for White (see

Game 44).

6...♗c5 7 ♘c3

The popular 7 ♘e2 allows Black to take the initiative immediately with 7...h5!, when 8...h4 cannot be stopped because 8 h4? ♘g4 9 0-0? (or 9 ♖f1 ♕f6!) 9...♘xh4! is awful for White, as is 8 ♗g5? ♗xf2+.

7...0-0

7...d6, 7...a5 and 7...h5 are also interesting, but castling is flexible and leads into the amusing miniature H.Titz-C.Rossi, Austrian Team Championship 2001: 8 ♘f3 d6 9 0-0 a6 10 ♕d3 b5 11 b3 ♗d7 12 a4 b4 13 ♘d1 ♕c8 14 ♗e3 ♘xe4 15 ♘xe5 ♘xe5 16 ♕xe4 ♗f5 17 ♕h4 ♘g6 0-1. White resigned because 18 ♕h5 ♗g4 19 ♕g5 h6 traps the queen.

As seen in this game, ...a7-a6 is often the best way to preserve the bishop in this variation, because with White's bishop fianchettoed, the advance ...b7-b5 is easy to achieve and likely to be effective.

A26: 5 a3 ♘f6 6 ♘c3 ♗c5

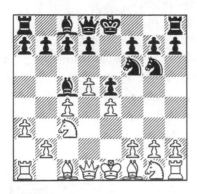

7 ♗d3

Other moves:

a) 7 ♘f3? ♘g4! or 7 ♘ge2? ♘g4! is terrible. Have you noticed that White needs to be careful on the *dark* squares? Eh?

b) I've seen White play 7 h3 here, after which he should have his right to play White permanently revoked – but the fact that he always loses here has as much to do with his obviously passive attitude as the defects of his position. 7...d6 8 ♘f3 a5 9 g3 0-0 10 ♗g2 c6 was C.Baluta-A.Cioara, Bucharest 1996 (see Game 45), in which White, an FM, got manhandled while Black demonstrated all the available ideas (...c7-c6, ...b7-b5, ...♘g4, ...f7-f5, etc).

c) 7 b4 certainly looks stupid and has lost all the games so far, but in analysis things are not so clear: 7...♗d4 8 ♘ge2 ♘xe4 (8...c5!? looks okay) 9 ♘xe4 (not 9 ♘xd4?? ♘xc3 10 ♕d3 exd4 11 ♕xd4 ♕e7+, winning) 9...♗xa1 10 d6! (stronger than 10 ♗e3?! ♗d4 11 ♘xd4 exd4, though after 12 ♕xd4! 0-0 13 d6 White still has some play) 10...b6

11 h4 ♗b7 12 dxc7 ♕xc7 13 ♘d6+ with full compensation and more than one way to pursue the attack. Against a dangerous and prepared (GM) opponent, Black would probably do well to avoid the whole mess with 8...c5, but otherwise it makes sense to pocket the material and let White try to figure out how to prove compensation.

7...a5

7...a6 has done well in practice, but I can't see the logic of allowing White to accelerate his queenside play.

8 ♖b1

Instead:

a) 8 ♘ge2?? is still terrible due to 8...♘g4 9 0-0?! ♕h4.

b) 8 ♘a4 is interesting, but not especially strong: 8...♗a7 9 c5 d6 10 ♗e3 was R.Staudte-M.Roth, Chemnitz 1998, when 10...♘h4! (instead of 10...♘g4?!) 11 ♔f1 ♘g4! 12 ♗d2 dxc5 already leaves White in poor condition. 9 d6 a little better, but 9...cxd6 and 10...d5 will be sufficient for easy equality.

8...d6 9 h3 0-0 10 b4 axb4 11 axb4 ♗a7

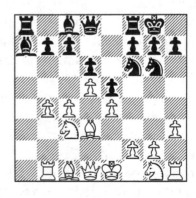

Black was already slightly more comfortable in Bu Xiangzhi-L.Christiansen, Deizisau 2000 (see Game 46), and Bu's 12 g3?! should have worsened White's situation after 12...c6 or 12...♗d7 (as opposed to Christiansen's 12...♘e8?!). Black, who was better throughout most of the opening and early middlegame, ...lost.

B: 3 dxe5 ♘xe5

White has:

> **B1: 4 ♘f3** *73*
> **B2: 4 f4** *76*

Instead, 4 ♘c3 ♗c5 5 ♘f3? (5 f4 ♘c6 transposes to line B22 below) 5...♘g4! 6 ♘d4 is like a Two Knights Defence (1 e4 e5 2 ♘f3 ♘c6 3 ♗c4 ♘f6 4 ♘g5 d5 5 exd5 ♘xd5) with reversed colours, except that Black's king's knight is at home instead of his queen's knight. This makes it harder to pressure the ♘d4, so the standard idea of 6...♘xf2 is less effective; e.g. 7 ♔xf2 ♕f6+ 8 ♔e3 ♘e7 9 ♘b5 ♕e5 10 c3 f5 11 ♔d2 fxe4 12 ♔c2 0-0 13 g3 d5 14 ♗f4 does not give Black

enough compensation. However, Black still has 6...d5!?; e.g. 7 ♘xd5 c6 8 f3 ♘e5 9 b4 ♗d6 10 ♘c3 ♗xb4 11 ♗b2 ♕h4+ 12 g3 ♕e7 and White is very loose. Alternatively, 6...♕h4 is less ambitious but much simpler: 7 g3 ♕f6 8 ♕xg4 ♗xd4 9 ♘d1 d5! (since the c8-bishop is defended!) 10 ♕e2 dxe4 11 ♕xe4+ ♘e7 and Black is a bit better.

B1: 4 ♘f3 ♘xf3 5 ♕xf3 ♘f6!

The usual move is 5...♕f6, but then White can either allow or avoid the queen trade as he pleases, with a pleasant position in either case. Although the text move has had no serious trials, analysis demonstrates its viability and none of the ideas previously tried have proven themselves reliable. In most cases, we intend to play like a Philidor, counting on the knight trade to ease our space disadvantage, while trying to show that White's queen is awkward on f3; and there are other possibilities depending on how White reacts. It is not possible to analyse exhaustively, but the following information should leave us a few steps ahead of the opponent, who has never even considered this position.

B11: 6 ♘c3 *74*
B12: 6 ♗c4 *74*
B13: 6 e5 *75*
B14: 6 ♗d3 *75*
B15: 6 ♗e2 *75*
B16: 6 ♗g5 *76*

B11: 6 ♘c3 ♗b4 7 ♗d3 ♗xc3+ 8 bxc3 0-0 9 0-0 d6 10 ♖e1

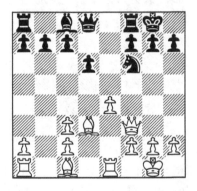

10 ♗g5 h6 11 ♗xf6 ♕xf6 12 ♕xf6 gxf6 is an equal endgame.

After 10 ♖e1, White is a little better in spite of his bad pawns. It is time for Black to reposition the knight with 10...♘d7, which steps out of the potential pin, prepares ...♕f6, and eventually ...♘c5 or ...♘e5, where it should have good prospects. Black further intends ...b7-b6, ...♗b7, and ...♖e8, targeting White's e-pawn, and may eventually try for ...f7-f5.

B12: 6 ♗c4

6...♗d6

6...d6!? is not bad, and keeps things very Philidor-esque, but I prefer the bishop to be more active if possible.

7 ♘c3 0-0 8 ♗g5

Or 8 0-0 ♕e7 9 ♗f4 (9 ♗g5?! ♕e5! 10 ♕g3 ♕c5 11 ♕h4! ♗e5! is level) 9...♗xf4 10 ♕xf4 d6 11 ♖ad1 ♖e8, intending ...♗e6 or ...♕e5. The exchanges have eased Black's space problem, and White's edge is tiny.

8...c6 9 ♗xf6 ♕xf6 10 ♕xf6 gxf6 11 0-0-0 ♗c5 12 f3 b5 13 ♗d3 d6

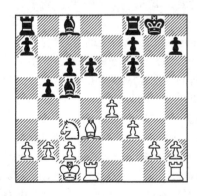

Black's powerful dark-squared bishop is (nearly) enough to balance his ugly pawn structure.

B13: 6 e5 ♕e7

7 ♗f4

7 ♕e2 ♘d5 8 c4 ♕b4+ 9 ♘d2 ♘f4 10 ♕e4 ♘e6 is equal.

7...c6 8 ♘d2

Other moves lead to equality:

a) 8 ♕e2 ♘d5 9 ♗g3 f5! 10 c4 ♘c7 11 ♘c3 ♘e6 12 f4 d6! 13 0-0-0 ♕c7 14 ♕c2 g6 15 ♔b1 dxe5 16 fxe5 ♗g7 (or 16...♗e7 or 16...f4!?).

b) 8 ♘c3 d6! 9 0-0-0 dxe5 10 ♖e1 ♘d7 11 ♗c4 f6 and Black keeps his extra pawn, although White has the appropriate compensation. Black intends ...♘b6 (or ...♘c5), ...♗d7 and ...0-0-0.

8...d5 9 0-0-0 ♘d7 10 ♕g3 ♘c5

On the surface, this looks bad for Black, who is still four or more moves away from completing his development – but he controls the e6-square, and White lacks the means to orchestrate a breakthrough, so White's advantage is small; e.g. 11 ♔b1 ♗f5 (11...h5!?) 12 ♘b3 ♘xb3 13 ♕xb3 0-0-0 14 ♗d3 ♗e6! with no real problems.

B14: 6 ♗d3 d6 7 0-0 ♗e7 8 ♘c3 0-0 9 ♗f4

9 ♘d5 ♘xd5 10 exd5 ♗f6 11 c3 ♖e8 gives White very little.

9...♗g4 10 ♕g3 ♗e6

The threat to trade off White's good bishop with 11...♘h5 is annoying. Assuming White defends against that, Black should consider the candidate moves ...c7-c6, ...♖e8, ...♘d7 (or ...♘g4), ...♘e5, ...♘xd3, ...♗h4, ...♗f6, and ...♕c7 (or ...♕e7). White is only slightly better.

B15: 6 ♗e2 d5 7 e5 ♘e4 8 ♘c3 ♘xc3 9 ♕xc3 c6 10 ♗e3 ♗e7 11 f4 0-0

And with 12...f6! coming, Black has equalized.

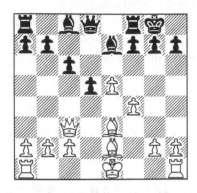

B16: 6 ♗g5 d6 7 ♘c3

As usual 7 ♗xf6?! ♕xf6 8 ♕xf6 gxf6 is equal.

7...♗e7

In principle, we can already notice that, compared to a regular Philidor, White's ♗g5 and ♕f3 are awkwardly placed, so White cannot expect much from the opening; e.g. 8 h3 0-0 9 0-0-0 c6 10 ♕g3 (10 e5 ♘e8 doesn't do anything, while after 10 ♗e2 ♕a5 11 ♗d2 ♕c7 12 ♕g3 b5 13 ♗h6 ♘e8 Black is certainly no worse) 10...♕a5 11 f4 ♗e6 leads to a wild race with approximately even chances.

B2: 4 f4

This is far less popular than 4 ♘f3 among the strongest players, but gives excellent results. Fortunately, it's easy to see where Black has been going wrong.

4...♘c6

White has:

> **B21: 5 ♗c4** 77
> **B22: 5 ♘f3** 78

Alternatively:

a) 5 ♘c3 ♗c5 6 ♘f3 transposes to line B22.

b) 5 ♗e3 prevents 5...♗c5, but Black is okay after 5...♗b4+ 6 c3 ♗a5 (R.Hübner-V.Hort, German League 1984, see Game 47). Even better is the unplayed novelty 5...d5! which brings equality; e.g. 6 exd5 ♘b4 7 ♗b5+ ♗d7 8 ♗xd7+ ♕xd7 9 ♘f3 ♘xd5 10 ♕e2 0-0-0 – come to think of it, White is much worse here, so 8 ♕e2 ♘xc2+ 9 ♕xc2 ♗xb5 10 ♘c3 ♗a6 11 ♘f3 ♗d6 12 0-0-0 ♘f6 13 ♖he1 0-0, when Black's bishop pair balances White's space advantage.

B21: 5 ♗c4

Preventing 5...♗c5 because of 6 ♗xf7+ ♔xf7 7 ♕d5+.

5...♘f6!

This strong move, from the IM-GM clash L.Shytaj-M.Godena, Italian Championship, Marta Franca 2008, leads to very sharp play, not unfavourable to Black. Before this, 5...♗b4+ was the standard reply, as played by E.Pedersen, Przewoznik, Miles and Hort, who scored one draw between them! (It was Miles.)

6 ♘c3

Shytaj's choice.

Only 6 e5 is critical, but Black has sufficient resources: 6...d5! 7 ♗b3 ♘g4 8 ♗xd5 ♗b4+ 9 ♘c3 (or 9 c3 ♗c5 10 ♗xc6+ bxc6 11 ♕xd8+ ♔xd8 12 ♘e2 ♗f2+ 13 ♔f1 ♗b6 14 ♘d4 f6 15 exf6 ♗a6+ 16 ♔g1 ♖e8 17 ♗d2 ♖e4 18 fxg7 ♔e7 19 g3 ♗d3 with dangerous play – Black's light-squared bishop is an absolute monster) 9...0-0! 10 ♗xc6 ♕xd1+ 11 ♔xd1 bxc6 12 ♔e2 f6! 13 h3 ♘h6 14 ♘f3 ♘f5 15 ♘e4 fxe5 16 fxe5 ♗e6 17 ♗d2 ♗xd2 18 ♔xd2 ♖ad8+ 19 ♔c3 ♘e3 20 ♘d4 ♗d5 21 ♘c5 ♗xg2 22 ♖hg1

♘d5+ 23 ♔c4 ♘e3+ 24 ♔c3 with a draw.

6...♗b4 7 ♘e2

Here 7 e5 d5 8 exf6 dxc4 9 ♕e2+?! ♔f8!? (9...♗e6 is also good) 10 ♗e3 ♕xf6 11 0-0-0 ♗e6 was better for Black, who went on to win in M.Orso-G.Bordas, Budapest 2000 (see Game 48). Go Bordas! 9 ♕xd8+ improves for White, when 9...♔xd8 10 fxg7 ♖g8 11 ♗e3 ♗xc3 12 bxc3 ♖xg7 13 ♔f2 ♗f5 14 ♖d1+ ♔c8 15 ♖d2 b6 is equal.

7...♘xe4!

7...d6 is equal; Godena finds more.

8 ♗xf7+ ♔xf7 9 ♕d5+ ♔f8 10 ♕xe4 d5

A sharp reversal of fortune has occurred in the centre, and this is far more important than any minor inconvenience suffered by Black's king.

11 ♕f3 ♕h4+! 12 g3 ♗g4!

After seeing this, Godena is my new hero.

13 ♕d3?

White, who is suffering badly, may as well take a pawn for his troubles. 13 ♕xd5 is not clearly losing, whereas the text move is.

13...♕h5 14 0-0

14...d4?!

14...♖e8! allows less counterplay: 15 ♗e3 d4! 16 ♘xd4 ♖xe3 17 ♕xe3 ♘xd4 18 ♕d3 ♘f3+ 19 ♖xf3 ♗xf3.

15 f5! dxc3 16 ♘f4! ♕f7 17 ♘e6+ ♔g8 18 bxc3 ♗d6 19 ♕e4 ♘e5 20 ♕xb7 ♖e8 21 ♘d4 c5 22 ♕a6 cxd4 23 ♕xd6 ♘f3+ 24 ♔g2 ♕b7

White has had enough. Did I mention that Godena is my new hero?

B22: 5 ♘f3

Rare at a high level, this lazy-looking move is White's best, apparently doing nothing to contest the a7-g1 diagonal.

5...♗c5 6 ♘c3

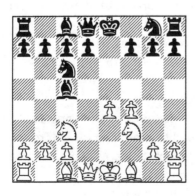

6...d6

Instead:

a) 6...a6?! 7 ♕e2! d6 8 ♗e3 ♗xe3 9 ♕xe3 ♘f6 10 0-0-0 is pleasant for White.

b) 6...♘f6!? leads to wild complications and is fully playable if you enjoy such positions. Here are some sample variations: 7 e5! ♘g4 8 ♗c4 (or 8 ♘e4! ♗b6 9 ♗c4 d5 10 ♕xd5 ♕e7 {10...♕xd5!?} 11 h3 ♗e6 12 ♕b5 a6 13 ♕a4 ♗xc4 14 ♕xc4 ♘e3 15 ♗xe3 ♗xe3 16 g3 0-0-0, when Black has compensation for most of a pawn) 8...d6 9 ♘g5 (or 9 ♘e4 ♗e3 10 exd6 0-0 {10...♗xc1!?} 11 ♗xe3 ♘xe3 12 ♕e2 ♘xc4 13 ♕xc4 cxd6 14 0-0-0 ♗e6 15 ♕b5 d5 16 f5 a6 17 ♕c5 ♗xf5 18 ♖xd5 ♕e7 19 ♘d6 ♗e6 20 ♖d2 ♗xa2! 21 b3 ♕f6 22 ♘d4 a5) 9...0-0 10 h3 ♘h6 11 ♘a4 ♗b6 12 ♘xb6 axb6 13 0-0 dxe5 14 ♕xd8 ♖xd8 15 fxe5 ♘xe5 16 ♗b3 c5 17 ♗f4 c4 with equality.

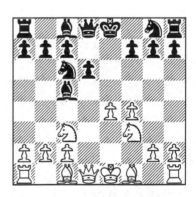

7 ♘a4! ♗b6 8 ♘xb6 axb6 9 ♗d3 ♘f6

9...d5 transposes to S.Fedorchuk-A.Miles, Ohrid 2001, which Miles won (see Game 49), but the idea does not merit the exclamation mark bestowed by Kalinin – the simple text is best.

10 0-0 0-0 11 ♖e1

So far we have followed M.Heyne-R.Vogel, Passau 1999, which actually started as an Englund Gambit! (1 d4 e5?!). Instead of 11...♖e8 (which could be met by 12 e5!), Black should have played 11...♘b4, an annoying attack on White's bishop pair, which he can no longer preserve (12 ♗c4 ♗e6!). After 12 ♗d2 ♘xd3 13 cxd3 Black's plan is to mobilize his queenside majority with 13...c5, ...b6-b5-b4 and ...b7-b5 (again!), develop the bishop with ...♗d7-c6, and restrain White's centre by ...♖e8. It is also important to prevent ♗g5, so if White plays f4-f5, then ...h7-h6 is the normal response. I cannot tell a lie – White has a tiny edge. Notice that 13...c5 14 a4 b5! is tactically possible (and desirable) because 15 axb5 ♖xa1 16 ♕xa1 ♗d7 recovers the pawn and activates the bishop.

If White prevents ...♘b4 with 11 ♗d2, the answer is 11...d5! 12 e5 ♘e4 13 ♗e1 ♘c5 14 f5 ♘xd3 15 ♕xd3 ♕e7

16 ♗c3 ♕c5+ 17 ♔h1 ♕c4 with equality.

White has also tried 11 b3!? ♗d7 12 ♗b2 ♘b4! 13 ♕d2 ♘xd3 14 cxd3 c5 15 f5 ♗c6 16 ♕g5 h6 17 ♗xf6 ♕xf6 18 ♕xf6 gxf6, when Black had equalized in J.R.Capablanca(!)-M.H.McGuire, New Orleans (simul) 1911. Black went on to win, outmanoeuvring Capablanca with his better minor and queenside pawn majority. Outrageous!

C: 3 ♘f3 exd4

Now White has:

C1: 4 ♘xd4 *80* – the Scotch Game
C2: 4 ♗c4 *88* – the Scotch Gambit

If 4 c3 (the Göring Gambit), we decline with 4...d5! 5 exd5 ♕xd5 6 cxd4 ♗g4 7 ♗e2 ♗b4+ 8 ♘c3 ♗xf3 9 ♗xf3 ♕c4 and White, who can't yet castle, has done terribly after 10 ♕b3 ♕xb3 11 axb3 with vile pawns, or 10 ♗xc6+ bxc6! 11 ♕e2+ ♕xe2+ 12 ♔xe2 0-0-0 13 ♗e3 ♘e7, when Black's king is safe and guards his weaknesses. White should really be okay, but has had serious problems in practice. One good idea for Black is ...♗a5-b6 to pressure White's d4-pawn and shore up the queenside.

C1: 4 ♘xd4 ♗c5!

We are allowed to play the normal move on occasion. There's always time for weirdness later.

White's main moves are:

> **C11: 5 ♗e3** *81*
> **C12: 5 ♘xc6** *85*

First let's take out the trash:

a) 5 ♘b3?! leaves our bishop uncontested on a strong diagonal: 5...♗b6 6 a4 a6 7 ♘c3.

The position is highly reminiscent of a Caro-Kann Classical Variation (in mirror image), but with a few advantages for us. We have saved a move on ...c7-c6 (i.e. ...f7-f6 here), it is hard for White to trade our strong dark-squared bishop, and we will find castling short to be far more efficient and effective than castling long in the Caro (where

...♔b8, ...♖c8, ...c6-c5 is time consuming).

If anyone tells you to let White play 8 ♘d5, don't believe them: 7...♘f6! (7...♘ge7 is good too, transposing to 6 ♘c3 ♘ge7 below, but not the insipid main variation with 7...d6?) 8 ♗g5 (8 ♗e2 is preferable) 8...h6 9 ♗h4 d6 and Black is better already.

Apparently Magnus Carlsen has had some good results with 6 ♕e2 d6 7 ♗e3 but, given the above comparison, it is clear that this should not be dangerous. Black simply needs to keep in mind the ...f7-f5 break: 7...♘ge7! 8 ♘c3 0-0 9 0-0-0 f5! – a few people have noticed this, and Black is +7 -4 =2 in this position (most of the games reached by transposition). Goh Wei Ming-F.Bellini, Turin Olympiad 2006, is a nice win by Black (see Game 50).

A cagier move order which is sometimes used is 6 ♘c3, when it is not yet clear whether White will be playing a2-a4 or ♕e2. It is more important to be prepared for the fashionable ♕e2, so 6...♘ge7 7 ♕e2 d6 8 ♗e3 transposes to the previous paragraph, while 7 a4 a6 8 ♗g5 f6 9 ♗h4 0-0 is absolutely fine for Black, who intends ...d7-d6, ...♞g6 and ...f6-f5, or else ...d7-d6, ...♗e6, ...♛d7 (or ...♛e8) and ...f6-f5.

b) 5 ♞f5?! performs well if Black doesn't know his stuff (he usually doesn't). Surprise the surpriser by knowing this short variation: 5...d5! 6 ♞xg7+ ♚f8 7 ♞h5 ♛h4 8 ♞g3 ♞f6! 9 ♗e2 dxe4 and Black has a small advantage with which he almost always wins.

c) 5 c3?! indicates that White has forgotten the move order. Don't lazily transpose with 5...♛f6?! 6 ♗e3, but play 5...♞f6! instead, with advantage.

C11: 5 ♗e3 ♛f6

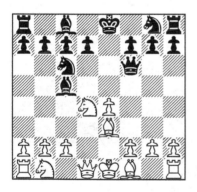

6 c3

White can try 6 ♞b5 here, but after 6...♗xe3 7 fxe3 ♛h4+ (this intermezzo forces a concession) 8 g3 ♛d8 9 ♛g4 g5! 10 ♞1c3 ♞e5 11 ♛e2 d6 12 h3 c6 13 ♞d4 ♞f6 14 0-0-0 ♛e7 15 ♛f2 ♗e6 16 ♗e2 0-0-0 Black was obviously fine and went on to win a marathon game

in P.Bontempi-O.Jovanic, Nova Gorica 2008 (see Game 51).

6...♛g6!?

From here the queen threatens e4, pressures g2, and clears the f6-square for the knight. Also, we steer clear of the most heavily analyzed continuations. Black has done very well with this move!

There are two main replies, and a bunch of minor ones.

> **C111: 7 ♞d2** *82*
> **C112: 7 ♞b5** *84*

Others:

a) The unlikely-looking 7 ♛e2 has also been popular. White hopes for 7...♛xe4?? 8 ♞xc6 ♗xe3 9 ♞d4, winning (this has yet to work, but hope springs eternal). Instead, 7...♞xd4! 8 cxd4 (or 8 ♗xd4 ♗xd4 9 cxd4 ♞e7 10 ♞c3 0-0 11 0-0-0 c6 and with 12...d5 coming, Black is slightly better) 8...♗b4+ 9 ♗d2 ♗xd2+ 10 ♞xd2 ♞e7 11 g3! (to discourage 11...d5) 11...0-0 12 ♗g2 ♛b6 and White will have compensation for the pawn he is losing, but no more than that.

b) 7 f3 a6!? (this is a novelty – it's time to put a stop to ♘b5 once and for all) 8 ♘d2 d6 9 ♕c2 ♘ge7 10 0-0-0 ♗a7 11 ♔b1 0-0 is equal; or 8 ♕d2 ♘ge7, transposing to S.Vajda-S.Skembris, Naujac 1999, which continued 9 ♘c2 ♗xe3 10 ♘xe3 d6 11 ♗e2 and Black found plenty of activity with 11...f5, going on to win (see Game 52).

c) Dembo and Palliser (D&P) like 7 ♕f3 pretty well,

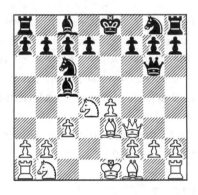

but after 7...d6 8 ♘b5 ♗g4 9 ♕f4 ♗xe3 10 ♕xe3 ♖c8 I don't agree that White is better; e.g. 11 f4 ♘f6 12 ♗d3 0-0 13 0-0 ♖fe8 14 ♘d2 ♗d7 and Black has no particular problems. 15 ♘xa7?! is met by 15...♘g4 16 f5 ♕h5 17 ♕g3 ♘xa7 18 ♖f4! ♕xh2+ (18...♘e5 19 ♖h4 ♕xh4 20 ♕xh4 ♘xd3 21 f6 is less clear) 19 ♕xh2 ♘xh2 20 ♔xh2 ♘c6 with a small but persistent endgame advantage for Black due to White's backward e-pawn, weak e5-square, and defensive bishop.

d) D&P also like 7 ♗e2, and it is in-deed dangerous to try to win a pawn, but in E.Stavropoulou-M.Ikonomo-poulou, Athens 2003, Black found an excellent alternative: 7...♘f6! 8 ♘d2 (8 0-0 d6 9 ♔h1 ♗d7 10 ♘d2 0-0 is equal) 8...d5! 9 exd5 ♘xd5 10 ♗f3 ♘xe3 11 fxe3 ♘e5! with a clear advantage.

C111: 7 ♘d2

This is pathetic, but it's played most of the time, so I guess that makes it the main line! I can't imagine why White would play the Scotch if this is his plan for dealing with 6...♕g6. The following draws significantly on Dembo and Palliser.

7...♘f6

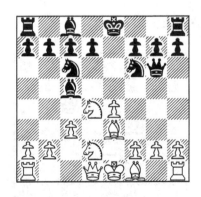

8 ♕f3

Other moves:

a) 8 f3 is more common, when Black should strike in the centre with 8...d5! 9 ♗b5! (stronger than 9 ♕c2?! ♗xd4 10 cxd4 0-0 11 0-0-0 dxe4 12 fxe4 ♖e8 13 a3 ♘xe4 14 ♗d3 ♗f5 15 d5 ♘d6 16 ♗xf5 ♕xf5 and Black keeps an extra pawn; or 9 ♘b5?! ♗xe3 10 ♘xc7 ♔f8 11 ♘xa8 dxe4 12 ♕e2 ♕h6 13 ♘xe4

♘xe4 14 fxe4 ♘e5 and White needs both to survive and to extricate the knight, which is more hard than easy) 9...♕xg2 10 ♖g1 ♕xh2 11 ♖xg7. Up until now we've been following E.Berg-I.Morovic Fernandez, European Championship, Saint Vincent 2000, which continued 11...♗d7 12 ♕b3 ♕h4+ 13 ♔d1 and D&P says favours Black, but *Houdini* calls even, and Black did go on to lose. Instead, I am recommending 11...♔f8!? 12 ♖g1 ♘xd4 13 cxd4 ♗e7 14 ♕b3 c6 15 e5! (after 15 ♗d3 dxe4 15 fxe4 ♕h4+ 16 ♗f2 ♕f4 17 ♖f1 ♗e6, White's compensation is insufficient) 15...cxb5 16 exf6 ♕h4+ 17 ♔e2 ♕xf6 18 ♕xd5 ♕f5 19 ♕e4 ♕xe4 20 fxe4 h5 21 ♘f3 ♗g4 with approximate equality in an unbalanced endgame.

b) 8 ♗e2 d5! transposes to Stavropoulou-Ikonomopoulou a few paragraphs above. I must say it's interesting that Black so rarely captures on e4 or g2. However, 6...♕g6 has other points to it, and White can't leave those pawns hanging forever.

c) 8 ♕c2?! ♘g4! 9 0-0-0 ♘xe3 10 fxe3 0-0 11 ♘2f3 d6 12 ♘f5 ♖e8 and Black is on top – D&P.

d) 8 ♕e2 ♘g4 9 ♘c2 ♘xe3 10 ♘xe3 ♘e7 11 ♘b3 ♗b6 12 ♘f5 ♕f6 13 ♘xe7 ♕xe7 14 g3 0-0 15 ♗g2 d6 with a small advantage in R.Roszkowski-A.Leniart, Grodzisk Mazowiecki 2007 – D&P.

e) 8 ♘f5 (or 8 ♘c2) 8...♗xe3 9 ♘xe3 0-0 10 ♗d3 d5 11 exd5 ♕xd3 12 dxc6 ♖e8 13 ♘b3 ♕b5 14 a4 occurred in J.Hoogendoorn-A.Van de Oudeweeter-ing, Leeuwarden 2001, which was equal after 14...♕xc6 15 0-0 (D&P), but Black can keep some pressure with 14...♕a6!, stubbornly denying White's castling rights. After 15 ♕e2 ♕xc6 16 0-0 ♘g4 17 ♘d4 ♕d6 White will soon have an isolated e-pawn and a somewhat worse position.

f) 8 f4 has worked very well for White in practice, so be careful! The careful response is 8...♘xd4 9 cxd4 ♗b4 10 f5 ♕g4 11 ♕xg4 ♘xg4 12 ♗f4 d5 13 h3 ♘f6 14 e5 ♘e4 15 g4 g6 16 fxg6 fxg6, which is slightly better for Black because of his imminent f-file control, though it was not enough to win in A.Motylev-S.Gligoric, Yugoslav Team Championship 2000 (see Game 53).

g) 8 h4 h5! is not helpful to White in any variation.

8...♘g4! 9 ♘f5

The unplayed 9 ♘b5!? is a better try, though after 9...♘xe3 10 fxe3 ♔d8, the position is balanced. And imbalanced. Go figure.

9...♘xe3 10 ♘xe3 0-0 11 ♘d5 ♘e5 12 ♕g3

So far this is B.Kharashkina-O.Stjazhkina, St. Petersburg 2001, and now instead of 12...♞g4?!, Black should have preferred 12...♛xg3 13 hxg3 c6, which D&P call "at least equal", though I think is safe to call a small advantage for Black.

C112: 7 ♞b5!?

This is the only critical move, but it is rarely played.

7...♝xe3 8 ♞xc7+

Just as often White wimps out with 8 fxe3 ♚d8, when White's structural problems are far more serious than Black's king position. Black wins virtually every game; e.g. 9 ♞d2 ♞f6 10 ♛f3 d6 11 h3 ♜e8 12 0-0-0 ♝d7 and Black can capture the e-pawn at his convenience. IM Rathnakaran somehow got caught behind the white pieces in this variation and tried 10 ♛b3 ♞g4!? 11 0-0-0? ♞f2 12 ♝e2 ♞xh1 (K.Rathnakaran-P.Negi, Indian Championship, Mangalore 2008), but the game is far too silly to put in my book.

8...♚d8 9 ♞xa8 ♝f4! 10 ♛f3 ♝h6!

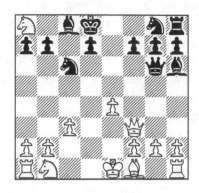

White's queen is lousy on the f3-square – it can't reach the queenside, it's vulnerable to ...♝g4, and makes it impossible for White to guard his e-pawn securely with f2-f3. The position is still extremely complicated, but approximately equal.

Some more analysis follows, though it is hardly practical to be exhaustive, so here are some bits to keep in mind:

1. The material imbalance (two minor pieces for a rook, once the a8-knight drops) is inherently the most useful for Black in the middlegame – the minor pieces are well suited for attack. This means that Black should not be eager for trades even though his king is a bit loose.

2. If an endgame is reached, it is far better for Black to retain his single rook than to trade it for one of White's two rooks.

3. Pawn exchanges favour White, whose rooks have the most to gain from an open board.

4. Naturally, Black will try to keep his bishop pair if possible. Even deep in

an endgame, two bishops are normally equal to a rook and two pawns.

Black had a chance to show the power of points #2 and #4 in P.Hromada-L.Ostrowski, Moravian Team Championship 2002 (see Game 54).

In D.Campora-V.Tkachiev, Biel 1995, White tried 11 ♕f5 ♕xf5 12 exf5 b6 13 ♘a3 ♗b7. As I just mentioned, a queen trade generally favours White, but the price was too high: a tempo, a crippled pawn majority, and a weakened centre position. Black had no problems after pocketing the knight, and had winning chances, although the game ended in a draw (see Game 55).

Dembo and Palliser recommend 11 ♗e2 ♘f6 12 0-0 ♘xe4 13 ♗d3 (end of analysis), but *Houdini* greatly prefers Black's position after 13...f5. Naturally, Black will play ...b7-b6 and ...♗b7 at his earliest convenience; e.g. 14 ♘a3 ♘e5! (14...♘d2 15 ♕d5 is not worth it) 15 ♕h3 (not 15 ♕e2? ♗f4! 16 g3?! ♘g5! 17 f3 ♖e8 with a brutal attack) 15...b6 15 ♖ad1 ♗b7 and it's still complicated, but Black is trapping the knight, activating his pieces, generating threats against the enemy king, and not being checkmated, which adds up to an excellent position.

C12: 5 ♘xc6

This move is popular among Extremely Boring GMs and people with no idea what's going on. (I'm thinking of taking it up myself.) Experience shows that in the endgames that are normally reached, White sometimes wins and just about never loses. Yuck! Don't worry, it's all taken care of.

5...♕f6 6 ♕d2

Apparently, 6 ♕f3!? is topical at the moment: 6...♕xf3 7 gxf3 bxc6 8 ♗e3 ♗xe3 9 fxe3

At first glance the position looks completely equal, which goes to show you that sometimes first glances are dead on. In practice White has a nagging edge (+13 -5 =21), but that's only because Black has not found the correct plan until this very moment: 9...d6! 10 ♘c3 (or 10 ♖g1 g6) 10...♘f6! (the novelty) 11 ♔f2 (or 11 0-0-0) 11...0-0 12 ♖d1 ♖e8.

The point is to immobilize White's centre pawns and prepare ...♖e5, from which the rook has quite a pleasant view! One obvious idea is ...♖h5, while under some circumstances ...d6-d5 can be played (especially if White has castled long). Black's activity is quite sufficient to neutralize the practical advantage White has been getting after 9...♘e7?!. This idea was inspired by I.Grynfeld-A.Bisguier, Helsinki Olympiad 1952! (see Game 56), though Bisguier in fact missed his chance to play ...♖e5.

6...dxc6

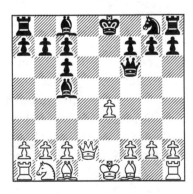

7 ♘c3

Or:

a) 7 ♕f4 ♗e6 8 ♘c3 0-0-0 9 ♗d3 h6!? – kingside expansion with 10...g5 will be useful whether the queens are traded or not. In any case, Black has activity in exchange for his crippled queenside majority. For the adventurous, 9...h5!? is also possible: 10 0-0 h4 11 h3 ♘e7 12 ♕xf6 gxf6 13 ♘e2 ♖hg8 with more weaknesses for more activity.

b) 7 ♗d3 ♗e6 and (to make a long story short) Black gets to castle long, with excellent development.

7...♗d4!

White intended 8 ♕f4 to enter an annoying endgame. The text move stops this insidious and somnolent plan and equalizes, according to Dembo and Palliser. In practical play, Black seems to do even better.

8 ♗d3 ♘e7 9 0-0 ♘g6

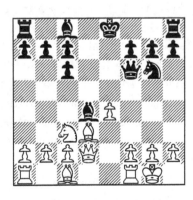

Black's knight is taking the scenic route to the g4-square, where it will be dangerous to the white king. If Black had tried to take a shortcut with

8...♘h6, White would have put a stop to it immediately with 9 h3!.

10 ♔h1

Since the main variation offers nothing, White sometimes tries 10 ♘e2!? which frees his position after 10...♗b6. So far, taking the pawn has performed badly for Black, but it is the critical move, and I do not believe in letting White off so easily: 10...♗xb2 11 ♗xb2 ♕xb2 12 f4 ♕a3 13 f5 ♘e5 14 ♕g5 ♗d7 is equal, as in J.Smeets-A.Beliavsky, Maribor (rapid) 2004 (see Game 57). Even better is 14...♕f8! followed by 15...f6, when White does not have quite enough for the pawn. If 15 f6?! ♕c5+ 16 ♔h1 g6, the threat of 17...♘xd3 gives Black time for ...♗d7 and ...0-0-0.

10...♘e5

The knight is strong, but if White tries to dislodge it with 11 f4, then 11...♘g4 12 ♕e1 (12 ♘d1?? ♘xh2) 12...♘xh2 (in B.Sultimov-N.Pokazanjev, Russia 2007, Black tried for and got more with the risky 12...♗d7!? – see Game 58) 13 ♔xh2 ♕h6+ 14 ♔g3 ♕g6+ is a draw by perpetual.

11 ♗e2 ♘g4 12 ♘d1 ♕d6

12...♗e6 is fine too, intending to castle long.

13 ♗xg4

After 13 g3 h5 14 c3 ♗b6 15 ♕g5 ♕e5 16 f3 ♕xg5 17 ♗xg5 ♘e5, Black had the initiative in D.Pavasovic-N.V.Pedersen, Bled Olympiad 2002; or if 13 f4, Black has the pleasant choice between 13...♘xh2, with another perpetual, and 13...h5!?, trying for more (Dembo and Palliser).

13...♗xg4

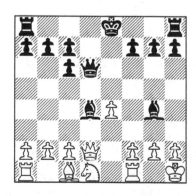

14 c3 ♗f6 15 ♕xd6 cxd6 is about equal, while the common 14 ♕g5 ♕g6 is a little better for Black.

C2: 4 ♗c4

The Scotch Gambit.

4...♘f6!

The Two Knights Defence. I have chosen sound sidelines for Black to simplify the study material.

White has:

> **C21: 5 0-0** *88*
> **C22: 5 e5** *89*

Or 5 ♘g5 d5! 6 exd5 ♕e7+ 7 ♔f1 ♘e5 8 ♕xd4 ♘xc4 9 ♕xc4 h6 10 ♘f3 ♕c5 11 ♕e2+ ♗e7 12 c4 ♘xd5 (12...b5!?) with an edge for Black.

C21: 5 0-0 ♘xe4 6 ♖e1 d5 7 ♗xd5 ♕xd5 8 ♘c3 ♕d8!?

This is rare but sound. The idea is to make it more difficult for White to recover the d-pawn.

9 ♖xe4+

Just as common is 9 ♘xe4?! ♗e7 10 ♗g5 f6! and White, down a pawn and lacking his light-squared bishop usually panics with 11 ♘xf6+ gxf6 12 ♗xf6 0-0 13 ♗xe7 ♘xe7, but there is no compensation for the sacrificed material.

9...♗e7 10 ♘xd4

10...f5! 11 ♖f4

Or 11 ♗h6!?, when Black can take a draw with 11...fxe4 12 ♗xg7 ♖f8 13 ♕h5+ ♖f7 14 ♖d1 ♕d6 15 ♘db5 ♕f4 16 ♘d5 ♕xf2+ 17 ♔h1 ♗d7 18 ♘f6+ ♗xf6 19 ♘xc7+ ♔e7 20 ♘d5+ ♔e6 21 ♘c7+, or play on with 11...0-0 12 ♘xc6 bxc6 13 ♖d4 ♕e8 14 ♗f4 ♗f6 with equal chances.

11...0-0 12 ♘xc6 ♕xd1+ 13 ♘xd1 bxc6 14 ♖c4 c5 15 ♗e3 ♖e8

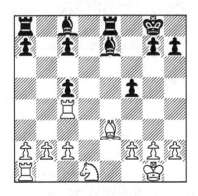

Black's bishops are strong enough that he is not worse.

C22: 5 e5 ♘g4!?

At first this seems insane because of 6 ♗xf7+ ♔xf7 7 ♘g5+, but as in so many similar positions, Black's king position is fine since White has traded off his most powerful attacking piece (the light-squared bishop). So 7...♔g8! 8 ♕xg4 (after 8 ♕f3 ♗b4+! 9 c3 ♕e7 10 ♕d5+ ♗f8 11 0-0 ♘gxe5 12 cxb4 ♘xb4 13 ♕b3 h6 White has nowhere near enough for two pawns) 8...h6! 9 ♘f3 d6 10 ♕e4 (or 10 e6 ♕f6) 10...dxe5 11 ♘xe5 and now 11...♕f6 12 ♘xc6 bxc6 13 0-0 ♗f5 is simplest, though *Houdini* likes 11...♕e7 12 f4 ♕h4+ 13 g3 ♕f6 14 0-0 ♗f5 15 ♕d5+ ♔h7 with a large advantage because White has a stupid position – or, to be more specific, due to Black's bishop pair and White's weak light squares.

White also has:

> **C221: 6 ♕e2** *89*
> **C222: 6 0-0** *90*

C221: 6 ♕e2

Most often played, but White struggles to equalize in the main lines.

6...♕e7 7 ♗f4 f6! 8 exf6 ♕xe2+!

This is the most forcing.

9 ♗xe2

9 ♔xe2?! is more common, when the brand new, never been opened, still in its original packaging 9...gxf6! gives Black the advantage; e.g. 10 ♖e1 ♘ge5 11 ♔f1 d6 12 ♘bd2 ♗d7 13 ♘e4 ♗g7, and although Black's position is far from perfect, White is having a hard time recovering the pawn. Or 10 ♖d1 ♘ge5 11 ♗d5 d3+ 12 cxd3 ♘xf3 13 ♗xf3 ♘d4+ 14 ♔d2 ♘xf3+ 15 gxf3 c6, when White has recovered the pawn, but wishes he hadn't.

9...♘xf6

There is still chess to be played, but the position is equal after (among others) 10 ♘bd2 d6 11 ♘b3 d3 12 ♗xd3 ♘b4 13 0-0-0 ♘xd3 14 ♖xd3 h6 and 15...♔f7, though Black has managed to stir things up a bit. Worse for White is 10 ♗xc7?! d6! 11 ♗b5 ♗d7 12 ♗xc6 ♗xc6 13 ♘xd4 ♗xg2 14 ♖g1, as in R.Stranz-K.Neumeier, Austrian Team Championship 2004, when Black should have continued 14...♗h3 with an edge.

C222: 6 0-0 ♗e7

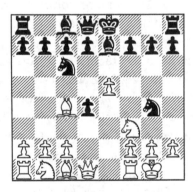

7 ♖e1

Or 7 ♗f4 g5! 8 ♘xg5 (8 ♗g3 h5! 9 h3 h4!, D.Von Wantoch Rekowski-J.Peric, Tivat 2001, was a strong case for Black – see Game 59) 8...d5! 9 e6 (9 exd6?! ♗xg5 10 dxc7 ♕f6 11 ♕e2+ ♔f8 doesn't give White enough for the piece) 9...♗xg5 10 ♕xg4 ♗xe6 11 ♗xg5 ♗xg4 12 ♗xd8 ♖xd8 and Black keeps a pawn, for which White has not nearly enough.

7...d6 8 exd6 cxd6!

Only 8...♕xd6 has been played, but

then 9 b3! 0-0 10 ♗a3 ♕d8 11 ♗xe7 ♘xe7 12 ♕xd4 ♕xd4 13 ♘xd4 gives White a good endgame.

Instead, the text move is very dynamic – a main idea is to use the g4-knight to harass White on the soft f2-square. Let's analyze: 9 ♘xd4 (not 9 h3?! ♘ge5 and Black is better already) 9...0-0 and now:

a) 10 h3 d5! 11 ♘xc6 (or 11 ♗b3?! ♗c5! 12 c3 ♘xf2! 13 ♔xf2 ♘xd4 14 cxd4 ♕h4+ 15 ♔f1 ♗xd4 16 ♗e3 ♕f6+ 17 ♔g1 ♗xb2 18 ♘d2 ♗xa1 19 ♕xa1 ♕xa1 20 ♖xa1 ♖e8 with advantage – quite a small one actually; the material balance very strongly suggests trades for Black, so if 21 ♔f2 ♗e6 22 ♘f3?! then 22...d4!! makes progress) 11...bxc6 12 hxg4 (12 ♗d3 ♘f6 is equal) 12...dxc4 13 ♕f3 ♗e6! 14 ♕xc6 ♗xg4! 15 ♕xc4 ♗e6 16 ♕e2 ♖e8 17 ♘c3 ♗f6 and the board is so open that the bishop pair offsets the missing pawn. White also lags in development.

b) 10 ♘c3 ♗h4! 11 g3 ♗f6 12 ♘db5 a6 13 ♘xd6 ♘xf2!

Wow! It's complicated, but at least

you won't be seeing the position for the first time, unlike your poor opponent. As it turns out, White has several acceptable routes to a draw, but no good way to play for a win:

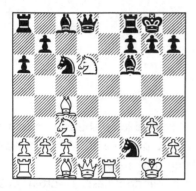

b1) 14 ♘xf7 ♕xd1 15 ♘xd1 ♘xd1 and White can repeat moves now with 16 ♘d6+ ♔h8 17 ♘f7+, or play 17 ♖xd1 ♗d4+ 18 ♖xd4 (18 ♔h1 ♗g4! is trouble for White, as is 18 ♔g2 ♖f2+ 19 ♔h1 ♗g4) 18...♘xd4 and repeat moves here with 19 ♘f7+ ♔g8 20 ♘g5+ etc.

b2) 14 ♕d5 ♗d4!, when White has a couple draws, but 15 ♖e8?! is not one of them: 15...♕xe8 16 ♘xe8 ♗e6! 17 ♕h5 ♗g4 18 ♘f6+ ♗xf6 19 ♕d5 ♖ad8 20 ♔xf2 ♖xd5 21 ♘xd5 ♗d4+ is better for Black, who is more active, and White's king is still a problem. Instead, 15 ♕xf7+ ♖xf7 16 ♘xf7 ♘d3+ 17 ♔h1 ♘f2+, and now it is Black who is best advised to repeat moves; or 15 ♘xf7 ♘d3+ 16 ♗e3 ♕xd5 17 ♗xd5 ♘xe1 18 ♖xe1 ♗f5 19 ♗xd4 ♘xd4 20 ♖e7 ♗xc2 21 ♖xb7 ♘f5 and the usual repetition follows.

b3) 14 ♗xf7+ ♔h8 15 ♔xf2 ♗d4+ 16 ♔g2 ♕xd6 17 ♗f4 ♕c5 18 ♘e4 ♕f5 and the complications are not over, but White's king position is far too fragile for him to have serious thoughts about winning – losing is quite attainable though!

b4) 14 ♔xf2?! doesn't make sense. 14...♗d4+ and 15...♕xd6 is not terrible for White, but he has nothing to compensate for his loose king.

Chapter Five
1 e4 ♘c6 2 ♘f3

With this move, White hopes to enter his favourite double-king-pawn position, which he will be happy to do after 2...e5. We are obligated to disappoint him, and in the resulting Pirc positions White may wish he had not committed his knight so soon – the Austrian Attack (f2-f4) and the Argentinean Attack (f2-f3) are no longer available to him, nor are several other aggressive variations.

2...d6 3 d4

After the premature 3 ♗b5 we have an extremely rare situation where it is fine to play 3...♘f6 4 ♘c3 ♗g4 – White

is unlikely to keep the bishop pair and he won't be able to stop Black from shifting his pawn structure to light squares. Nonetheless, 3...♘f6 4 ♘c3 g6 5 d4 a6 is simpler, especially since we will need to know this position anyway. **3...♘f6**

4 ♘c3

Other moves:

a) 4 c3 is possible and does not actually drop a pawn: 4...♘xe4?? 5 d5 ♘b8 6 ♕a4+ picks up the e4-knight. However, 4...g6 is fine for Black. Miles downed GMs Becerra Rivero and Zelcic starting with this move (see Games 60 and 61). Mestrovic is also 2-0 with 4...g6 here. To continue: 5 ♗d3 ♗g7 6 0-0 0-0 7 h3 e5 8 ♖e1.

Although Black has tried many things in hundreds of games, I am recommending 8...b6!, as played once in I.Vasilevich-M.Allakhinova, Russian Team Championship 2002. One point is that, after 9 d5 ♘e7, Black's pawn holds up White's queenside play; while 9 ♗e3 exd4! 10 cxd4 ♘b4 picks up the bishop pair: 11 ♘c3 ♘xd3 12 ♕xd3 ♖e8 13 ♖ad1 (or 13 ♖ac1 c5) 13...♗b7 14 d5 ♖c8 with only a small advantage to White; ...♖c8 helps prepare an eventual ...c7-c6, and pre-empts any White pressure down the c-file.

The game continuation should not have been too dangerous either: 9 ♕a4 ♗d7 10 ♗b5 ♕e8 11 d5 ♘e7 (11...♘b8!) 12 ♗xd7 ♘xd7 (12...♕xd7!) 13 ♕c4 ♘c5 14 b4 b5 15 ♕e2 ♘a4 16 ♗d2 and now, instead of 16...c5?! as played, 16...f5!! 17 ♘g5 fxe4 18 ♘e6 ♕f7 19 ♘xc7 ♖ab8 20 ♘e6 ♖fc8 21 ♕xe4 ♗f6! is good for Black, who plans 22...♘b6 and 23...♘bxd5.

White tried 8 ♘a3 in L.Rozman-

J.Schuyler, Washington 2012: 8...d5! 9 ♗g5?! (9 exd5 ♘xd5 10 dxe5 ♘xe5 11 ♘xe5 ♗xe5 12 ♖e1 ♗g7 is equal) 9...dxe4 10 ♗xe4 exd4 11 ♗xc6?! (11 cxd4 is still fairly level) 11...dxc3! with great complications favouring Black (see Game 62).

b) 4 ♘bd2 is similarly met by 4...g6.

Miles took down GMs Zapata and Nijboer with this move (see Games 63 and 64). Given his successes with this fianchetto, it is surprising to me that Miles was never willing to play 4...g6 against 4 ♘c3, even when other moves were giving him trouble.

c) 4 ♗d3 doesn't look right because Black can pick up the bishop pair with 4...♘b4. My first inclination was that this must equalize immediately, but apparently tempi sometimes matter in chess! After 5 0-0 ♘xd3 6 ♕xd3 g6 7 c4 ♗g7 8 ♘c3 it will be difficult for Black to disrupt White's huge centre. Therefore, 4...g6 here too! All three of White's fourth move sidelines may transpose into each other.

4...g6!

4...♗g4 is by far the most common move, ensuring that Black reaches positions unique to 1...♘c6, but Black has both objective and practical problems after White's most accurate reply 5 ♗e3. Then Miles always played 5...e6 and, when that stopped working, 5...a6, which was worse, while Mestrovic has repeatedly but unsuccessfully tried to uphold 5...e5. After 6 ♗b5, his record speaks for itself (+2 -9 =3).

On the other hand, our standard fianchetto with 4...g6 is reliable, transposing to a Classical Pirc (1 e4 d6 2 d4 ♘f6 3 ♘c3 g6 4 ♘f3) with the odd 4...♘c6. There are many strong players happy to use this placement for the knight; for instance, GMs Smirin and Adorjan have played (4...♗g7 5 ♗e2 0-0 6 0-0) 6...♘c6 twenty times between them, with seven wins and one loss. Of course, 6...♘c6 is not precisely 4...♘c6, but I intend to show that the differences are not critical.

White has many moves here, so I will divide the material into three groups:

A: 5 ♗b5 *94*
B: 5 d5 *96*
C: Others (without d4-d5) *102*

A: 5 ♗b5 a6

6 ♗xc6+

6 ♗a4 doesn't make much sense, but it has been played several times, most significantly in M.Kozakov-A.Zajarnyi, Lvov 1998, which continued 6...b5 7 ♗b3 ♗g7 8 h3 0-0 9 0-0 e6 10 a3 ♗b7 11 ♖e1 ♘a5 12 ♗a2 c5 13 d5

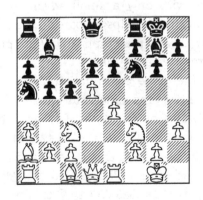

and now after 13...e5?! 14 b4! cxb4 15 axb4 ♕c7 16 bxa5 ♕xc3 17 ♗d2 ♕c7 18 c4! White eventually converted his advantage. Instead, Black could have kept the balance with 13...exd5! 14 ♘xd5 ♗xd5 15 ♗xd5 ♘xd5 16 ♕xd5 ♘c4. The important feature of the position from Black's standpoint is the active g7-bishop.

The simple 8...♘a5, picking up the bishop pair, also brings equality; e.g. 9 0-0 ♗b7 10 e5 dxe5 11 dxe5 ♘xb3 12 axb3 ♘e4 13 ♕xd8+ ♖xd8 14 ♘xe4 ♗xe4 15 ♖xa6 ♗xf3 16 gxf3 ♗xe5 and if you're still awake after all these trades, you'll notice that White's disgusting pawn structure is balanced by some extra rook activity.

Based on the Kozakov game, 6 ♗a4 is recommended (sort of) by Andrew Greet in *Beating Unusual Chess Defences: 1 e4*, so it is a good idea to be prepared.

6...bxc6 7 0-0 ♗g7

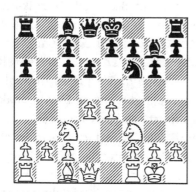

8 h3

White usually plays this move sooner or later in the Dark Knight Pirc, as he gets tired of worrying about ...♗g4. Others:

a) 8 e5!? ♘d5 9 ♘e4 0-0 10 ♖e1 was

equal in O.Biti-G.Belamaric, Portoroz 2005. White's lunge has pushed into where Black is strong and opened up squares for the c8-bishop. Black should play 10...a5 11 h3 c5!? 12 exd6 cxd6 13 dxc5 dxc5 14 ♘xc5 ♕d6 15 ♘e4 ♕c6 16 c3 a4 and in this open position, the bishop pair and queenside pressure are fully worth the sacrificed pawn.

b) 8 ♕e2 0-0 9 ♖d1 ♗g4 (9...a5! equalizes) 10 h3 ♗xf3 11 ♕xf3 ♘d7 12 ♗e3 e5 with a small edge for White in E.Sveshnikov-T.Gelashvili, Cappelle la Grande 2009, albeit one he was unable to convert (see Game 65).

8...0-0 9 ♖e1 ♖b8 10 ♖b1 ♘d7

11 ♗g5?!

The strong White and Black players to hold this position were focused on the ...e7-e5 break when they should be preparing for ...c6-c5.

11 ♗e3 is a bit better, though it still doesn't stop 11...c5!; e.g. 12 dxc5 ♖xb2! 13 ♖xb2 ♗xc3 14 ♖b3 ♗xe1 15 ♕xe1 ♘xc5 16 ♗xc5 dxc5 equal, or 12 ♕d2 cxd4 13 ♗xd4 ♘f6 14 e5 ♘h5 15 exd6 cxd6 16 ♗xg7 ♘xg7 with equality.

11...c5!

After 11...h6 12 ♗h4 g5 13 ♗g3 e5?! (13...c5 or 13...f5!? is better) 14 dxe5 dxe5, as in B.Vuckovic-Z.Petronijevic and D.Nestorovic-N.Ristic (from the 2003 Serbian Team Championship), White enjoys a large structural advantage which is not compensated for by Black's inactive bishop pair.

Whereas 11...c5! 12 e5 ♖e8 13 exd6 cxd6 14 ♘d5 f6 15 dxc5 ♘xc5 sees Black starting to get the better of it. Of course, White could swallow his pride and play 12 ♗e3, which is equal after 12...e6.

B: 5 d5 ♘b8

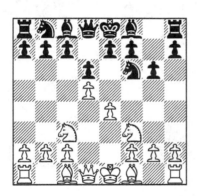

As I have mentioned before, one of the significant benefits of the fianchetto is that 5 d5 opens the diagonal for the g7-bishop. It would be a shame to close it with 5...♘e5 6 ♘xe5 dxe5.

6 ♗e2

Other moves:

a) 6 ♗c4 isn't as stupid as it looks – after all, when Black plays ...c7-c6 White will enjoy having the option to open the a2-g8 diagonal whenever he wants. However, Black is allowed to change his plans too: 6...♗g7 7 0-0 0-0 8 h3 (this is usually played by this stage, on moves 5, 6, 7 or 8; otherwise White has to worry about both ...♗g4 and ...♘g4) 8...e5!? (this is a new move intended to punish ♗c4 and h2-h3; if White refuses to open the position, the c4-bishop is atrocious – both passive and hindering White's natural plan of c2-c4-c5) 9 ♗e3 (or 9 dxe6 ♗xe6 10 ♗xe6 fxe6 11 e5 dxe5 12 ♕e2 ♘c6, and with the knights jumping to the d5- and d4-squares, Black has full compensation for his weakness on e6) 9...a6 10 b4 (if 10 a4 then 10...a5 and 11...♘a6) 10...♘h5 11 ♕d2 ♘d7 12 ♘e2 ♕e7 and with ...f7-f5 coming, Black has reached a good King's Indian-type position.

Instead of 8...e5!?, N.Praznik-A.Beliavsky, Bled 1999, continued 8...c6 9 a4 a5 10 ♖e1 ♘fd7 11 ♗e3 ♘a6. Though White was better, Black played effectively on the dark squares throughout the game and went on to win, making this a must-see (see Game 66).

b) 6 ♗g5 is in fact the most often played. White intends long castling and a quick attack, but despite the time gained against Black's knight, this strategy is questionable – Black's counterplay with ...c7-c6 is very fast: 6...♗g7 7 ♕d2 c6 8 ♗h6 (after 8 0-0-0, Black courageously castled in F.Lukez-S.Lejlic, Rodeby 1998, and equalized with 8...0-0 9 ♗h6 ♗g4 10 ♗xg7 ♔xg7 11 ♗e2

♘bd7 – White's "attack" is going nowhere; e.g. 12 h3 ♗xf3 13 ♗xf3 ♕b6 14 h4?! ♘e5, threatening ...♘c4) 8...♗xh6! 9 ♕xh6 ♕b6 10 0-0-0 ♗g4 is an interesting position, not at all unfavourable for Black; e.g. 11 ♖d2 ♗xf3 12 gxf3 ♘bd7 13 f4 cxd5 14 exd5 ♖c8 (14...0-0-0!? and 15...♔b8) with great interest in ...♖xc3; or 11 ♗e2 ♕xf2 12 ♖hf1 ♕c5 and while White is certainly well developed, he has nothing concrete for the pawn. In N.Sulava-M.Muse, Croatian Team Championship 2002, White changed the course of the game with 11 e5?! dxe5 12 d6, but had Black spotted 12...♘bd7 13 dxe7 ♕b4, followed by 14...♕xe7 and 15...0-0-0, White would have found himself without sufficient compensation.

c) 6 ♗e3 is very similar to 6 ♗g5, into which it often transposes (i.e. after ♗e3-h6). One time that didn't happen was in K.Nemcova-F.Olafsson, Marianske Lazne 2008, which went 6...♗g7 7 ♕d2 c6 (by transposition) 8 h3 b5?! (8...0-0 9 ♗e2 b5!, as in J.Hjartarson-F.Olafsson, Reykjavik 1995, was a better move order – see Game 68) 9 a3?! (9 dxc6! b4 10 ♗b5! is unpleasant for Black) 9...a6 10 dxc6 ♘xc6 11 ♗d3 0-0 12 0-0 ♗b7, resulting in an equal Dragodorf type of position which Black went on to win (see Game 67).

d) 6 h3! is the most accurate move, reaching line B1 below after 6...♗g7 7 ♗e2 0-0 8 0-0.

6...♗g7

There is something to be said for 6...♗g4 (or 7...♗g4), with a likely transposition to B2. Of course White could have played 6 h3, insisting on B1.

7 0-0 0-0

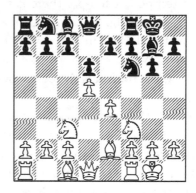

White has:

B1: 8 h3 97
B2: Others 99

Or 8 a4 a5! – Black cannot allow himself to become further cramped. The insertion of the two a-pawn moves is helpful to Black though, since it helps him to establish knight outposts on the c5- and b4-squares.

B1: 8 h3

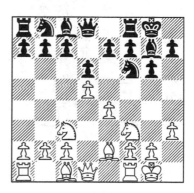

This is played most often, spending a tempo to stop 8...♗g4. As we will see, 8...♗g4 was indeed Black's intention, but a tempo is a tempo. There is some disagreement about the merits of 8 h3 – Alburt and Chernin adorn it with an (!), while Nunn says it is "not really necessary". I think it is the best move in the position.

8...e5!

Smirin and Gulko have each chosen 8...e5 three times, with an even (total) score, while Finkel, Urban, and Gufeld have four wins and three draws with 8...c6, but against this, Benjamin's plan (9 a4 a5 10 ♖e1 ♘a6 11 ♗xa6! – see the note on 8...c6 in line B2) is very strong for White.

For those interested in making ...c7-c6 work, I suggest 8...a6 (or 8...b6) 9 a4 b6 10 ♗e3 ♗b7 11 ♕d2 c6 12 ♖ad1 ♕c7 13 ♗h6 ♘bd7 as in A.Bachofner-P.Hopman, Amsterdam 2006, when White is only slightly better.

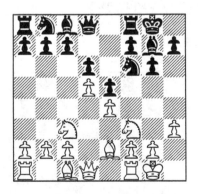

9 dxe6

If White does not play this move, he winds up in a King's Indian type of po-

sition where his normal play (with c2-c4-c5) is blocked by the c3-knight. This problem is serious for White, more so than Black's funny knight on b8 (which is normally on the e7-square). Black will play carefully for ...f7-f5. Part of being careful is considering ...h7-h6 to prevent White's ♘g5-e6.

9...♗xe6

Black has caught up in development and now has only to worry about a small space disadvantage. If White is not alert, Black will fix this with a quick ...d6-d5.

White has now only showed interest in:

> **B11: 10 ♗g5** 98
> **B12: 10 ♘d4** 99

B11: 10 ♗g5!

Dubious according to Nunn, in his 1989 *The Complete Pirc*, this has been by far the more dangerous move in practice.

10...h6

11 ♗e3

Instead:

a) 11 ♗h4 ♘c6 12 ♕d2 g5 13 ♗g3 d5 equalizes.

b) 11 ♗f4 ♘c6 12 ♕d2 g5 13 ♗h2 ♖e8 14 ♖ad1 ♘d7 offers White a tiny edge, but typical dark-square play for Black.

11...♘c6 12 ♕d2 ♔h7 13 ♖ad1 ♖e8 14 ♖fe1 a6 15 a4

So far we have followed J.Piket-B.Gulko, Amsterdam 1989, which continued 15...♗d7 16 ♗c4 ♗e6 17 ♗e2 ♕e7 18 ♘d5 ♕d8 19 ♘c3, indicating that nobody could come up with a plan – this is already a threefold repetition,

but somehow the game continued and Gulko contrived to lose, even after a later repetition.

Alternatively, 15...♕e7 is fine to test the opponent for a draw (16 ♘d5 ♕d8 17 ♘c3), but if one wants to continue, there is 15...♘d7!? 16 ♗f1 b6, intending 17...♘c5, while ...♘de5 is also a possibility, as is the manoeuvre ...♕c8-b7. White is a little better.

Y.Gruenfeld-I.Smirin, Israeli Team Championship 1997 (see Game 69), shows what happens if White does not play a2-a4 to contain Black's queenside expansion – Black's counterplay was more than sufficient.

B12: 10 ♘d4 ♗d7

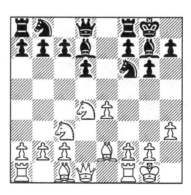

The insertion of these moves makes it easier for Black to pressure the e4-pawn.

11 ♖e1 ♘c6

Now White either loses time retreating the knight or agrees to an exchange that will ease Black's position. Similar is 11...♖e8 12 ♗f1 ♘c6 13 ♘b3 a5 14 a3 a4 15 ♘d2, and instead of

15...♘a5?! 16 ♘f3, which was good for White in K.Hulak-S.Marangunic, Yugoslavia 1977, Black should play 15...♘d4! 16 ♘f3 ♘xf3+ 17 ♕xf3 ♗c6 with an equal position.

12 ♘f3 ♖e8 13 ♗c4 ♗e6 14 ♘d5 ♕d7 15 c3 ♗xd5 16 exd5 ♖xe1+ 17 ♕xe1 ♘e5! 18 ♘xe5 dxe5

The position is equal, White's bishops being offset by his poor development and the inconvenience of guarding the d5-pawn. If 19 ♕xe5, then after 19...♖e8 and 20...♖e1+, White will never complete his development.

B2: Others (besides 8 h3)

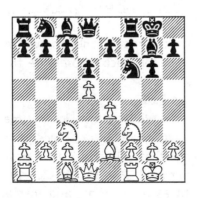

If White is going to refrain from 8 h3, it makes very little difference which move he chooses, but we'll take the following as the main line:

8 ♗e3

Alternatively:

a) 8 ♗g5 should be treated similarly: 8...♗g4! 9 h3 ♗xf3 10 ♗xf3 c6 11 ♕d2 ♘bd7 and Black follows with ...♕b6, ...a7-a5, ...♘c5 and ...♘fd7, with typical dark-square play, even if White is still slightly better.

White can also try to do without h2-h3. For instance, 9 ♕d2 c6 10 ♖fe1 ♘bd7 transposes to L.Vajda-M.Marin, Rumanian Championship, Bucharest 1998, and M.Kolosowski-Dan.Fraczek, Legnica 2011, which both continued 11 dxc6!? bxc6 12 ♘d4 ♖c8?! 13 f3 ♗e6 14 ♘xe6 fxe6 with advantage to White. According to *Houdini*, Black can equalize in this line with 12...♕b6! 13 ♘a4 ♕c7 14 ♗xg4 ♘xg4 15 ♗xe7 d5 16 f4 (16 ♘f3?! ♘de5! 17 ♗xf8 ♘xf3+ 18 gxf3 ♕xh2+ 19 ♔f1 ♖xf8 20 fxg4 ♕h1+ 21 ♔e2 ♕xe4+ 22 ♔f1 ♕xa4 is good for Black) 16...♖fe8 17 exd5 cxd5 18 h3 ♘ge5 19 dxe5 ♖xe7.

b) 8 ♖e1 ♗g4 (of course) 9 h3 ♗xf3 10 ♗xf3 ♘fd7! 11 ♗e3 c6 was D.Rogozenco-V.Nevednichy, Rumanian Team Championship 2005, where White went wrong immediately with 12 ♗d4?!, initiating an exchange beneficial to Black; e.g. 12...♗xd4 13 ♕xd4 ♕b6 is equal. Without this mistake White is a little better, but Black's minor pieces are all good, and he has the simple plan of ...a7-a5, ...♘a6, ...♘ac5, ...a5-a4-a3 (if possible), and ...♕b6 or ...♕c7.

8...♗g4

Black has done very well with 8...c6, but Joel Benjamin (who played 1...♘c6 frequently in the 1990s) warned me that Black's position is difficult after 9 a4! a5 10 h3 (otherwise 10...♗g4) 10...♘a6 11 ♗xa6! (an idea I have not been able to find in any published games – the point is to stop Black's active 11...♘b4) 11...♖xa6, when it is hard to find a constructive plan for Black, whereas White can still build; e.g. 12 ♕d2 ♖a8 13 ♖ad1 ♖e8 14 ♗d4 ♕c7 15 ♖fe1. Black lacks space, development and pawn play, while his only "asset", the light-squared bishop, is more of a problem than anything else. Indeed, this type of position acts more closed than open, in part because nobody wants to relieve the tension between the d5- and c6-pawns – for White to trade would assist Black greatly in the central battle, while if Black trades, he has accessible weaknesses on the b5- and e7-squares.

A possible antidote is 8...a5!? 9 a4 ♘a6, when White should be less eager to snap off the knight. Notice that since Black has not yet played ...c7-c6, he can later try ...e7-e6 or ...e7-e5 instead. However, there are other moves to worry about besides 9 a4.

8...♗g4 is simplest, transposing to a favourite line of the great Pirc expert Alexander Chernin, who used it with great success in the 1990s (three draws, three wins, all against GMs). The normal move order to reach this position is 1 e4 d6 2 d4 ♘f6 3 ♘c3 g6 4 ♘f3 ♗g7 5 ♗e2 0-0 6 0-0 ♗g4 7 ♗e3 ♘c6 8 d5 ♘b8. (8...♗xf3 is the traditional main line, but it is not stronger.)

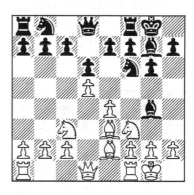

9 h3

White must play this sooner or later unless he is intending to allow the exchange of light-squared bishops. White should at least retain the bishop pair if he is hoping to keep an advantage:

a) 9 ♘d2 ♗xe2 10 ♕xe2, and now Chernin's recommendation 10...♖e8 11 f4 e6 has been tested only once, in A.Czebe-N.Resika, Budapest 2000 – Black, an FM, held the draw against the GM.

b) 9 ♘d4 ♗xe2 10 ♕xe2 c5 11 ♘f3 ♕b6 12 ♖ab1 ♕a6 13 ♕d2 ♘g4 14 ♗g5 ♖e8 with equality in B.Chatalbashev-M.Popchev, Cacak 1991 (see Game 70).

c) 9 ♗g5 ♗xe2 10 ♕xe2 c6 11 ♖ad1 ♕a5 12 f4 ♕a6 13 ♕f3 ♘bd7 with equality. Black, with more experience in this type of position, went on to win in R.Ziatdinov-A.Chernin, New York Open 1998 (see Game 71).

d) 9 ♕d2 ("Here the 'threat' of ♗e3-h6 is a fiction because the exchange of bishops is in Black's favour. But what other plan can White try?" – Chernin) 9...c6 10 ♖ad1 ♕a5 11 a3 ♖c8 12 b4 ♕c7 13 ♗d4 ♘bd7 14 ♖fe1 a5 was equal in P.Blatny-A.Chernin, Pardubice 1993, and ended as a draw.

9...♗xf3 10 ♗xf3 c6 11 a4 a5

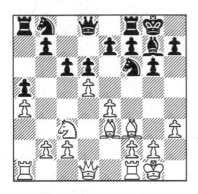

The GM to hold this position as White found nothing better than 12 ♘b1?!. To me, this is a good indication of the health of Black's position. 12...♘bd7 13 g3 was V.Arbakov-A.Chernin, Bern 1995, where Black can equalize with 13...♘e5 14 ♗g2 ♘c4 15 ♗d4 ♘h5 or 13...♘c5 14 ♗xc5 dxc5 15 dxc6 bxc6, as well as Chernin's 13...♘b6 14 ♗g2 ♕c7.

Instead, in D.Primel-A.Nowocien, French Team Championship 2007, White tried 12 ♕d2 ♕c7 13 ♖ad1 ♘a6 14 ♖fe1 ♘b4 15 ♗d4 ♘d7 16 ♗xg7 ♔xg7, again with equality; while R.Kashtanov-A.Lugovoi, St. Petersburg

2000, saw 12 ♗e2 ♕c7 13 f4 ♘a6 14 ♗c4 ♘d7 15 ♕e2 ♘b4 (15...♗xc3!?) 16 dxc6 bxc6 17 ♖ad1, and now Black took a break from his dark-square strategy to play 17...e6! 18 ♗b3 d5!.

If there is a way to an advantage in this variation, White has yet to find it.

C: Others (without d4-d5)

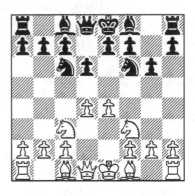

In these lines White chooses to play a regular-ish Pirc instead of trying to challenge the correctness of Black's early ...♘c6 with 5 d5 or 5 ♗b5.

There are a few choices:

C1: 5 h3 *102*
C2: 5 ♗e2 *106*
C3: 5 ♗e3 *108*
C4: 5 ♗c4 *109*
C5: 5 ♗g5 *112*

C1: 5 h3

This is the most frequently played move here. White does not want to be bothered by ...♗g4 or ...♘g4. Nevertheless, a tempo is a tempo, however well motivated.

5...♗g7 6 ♗e3

By far the most common, but also seen are:

a) 6 ♗g5 0-0 7 ♕d2, when both 7...a6 and the surprising 7...d5 have worked extremely well for Black.

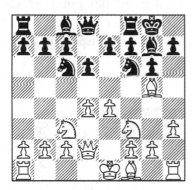

a1) 7...d5 8 exd5 ♘xd5 9 ♗h6 (9 0-0-0 ♘xc3 10 ♕xc3 ♕d6 11 ♗c4 ♗f5 12 ♖he1 ♖ad8 13 ♕e3 ♘a5 14 ♗d3 ♗e6 gives White a tiny edge) 9...♘xc3 (9...♗e6! is equal) 10 ♗xg7 ♔xg7 11 ♕xc3 ♕d5 12 0-0-0 ♗e6 13 b3 ♗f5 and Black converted White's advantage (har!) in So.Polgar-J.Fries Nielsen, Rimavska Sobota 1991 (see Game 72).

a2) 7...a6 8 0-0-0 b5 (8...d5!?) 9 a3 (9 ♗d3 ♗b7 10 ♔b1 ♖e8 11 ♖he1 e5 12 d5 ♘e7 is slightly better for White) 9...♖b8 10 ♗h6 b4 11 axb4 ♘xb4 12 ♗xg7 ♔xg7 13 e5 ♘fd5 was equal in M.Yilmazyerli-D.Arutinian, Istanbul 2007, though the stronger player (Black) went on to win (see Game 73).

b) 6 ♗e2 is not very consistent with 5 h3 because the pin has been prevented already – White is normally hoping to retain the option of ♗c4.

Then 6...0-0 7 0-0 (7 ♗e3 transposes to 7 ♗e2 in the notes to the main line) 7...e5 (7...a6!? is more combative, and was tried successfully in N.Ryba-J.Schuyler, Washington 2012 – see Game 74) and now:

b1) 8 dxe5

Hold on! Seriously, how do we decide how to recapture in this position (and similar positions)?

First of all, it is safe to assume that if White took once on e5 he will take again given the opportunity, so we will wind up with the same pawn structure in either case – the only difference being the c6- and f3-knights. Do we like having them there or not? The main factor if the knights are on is that White can play ♘d5 without having to worry about being evicted by ...c7-c6, but sometimes Black's ...♘d4 is useful, too. If the knights are off, White has the possibility to pressure Black's centre and activate his rook with f2-f4, but this also frees Black's g7-bishop. In general, the ability to play ...c7-c6 is the most important factor, so ...♘xe5 is the normal choice. The reader would be well advised to take special note of any exceptions.

Here 8...♘xe5 9 ♘xe5 dxe5 10 ♗g5 c6 is equal, when 11 ♗c4 b5 allows Black free expansion on the queenside.

b2) 8 ♗e3 is a bad version of 7 ♗e2 e5 in the main line – if White is castled kingside he has no attack to compensate for his troubles; i.e. 8...exd4 9 ♘xd4 ♖e8 and White already lacks a comfortable way to defend his e-pawn. 10 ♘xc6 bxc6 11 ♗f3 is most common, when Black plays ...♗a6, ...♘d7, and can consider ...♖b8, ...♕b8, ...♘e5, and/or ...♘b6. White is equal according to Mr. H, but Black wins most of the games. There are no worthy examples because White can't seem to hold onto his pieces.

b3) 8 d5 ♘e7 9 ♗e3 is similar to the main line – except that White is not fast enough with his pressure on the d-file, so 9...c6 is already equal, and after 10 dxc6 bxc6 11 ♕d2 ♕c7 12 ♖ad1 d5 13 exd5 ♘exd5 14 ♘xd5?! cxd5 Black took over the centre in N.Jhunjh-nuwala-S.Gligoric, Lucerne Olympiad 1982 (see Game 75).

c) On 6 ♗c4 Black could proceed "normally" with 6...0-0 (cf line C41 below), but the immediate 6...♘xe4! is an equalizer: 7 ♗xf7+ ♔xf7 8 ♘xe4 d5 9 ♘c5 ♕d6, threatening 10...♘xd4 or 10...e5. White can sacrifice a pawn with 10 ♘d3, when 10...♘xd4 11 ♗f4 ♘xf3+ 12 ♕xf3 ♕e6+ 13 ♗e5+ ♔g8 14 ♕g3 ♗xe5 15 ♘xe5 ♕a6 leaves him with enough compensation but no more. Or

Black can decline the gift: 10...♖f8 11 c3 (11 ♗f4 ♕e6+ 12 ♗e5 ♔g8 13 c3 ♘xe5 14 ♘dxe5 ♕d6 is equal) 11...♔g8 12 0-0 h6 13 ♖e1 g5, though White is slightly better here.

d) 6 ♗b5 looks silly since Black can castle out of the pin, but after 6...0-0 7 0-0 Black has nothing better than 7...a6 8 ♗xc6 bxc6, transposing to line A above.

6...0-0

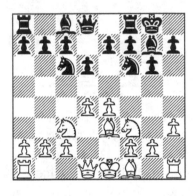

7 ♕d2

Or 7 ♗e2 e5 (7...a6 is more aggressive, but riskier) 8 dxe5 (other moves transpose elsewhere: 8 d5 ♘e7 9 ♕d2 is 9 ♗e2 in the main line, while 9 0-0 and 8 0-0 are respectively notes 'b3' and 'b2' above) 8...dxe5 (Didn't I just say this was wrong? – this is one of those exceptions; actually, 8...♘xe5 is fine too, but the text move has performed much better, so why not?) 9 0-0 ♕e7 with equal chances. The point is that 10 ♘d5 is not dangerous because of 10...♘xd5 11 exd5 ♘d4! 12 ♖e1 ♘f5! (chasing the more dangerous bishop) and Black is comfortably equal.

7...e5 8 d5

Others:

a) 8 0-0-0 exd4 9 ♘xd4 ♖e8 10 f3 – Black wins nearly every game from this position. Indeed, White's pawns on h3 and f3 make a ludicrous impression (he is essentially down a full tempo in a Philidor Defence Larsen Variation), though White should not actually be worse. 10...♘xd4 11 ♗xd4 ♗e6 12 g4 (12 ♗f2 a6 13 ♔b1 b5 14 h4 c5! was about equal in G.Bastrikov-E.Geller, Tashkent 1958 – see Game 76) 12...c5! 13 ♗e3 ♕a5!? (13...d5! equalizes) 14 ♕xd6?! (14 ♗h6! ♗xh6 15 ♕xh6 ♗xa2 16 ♖xd6 ♖e6 is slightly better for White) 14...♘xe4! 15 fxe4 ♗xc3 16 ♕xc5? ♗xb2+ 17 ♔xb2 ♕xa2+ 18 ♔c1 ♖ac8 and White soon called it quits in D.Bescos Cortes-S.Garza Marco, San Jose 1998. 16 bxc3? ♕a3+ 17 ♔d2 ♖ad8 wouldn't have worked either; instead after 16 ♗d3, closing the d-file, the game still continues, though Black is clearly better.

b) 8 dxe5 seems like it is headed for dullness, but things could get interesting if nobody trades those queens; e.g. 8...♘xe5 9 ♘xe5 dxe5 10 0-0-0 ♗e6 11 g4 c6 12 g5 (12 ♕xd8 ♖fxd8 13 ♖xd8 ♖xd8 14 ♗xa7 ♗h6+ 15 ♗e3 ♗xe3+ 16 fxe3 h5 17 g5 ♘h7 18 h4 f6 19 gxf6 ♘xf6 is equal despite the slight pawn deficit: Black's activity and future passed h-pawn are sufficient) 12...♘d7 13 h4 ♕a5 and the race is on. Black has no reason to be pessimistic about his prospects.

8...♘e7

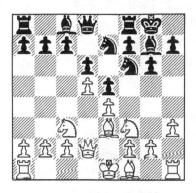

8...♘b8 is also quite reasonable. The e7-knight supports the ...c7-c6 break, but with White likely to castle long and form a battery on the d-file, the usefulness of this option is reduced.

9 0-0-0

Instead:

a) 9 ♗h6 is statistically the most dangerous, scoring 6/7 for White, but Black was heavily outrated and his play quite uninspired. Artashes Minasian shows us the way in D.Saduakassova-Art.Minasian, Dubai 2011: 9...♗d7! 10 ♗d3 (10 0-0-0?! b5!) 10...c6 (or 10...b5 11 a3 a5 12 0-0 b4 intending ...c7-c6 with counterplay) 11 dxc6 ♗xc6 (taking firm control over the d5-square; backward pawn? what backward pawn?) 12 ♗xg7 ♔xg7 13 0-0 ♕c7 (13...b5!?) with easy equality (see Game 77).

b) 9 ♗e2 ♗d7 (9...♘xe4!? 10 ♘xe4 f5 11 ♘c3 f4 12 0-0-0 is slightly better for White) 10 g4 (not 10 ♗h6?! c6! 11 dxc6 ♗xc6 with advantage) 10...b5! 11 g5 (11 ♗d3?! b4 12 ♘e2 c6 13 dxc6 ♗xc6 14 ♘g3 ♘xe4! is good for Black; while 11 a3 ♖b8 is equal, since 12 ♗xa7? runs into 12...♖a8! 13 ♗e3 b4) 11...b4 12 gxf6 bxc3 13 ♕xc3 ♗xf6 with a level position.

c) 9 ♖d1 ♘h5 10 g4 ♘f4 (this aggression is called for because White can no longer tuck his king away on the queenside) 11 ♗xf4 exf4 12 ♕xf4 f5 13 exf5 gxf5 14 g5 ♗xc3+ 15 bxc3 ♖e8 16 ♗e2 ♘g6 with compensation.

d) 9 g4 a6 should transpose to the main line once White castles long.

9...a6 10 g4 b5 11 g5

11 ♗d3 ♗b7?! 12 ♘e2?! (better 12 a3 or 12 g5 with an edge) 12...c6?! was equal in K.Haznedaroglu-T.Gelashvili, Antalya 2009; but Black could have blown it open with 11...b4 12 ♘e2 ♘exd5! 13 exd5 e4 14 ♗xe4 ♘xe4 15 ♕xb4 ♖e8, when White has a great deal to worry about for his extra pawn. In the actual game 12...♘fxd5! would have been even stronger, giving Black a comfortable advantage, but White need not have allowed that.

11...♘h5

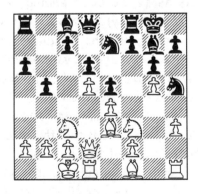

A race scenario is developing in which Black's chances are no worse –

White has a hard time evicting the h5-knight, and will also find it hard to profit even if the h-file opens. One continuation of many: 12 ♔b1 ♗d7 13 ♘h2 ♘c8!? 14 ♘g4 ♘b6 15 b3 b4 16 ♘e2 a5, still with approximately even chances.

C2: 5 ♗e2 ♗g7 6 0-0 0-0

Azmaiparashvili plays 6...♗g4 here, making sure White can't change his mind and play 7 d5 and 8 h3. Black may even have considered 5...♗g4!?. It is not clear which is the most accurate. Besides, why should White change his mind?

7 ♗e3

White tries to make do without h2-h3. Is he inviting trouble or saving a tempo? The alternative is 7 ♗g5 h6 and then:

a) 8 ♗h4 g5 9 ♗g3 ♘h5 10 d5 ♘xg3 11 hxg3 ♘e5 is equal; e.g. 12 ♘d4 c6 13 ♘f5 ♗xf5 14 exf5 ♕b6 15 ♖b1 ♘d7 16 ♗f3 ♖fe8 17 g4 ♘f6.

b) 8 ♗e3 ♘g4 9 ♗d2 e5 10 d5 ♘e7 11 h3 ♘f6 12 ♗e3 ♘d7 13 ♕d2 ♔h7 14

♘e1 f5 most closely resembles a King's Indian, where White's attack will be greatly delayed by his pawn stuck on the c2-square.

c) 8 ♗f4 ♘g4! 9 h3 (if White does not play h2-h3, the game will transpose to note 'b' just above; e.g. 9 d5 e5 10 ♗d2 ♘e7, or 9 ♗d2 e5, or even 9 ♗c1 e5 10 d5 etc) 9...e5 10 dxe5 ♘gxe5 11 ♘xe5?! (11 ♕d2 is better, retaining a tiny edge after 11...♔h7; Black can consider ...♘xf3+ and ...♘d4, or ...♗e6, or ...f7-f5, or ...♖e8) 11...dxe5 was level in A.Sakharov-A.Adorjan, Sochi 1976, though Black went on to win a wild game (see Game 78).

7...e5!

As usual, 7...a6 can be tried – the main line is a bit drawish – but then 8 d5 ♘b8 9 a4 is an excellent answer. Alternatively, 7...♗g4 8 d5 ♘b8 transposes to line B2 (8...♗xf3 9 ♗xf3 ♘e5 10 ♗e2 c6 is a main line Classical Pirc which will not be covered).

8 dxe5

От:

a) 8 d5 ♘e7 9 ♕d2 ♘g4 10 ♗g5 h6 11 ♗h4 g5 12 ♗g3 f5 13 h3 ♘f6 14 exf5 ♘xf5 15 ♗h2 ♕e8 with a tiny edge as Black considers a kingside attack based on his space advantage there, or the ...e5-e4-e3 lunge, or ...♕f7 and ...♘e7, building pressure on White's d-pawn. White is not well situated to use his asset – the e4-square.

b) 8 ♕d2 (as usual, it is a bad idea for White to try to maintain the tension – this only works if Black is not happy to take!) 8...exd4 9 ♘xd4 ♖e8 10 f3 (10 ♘xc6 bxc6 11 f3 d5 transposes; 11...♕e7 is also fine) 10...d5! 11 ♘xc6 bxc6 12 ♖ad1 ♕e7 13 ♗d4 dxe4 14 fxe4 ♘xe4 15 ♘xe4 ♕xe4 16 ♗xg7 ♔xg7 17 ♗f3 ♕e3+ 18 ♕xe3 ♖xe3 19 ♗xc6 ♖b8 20 ♖d8 ♖b6 with a level endgame.

8...♘xe5

8...dxe5 is also playable. Z.Bratanov-B.Chatalbashev, Bulgarian Championship 2004, continued 9 ♕xd8 ♖xd8 10 ♗c4 h6 11 h3 b6 12 ♘d5 ♘a5! 13 ♘xf6+ ♗xf6 14 ♗e2 ♗b7 15 b4 ♘c6 16 c3 a5 17 a3 ♘e7 18 ♘d2 ♗g5! and Black went on to win (see Game 79).

9 ♘xe5 dxe5 10 ♕xd8 ♖xd8

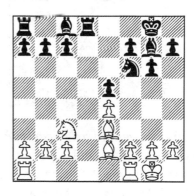

In practice this is equal, but White can try to extract a little something:

a) By far the most common is 11 ♖fd1 (or 11 ♖ad1 – it doesn't much matter) 11...♗e6 12 ♘b5, when the new move 12...♖dc8! keeps things level; e.g. 13 ♘xa7 ♖xa7 14 ♗xa7 b6 15 ♖d3 ♖a8 16 ♖a3 ♗f8 17 ♖a6 ♗c8 18 ♖a4 ♗d7 etc.

b) 11 ♘b5 ♗d7 12 f3 looks scary,

and both 12...b6 and 12...♗xb5 give White something to work with. The novelty 12...a6 13 ♘xc7 ♖ac8 14 ♗b6 ♗c6 15 ♘xa6 ♖d2 16 ♗d3 bxa6 17 ♗e3 ♖xd3 18 cxd3 is a tiny edge for White, but the imbalances should provide Black some winning chances as well.

c) 11 ♗c4 c6 12 ♖ad1 ♖e8 13 a4 ♗f8 14 f3 ♔g7 15 ♖d2 ♗b4 16 ♖fd1 ♖e7 17 ♔f2 ♖d7 and White is running out of things to play for.

C3: 5 ♗e3 ♗g7 6 ♕d2

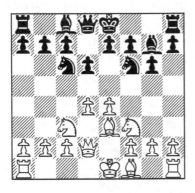

Other moves are covered elsewhere: 6 d5 ♘b8, 6 h3 0-0, and 6 ♗e2 0-0 7 0-0 were seen in lines B, C1 and C2 respectively, while 6 ♗c4 is C43 below.

6...0-0!

6...♘g4?! should not work here. 7 ♗f4 e5 8 ♗g5 f6 9 ♗h4 0-0 10 ♗c4+ ♔h8 11 d5 ♘e7 12 h3 ♘h6, intending 13...♘hg8, 14...h6 and 15...f5 is satisfactory for Black, but after 7 ♗g5 h6 8 ♗h4 the bishop chase is not paying dividends and White wins nearly every game.

7 ♗h6

7 h3 is C1 again, and 7 d5 ♘b8 8 h3 c6 is in the notes to line B. Others:

a) 7 0-0-0 has not scored well, but White's set-up is challenging – he has managed to omit h2-h3 and stop ...e7-e5, while 7...♘g4?! 8 ♗f4 e5 9 dxe5 ♘gxe5 10 ♘xe5 ♘xe5 11 h4 is still not convincing.

However, White has committed his king, so: 7...a6! 8 ♗h6 b5 9 ♗xg7 (9 ♗d3 allows 9...e5!) 9...♔xg7 and the annoying threat of 10...b4 already forces some sort of concession (such as the weakening 10 a3 or an awkward defence of the e-pawn). White is only slightly better.

b) 7 ♗e2 e5 (7...a6 8 d5! ♘b8 9 a4 was K.Wang-J.Schuyler, Washington 2012; I felt my a-pawn was misplaced, and I did go on to lose, but I was not without chances – see Game 80) 8 dxe5 (or 8 0-0-0 ♘g4 9 dxe5 dxe5 10 ♕xd8 ♘xd8 11 ♘d5 ♘e6 with an even position, while 10 ♕e1!? ♘d4 11 ♔b1 c6 12 ♗xd4 exd4 13 h3 ♕f6 is unclear) 8...dxe5 is equal. With White's queen on d2 and his passive bishops, this is not the time for the exchange variation, and 9 0-0-0 ♕e7 (or 9...♘g4) 10 ♗g5 ♗e6 11 ♘d5?! ♗xd5 12 exd5 ♖fd8 just makes matters worse for White.

c) 7 ♗c4 ♘g4 8 ♗g5 h6 9 ♗h4 g5 10 ♗g3 e5 11 d5 ♘d4 is about equal, but not a very rational position – the tactics would take pages. Instead, 7...♗g4!? keeps things under control; e.g. 8 d5 ♗xf3 9 gxf3 ♘e5 10 ♗e2 c5 11 0-0-0 ♕a5 12 ♔b1 ♖ab8, or 8 0-0-0 ♘xe4 9 ♘xe4 d5 10 ♗d3 dxe4 11 ♗xe4 ♕d7 12 d5 ♗xf3 13 ♗xf3 ♘e5 14 ♗e2 ♘g4 15 ♗d4 e5 16 dxe6 ♕xe6 17 ♗xg7 ♔xg7 with near equality.

7...e5!

Centre play beats wing play.

8 ♗xg7 ♔xg7 9 0-0-0

After 9 d5 ♘e7 10 0-0-0 ♖b8 11 ♗d3 (if 11 h4 ♗g4, or 11 ♔b1 b5) 11...b5, 11...c6 or 11...♗g4, Black has full counterplay.

9...♗g4 10 dxe5 dxe5

This position has led to three draws, but Black has a slight advantage based on White's weak bishop. For instance, 11 ♕e3 ♘d4 12 ♘b5?! was F.Saez-

A.Safranska, Grenoble 2003, when 12...c5 13 c3 ♕a5! 14 ♘a3 (14 cxd4? cxd4 15 ♕a3 ♖ac8+ 16 ♔b1 ♕xa3 17 ♘xa3 ♘xe4 18 ♖e1 ♘xf2 19 ♖g1 ♗xf3 20 gxf3 d3 21 ♖xe5 d2 22 ♗e2 ♖fe8 23 ♘c4 b5 is nearly winning) 14...♗xf3 15 gxf3 ♘e6 would have given Black a large positional advantage.

C4: 5 ♗c4 ♗g7

And now:

C41: 6 0-0 *110*
C42: 6 ♕e2 *110*
C43: 6 ♗e3 *112*

Instead:

a) 6 ♗g5?! ♘xe4! 7 ♘xe4 (or 7 ♗xf7+ ♔xf7 8 ♘xe4 d5 9 ♘c5 ♖f8) 7...d5 8 c3!? dxc4 9 d5 f5! 10 dxc6 ♕xd1+ 11 ♖xd1 fxe4 12 ♘d2 bxc6 13 ♘xe4 ♖b8 is good for Black.

b) 6 ♗f4 – As a novice, I remember thinking that this was some kind of ideal position for White. Nowadays, it looks like White is begging for trouble, as the bishops are vulnerable and do not defend his centre. Indeed, my research uncovered a large collection of games by some of the lowest-rated players I have ever seen in any database. – 6...♘xe4 (6...♗g4 is more combative) 7 ♘xe4 (7 ♗xf7+ ♔xf7 8 ♘xe4 ♖f8 9 d5 ♔g8! 10 ♕d2 ♕d7!! 11 dxc6?! ♕g4! or 10 ♗g5 ♘e5 with a tiny edge) 7...d5 8 ♗d3 dxe4 9 ♗xe4 ♘xd4 10 ♘xd4 ♕xd4 11 ♕xd4 ♗xd4 12 ♗xc7 ♗xb2 13 ♖b1 f5 14 ♗f3 ♗d4 with a level endgame.

C41: 6 0-0

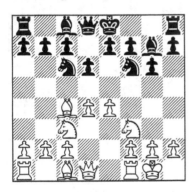

6...0-0

6...♗g4 is also good; e.g. 7 ♗e3 0-0 8 h3 ♗xf3 9 ♕xf3 e5 10 dxe5 (or 10 d5 ♘e7) 10...♘xe5 11 ♕e2 ♘xc4 with equality.

7 h3?!

This is no good, but it is the most common, and other moves are either met by ...♗g4 or else are covered elsewhere: 7 d5 ♘b8 is line B again, while 7 ♗e3 ♘g4 is C43 below.

7...♘xe4 8 ♗xf7+

8 ♘xe4?! d5 9 ♗d3 (9 c3! dxc4 is

only a little worse for White) 9...dxe4 10 ♗xe4 ♘xd4 is clearly unsatisfactory for White.

8...♖xf7 9 ♘xe4 d5!

White has four knight retreats and they're all bad – he has reached an inferior version of 5 h3 ♗g7 6 ♗c4 ♘xe4! etc in line C1 (see note 'c' to White's 6th move). The most frequent is 10 ♘c5?! and now, rather than 10...♕d6?! as always played, 10...b6! 11 ♘b3 ♕d6 12 ♘g5 ♖f8 13 ♖e1 e5 gives Black a comfortable advantage.

C42: 6 ♕e2 ♗g4!

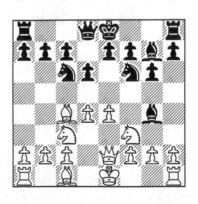

7 ♗e3

GM Robert Zelcik has twice played 7 e5 and won (against much weaker opponents). If Black takes the bull by the horns with 7...♗xf3 8 gxf3 ♘xd4 9 exf6 ♘xe2 10 fxg7 ♖g8 11 ♔xe2!? (or similarly 11 ♗xe2 – White is 2-0 here as well) 11...♖xg7 we reach this mess:

Queen and two pawns is a lot for three minor pieces, even three pieces that include the bishop pair. Is there really no way to use the material? The key to the position is to make sure the pawns stay mobile. It is not bad to sacrifice a pawn if it helps to open files, trade rooks, disorganize the white pieces, or expose the enemy king. A close look at the games shows that one of the candidate masters was crushing the GM, so we should not despair, and instead resolve to emulate Black (up to a point) in R.Zelcik-M.Djurkovic, Pula 2001 (see Game 81).

Anyway, if this is not to your taste, Black can chicken out without adverse consequences; e.g. 7...dxe5 8 dxe5 ♗xf3 9 gxf3 ♘h5 10 f4 ♗h6 which is equal, though still not simple.

7...e5 8 dxe5

8 d5?! ♘d4! 9 ♗xd4 (or 9 ♕d1 ♗xf3 10 gxf3 0-0) 9...exd4 10 ♘b5 (10 e5? 0-0! 11 exf6 dxc3 wins) 10...0-0 11 0-0 ♖e8 was much better for Black in M.Strubreiter-K.Rogetzer, Austrian Team Championship 2004, and after 12 ♘bxd4?! ♘xe4 13 ♕d3 ♘c5 14 ♕d2 Black should have cashed out: 14...♗xf3 15 ♘xf3 ♗xb2, with a squeaky-clean extra pawn to go with his positional advantages.

8...♘xe5 9 ♗b3 0-0 10 0-0-0

10 h3 ♗h5 11 0-0-0 a5 simply transposes.

10...a5

This is a new move. Black has equalized and should start thinking about how to exert the most pressure. White will not enjoy playing a2-a4, but it is necessary: 11 h3 ♗h5! 12 a4 (not 12 g4? ♘fxg4 13 hxg4 ♗xg4 and 14...♗xf3) 12...♘xf3 13 gxf3 ♘d7 14 ♖hg1 ♘e5 15 ♖g3 c6 is still equal, Then 16 ♗c5 ♗h6+ 17 ♗e3! ♗g7 repeats, since 17 ♔b1? dxc5! 18 ♖xd8 ♖axd8 should terrify White.

C43: 6 ♗e3 0-0

7 0-0

7 ♕d2 transposes to 7 ♗c4 in line C3 (see note 'c' to White's 7th move).

7...♘g4 8 ♗g5

Instead:

a) 8 ♗f4?! ♘xd4! (fork tricks everywhere!) 9 ♘xd4 e5 10 ♗e3 ♘xe3 11 fxe3 exd4 12 exd4 ♗e6 was H.Hughes-K.Richardson, British League 2004. Black had the edge and went on to win (see Game 82), although 12...c6! was simpler with a comfortable advantage.

b) I don't know who would play it, but *Houdini* likes 8 ♗c1, when 8...e5 allows White a small advantage after 9 ♗g5! ♗f6 10 ♗xf6 ♘xf6 11 d5 ♘b8. Instead, 8...♘f6 returns to 6...0-0 in line C41 and offers (or bluffs) a repetition.

8...h6 9 ♗h4

On 9 ♗f4?! ♘xd4! is best, as in the previous note, even though White has the extra possibility 10 ♘xd4 e5 11 ♗xh6! (after 11 ♘e6!? fxe6 12 ♕xg4 exf4 13 ♗xe6+ ♔h7 14 ♗xc8 ♕xc8 Black's active bishop allows him a small plus – which he may convert to a struc-

tural advantage with ...♗xc3) 11...♗xh6 12 ♘f3 c6 and White is only slightly worse.

9...g5

This potentially king-weakening move is acceptable because White has also castled short.

10 ♗g3 ♘f6

Chances are equal; e.g. 11 h3 ♘xe4, or 11 ♗b3 ♗g4 12 d5 ♘a5 13 h3 ♗h5 14 ♕d3 ♗g6.

C5: 5 ♗g5 ♗g7 6 ♕d2 h6!

This bishop hunt does work.

7 ♗f4

Others:

a) 7 ♗h4 g5 8 ♗g3 ♘h5 9 d5 ♘b8 (it is good form to delay ...♘xg3 until the last moment, even without any specific idea in mind) 10 ♘d4 c5 11 ♗b5+ ♔f8 was equal in A.Grilc-G.Mohr, Slovenian Team Championship 2008, though the better player (Black) went on to win because White could not control the dark squares (see Game 83).

b) 7 ♗e3 ♘g4 (8 ♗f4 ♘xd4! 9 ♘xd4 e5 equalizes; e.g. 10 h3 exd4 11 ♘b5 ♘e5 12 ♘xd4 ♕e7 13 ♗b5+ ♗d7 14 ♗xd7+ ♘xd7 15 0-0-0 0-0-0) 8 0-0-0 ♘xe3 9 ♕xe3 0-0 10 h3 a6 11 g4 b5 was equal in D.Janowski-F.Yates, Marienbad 1925(!), a wild game that ended in a draw (see Game 84).

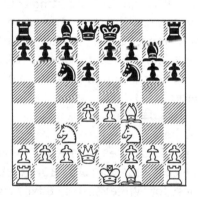

7...d5!

Abruptly, Black aborts the bishop chase in order to seize this opportunity for an unexpected central thrust. This is a new move.

8 exd5

Or 8 ♗b5 ♘xe4 9 ♘xe4 dxe4 10 ♘e5 ♗d7 11 ♗xc6 ♗xc6 12 ♘xc6 bxc6 13 0-0-0 ♕d5 14 ♔b1 0-0-0 15 c3 g5 16 ♗e3 f5 17 g3 e5 18 ♕e2 ♕b5 19 ♕xb5 cxb5 20 dxe5 ♗xe5 21 ♗xa7 ♔b7 with some chances in the endgame for Black due to his extra space, superior bishop, and "queenside" (i.e. away from the kings) pawn majority.

8...♘xd5 9 ♘xd5 ♕xd5 10 c3

10 ♗xc7 is too greedy; e.g. 10...♗g4 11 c3 (11 ♗e2 ♖c8 12 ♗g3 ♗xf3 13 ♗xf3 ♕e6+ 14 ♕e3 ♘xd4 15 ♕xe6 ♘xf3+ 16 gxf3 fxe6 is equal) 11...♗xf3 12 gxf3 ♖c8 13 ♗f4 ♕xf3 14 ♖g1 e5 15 dxe5 ♗xe5 16 ♗xe5 ♘xe5 17 ♗b5+ ♔e7 and Black has slightly fewer king problems than White.

10...♗g4 11 ♗e2 0-0-0

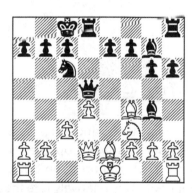

Black has reached a very satisfactory cross between a Modern and a Scandinavian, and has excellent activity to compensate for White's extra pawn presence in the centre, with ...g6-g5 and/or ...e7-e5 to follow. Now 12 0-0 e5?! 13 ♘xe5 doesn't quite work because the g4-bishop is hanging, but 12...♗h5! threatens both 13...e5 and 13...g5 14 ♗g3(?!) f5, with the initiative.

Chapter Six

1 e4 ♘c6 2 ♘c3

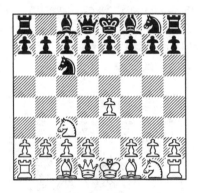

To play the Dark Knight against both 1 e4 and 1 d4 (as opposed to just against 1 d4) requires some plan for dealing with this relatively rare move.

As with 2 ♘f3, White hopes to return to familiar territory with 2...e5, and while this is fine theoretically, learning the Spanish Four Knights, Belgrade Gambit, Vienna Game, Vienna Gambit, and Scotch Four Knights is not a practical answer to an "uncommon" variation.

Another possibility is 2...e6 3 d4 d5, transposing to a French sideline covered in Wisnewski's *Play 1...♘c6!*.

Ideally we should find something that resembles – and is likely to transpose into – positions we already know, but we need to be careful of our move order because the Dark Knight Pirc is not well suited for generating counterplay against the Argentinean Attack. (For instance, 2...g6 3 d4 ♗g7 4 ♗e3 d6 5 ♕d2 ♘f6 6 f3 e5 7 ♘ge2 is tricky for Black at best, though 7...a6 8 0-0-0 b5 is a decent try.)

2...♘f6 3 d4

Others:

a) 3 f4 d5 4 e5 d4 5 exf6 (5 ♘ce2?! d3! 6 cxd3 ♘d5 7 a3 ♗g4 8 ♕b3 ♘b6 is a mess for White) 5...dxc3 6 fxg7 cxd2+ 7 ♕xd2 ♕xd2+ (or 7...♗xg7 8 ♕xd8+ ♘xd8) 8 ♗xd2 ♗xg7 is just equal.

b) 3 ♘f3 d6 followed by ...g7-g6 will be a Dark Knight Pirc.

3...d6

We intend to fianchetto but we are not yet committed, so it is impossible for White to start an Argentinean Attack. The most common reply by far is 4 ♘f3, transposing to Chapter Five.

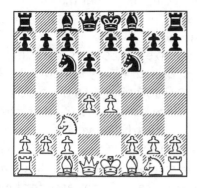

Here, we will take a close look at:

A: 4 f4 *115*
B: 4 d5 *117*

But first:

a) 4 ♗e3 makes no sense because of 4...♘g4!. If 5 ♗g5 h6 6 ♗h4 g5 7 ♗g3 ♗g7, we have gotten our fianchetto with gain of time, reaching positions similar to Chapter Five. While this does not actually give easy equality, it is certainly satisfactory – 4 ♗e3 is almost never played.

b) 4 f3 e5 5 ♘ge2 exd4 6 ♘xd4 ♗e7 is a kind of Philidor where White's f-pawn does not belong on f3. White normally continues in "Argentinean" style with 7 ♗e3 0-0 8 ♕d2, when Black has 8...♘xd4 (8...d5!? 9 0-0-0 dxe4 10 ♘xc6 ♕xd2+ 11 ♖xd2 bxc6 12 ♘xe4 ♘xe4 13 fxe4 offers a tiny endgame advantage for White) 9 ♗xd4 c6 10 0-0-0 and now 10...b5 with an equal game (though perhaps we should call such a position unclear), or 10...♗e6, which transposes to A.Mista-M.Szelag,

Koszalin 1999 (see Game 85).

c) 4 ♗g5 h6! (Mestrovic's move, which he has had a chance to use four times, with two wins and two draws against very strong opposition) 5 ♗h4 (this doesn't seem consistent, but it is the most common; also, if 5 ♗xf6 exf6! 6 d5 ♘e7, White has little to combat the incredibly slow but effective plan of 7...a6, 8...g6, 9...♗g7, 10...0-0 and 11...f5, with approximate equality) 5...g5 6 ♗g3 ♗g7 (6...e6!?) is also equal. White tried 7 h4 g4 8 h5 in I.Jakic-Z.Mestrovic, Zadar 2001 (see Game 86), where 8...e5 9 d5 ♘d4 was quite sufficient; while R.Zelcic-Z.Mestrovic, Nova Gorica 2003, saw 7 f3 0-0 8 ♗f2, but Black used the same idea, taking advantage of White's slow play: 8...e5 9 d5 ♘d4! 10 ♘ge2 c5! 11 dxc6 bxc6 12 ♘xd4 exd4 13 ♗xd4 and although Mestrovic was successful with 13...c5?! (see Game 87), 13...♖b8! is stronger, with excellent compensation.

A: 4 f4 e5

5 dxe5
Other moves don't offer much:

a) 5 ♘f3 exd4 6 ♘xd4 is some sort of Philidor where White's 4 f4 is premature.

Black must be alert in order to prove this – and it is worth noting that, until now, he has not been up to the task: 6...♗e7 7 ♗e2 0-0 8 ♗e3 ♘xd4 9 ♗xd4 and here the new move 9...d5! 10 ♗xf6 ♗xf6 11 ♕xd5 ♗xc3+ 12 bxc3 ♕f6 13 ♕d2 ♖d8 14 ♗d3 (14 ♕e3 is met by 14...♕h4+ 15 ♕f2 ♕f6 16 e5 ♕c6, or 15 g3 ♕h3 and White has some trouble getting his king safe and activating his h1-rook; e.g. 16 ♗f3 b6 17 e5 ♖b8 18 ♕e2 ♗b7 19 ♗xb7 ♖xb7 20 ♖d1 ♖bb8 with compensation) 14...♕b6 15 ♕f2 ♕b2 16 0-0 ♕xc3 17 e5 ♕d4 18 ♕xd4 ♖xd4 19 ♖ad1 ♔f8 20 c3 ♖d7 21 ♗e4 ♖b8 and Black unravels safely.

b) 5 d5 ♘e7 6 ♘f3 (6 fxe5 dxe5 7 ♗e3 ♘g6 8 a3 ♗d6 is fine for Black; or 6 f5 c6! 7 dxc6 bxc6 8 ♘f3 ♕c7 with usually ...d6-d5 coming soon, and sometimes ...♖b8 and/or ...g7-g6) 6...exf4 7 ♗xf4 ♘g6 8 ♗g3 ♗e7 9 ♕d2 0-0 10 0-0-0 ♘d7 intending ...♗f6, ...♖e8, ...a7-a6, ...b7-b5, ...♘c5, ...♗b7. White's h2-h4 must be

met by ...h7-h6 so that the enemy pawn does not reach the h6-square. The position is equal.

c) 5 fxe5 dxe5 6 d5 ♘d4! (6...♘e7 transposes to 6 fxe5 in note 'b') 7 ♘f3 ♗c5 8 ♘a4!? (or 8 ♗g5 0-0 9 ♕d3 ♕d6 and since 10 0-0-0?! ♘g4! is strong, White is clearly worse) 8...♘xe4 9 ♘xc5 ♘xc5 10 ♘xd4 ♕h4+ 11 g3 ♕xd4 12 ♕xd4 exd4 and although White's bishops are nice, it is not easy for him to recover the pawn with a good position – Black is a little better.

d) 5 ♗b5?! exd4 6 ♕xd4 ♗e7 7 ♘f3 0-0 8 ♗xc6 bxc6 9 0-0 ♖e8 10 ♖d1 ♗b7 with two bishops and a big bull's-eye on the e4-pawn – more than enough to make up for our space disadvantage.

5...dxe5

Black often throws in 5...♗g4 6 ♘f3, but this does not help the situation.

6 ♕xd8 ♔xd8 7 ♘f3 ♗b4 8 ♗d3 ♖e8

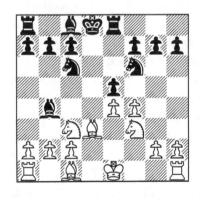

This position has been reached only once: in Ma.Tseitlin-C.Barlocco, World Seniors Championship, Port Erin 2004, which continued 9 0-0 exf4 10 ♘d5 ♘xd5 11 exd5 ♘e7, and White went on to win. However, Black can equalize with 9...h6! 10 fxe5 ♘g4 11 h3 (or 11 ♖d1 ♗c5+ 12 ♔f1 ♗d7) 11...♘gxe5 12 ♗f4 (or 12 ♗b5 ♗d7 13 ♘d5 ♘xf3+ 14 gxf3 ♗d6) 12...♘xd3 13 cxd3 ♗e6.

B: 4 d5 ♘b8

Don't get any funny ideas. 4...♘e5?! 5 f4 ♘ed7 6 ♘f3 c6 7 dxc6 bxc6 8 e5 is no good for Black.

After 4...♘b8, White will usually play ♘f3 soon (and Black ...g7-g6), transposing to line B in Chapter Five. Here we investigate some independent set-ups by White.

5 f4

The most often played, but it is not a strong move. The problem is that, after 5...c6, White will be unable to maintain the e4/f4 pawn duo, unless he plays the otherwise undesirable 6 dxc6. Instead:

a) 5 ♗g5 g6 6 ♗xf6 exf6 7 ♗d3 (to hinder ...f6-f5) 7...♗g7 8 ♕d2 0-0 9 0-0-0 ♘d7 10 h4 ♘c5 11 h5 f5 with full counterplay.

b) 5 ♗e3 (this logical move has had

only one obscure trial) 5...c6 6 ♕d2 ♘bd7 7 0-0-0 cxd5 8 exd5 a6 should make for a lively game, with ...b7-b5 and ...♗b7 coming, and probably ...g7-g6 and ...♗g7, with maybe ...♖c8, ...♕c7 and/or ...♘b6. White will be unable to organize the rapid pressure on the e-file that would make this uncomfortable for Black.

5...c6

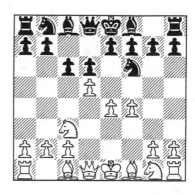

6 dxc6

Other moves:

a) 6 ♘f3 cxd5 7 exd5 g6 8 ♗e3 ♗g7 is equal. Black will continue with ...0-0, ...♘bd7, ...♕c7, ...a7-a6, ...b7-b5, ...♘c5 (or ...♘b6), and ....♗b7 (or ....♗d7). Since White's central pawns are split, the f-pawn is mainly a weakness. Then 9 ♗e2 0-0 10 0-0 ♘bd7 transposes to M.Drasko-Z.Mestrovic, Bosnian Team Championship 2003 (see Game 24).

b) 6 ♗e2 g6 will probably transpose to 6 ♘f3, after 7 ♘f3 cxd5 8 exd5 ♗g7 9 ♗e3 for instance. Instead, A.Stefanova-M.Zielinska, Dresden 2004, continued 7 ♗e3 ♕a5 8 ♗f3!? ♗g7 9 ♘e2 cxd5 10 exd5 ♗g4, which was about equal, but

Black did go on to lose. He can improve slightly by 7...♗g7 and 8...0-0, rather than committing the queen so early.

6...♘xc6 7 ♘f3 g6

8 ♗c4

Alternatively:

a) 8 e5!? is a good try, though it has never been played: 8...♘h5 (or 8...♘d7!? 9 exd6 ♗g7! 10 dxe7 ♕xe7+ 11 ♕e2 ♘b4 12 ♕xe7+ ♔xe7 13 ♔d1 ♖d8 with compensation) 9 exd6 ♗g7 10 ♗c4 0-0 11 0-0 exd6 and White's holes balance Black's holes.

b) 8 ♗e3 ♗g7 9 ♕d2 0-0 10 0-0-0 ♘g4 11 ♗g1 ♕a5 12 h3 ♗xc3 13 ♕xc3 ♕xc3 14 bxc3 ♘f6 with slightly the more comfortable game for Black.

8...♗g7 9 0-0 0-0 10 ♔h1 ♗g4 11 ♗e3 ♖c8 12 ♗b3

The position is equal, but Black needs to find something more active than 12...a6?! 13 h3 ♗d7 14 ♕e1 b5?! 15 e5!, after which White was much better in N.Raghavi-K.Szczepkowska, World Junior Championships, Istanbul 2005.

Black can choose between 12...♘d7, 12...♕d7, 12...♘h5, and 12...♘a5 (since the complications after 13 ♗xa7?! b6 14 e5 ♘d7! 15 h3 ♗xf3 16 ♕xf3 ♘c6 17 ♘b5 dxe5 favour Black).

Section Three
Others

This section deals with almost everything except the opening moves 1 e4 and 1 d4, including some quite unusual openings. Except for 1 c4, which needs to be taken seriously, the challenge for Black is to give himself chances to wrest the initiative early, and/or make sure that White does not reach the type of position with which he is experienced and comfortable. In a few cases, I am forced to admit that 1...♘c6 is not suitable, in which case I like 1...g6. I choose to believe that this is not too much of a departure, since the fianchetto is so common in the Dark Knight System.

I will warn the reader that the coverage in section 3 is less detailed than in the other sections. This is because these openings are far less common, and also because you may already have your own systems of defence, which there is no need to abandon.

Chapter Seven
1 c4 ♞c6

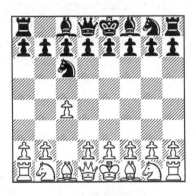

You could play the Dark Knight against 1 e4 and 1 d4 and then play any favourite system against 1 c4, but it makes some sense to use 1...♞c6 here too, since there is a fair chance of reaching positions you already need to know to meet 1 d4.

2 ♞c3

Others:

a) 2 d4 e5 returns to Chapter Two.

b) 2 g3 e5 3 ♝g2 f5 will transpose to line A below once White (inevitably) plays ♞c3.

c) 2 ♞f3 e5 3 d4 e4 4 ♞g5 (4 ♞fd2 f5 5 ♞c3 ♞f6 6 e3 is line B2) 4...♝b4+ 5

♞c3 and now Black can certainly play 5...f5, transposing to line B1; but 5...d5! is even better, as in Ge.Lambert-A.Labarthe, Vichy 2000. Not without reason, White worried about the centre opening up and played 6 c5?, when 6...h6 7 ♞h3 ♝xh3 or 6...b6! would have been strong; but even after 6 a3 ♝xc3 7 bxc3 ♞f6 8 cxd5 ♛xd5 9 f3 0-0 10 fxe4 ♞xe4 11 ♞xe4 ♛xe4 12 ♛d3 ♝f5 Black maintains an advantage along with his grip on the e4-square.

2...e5

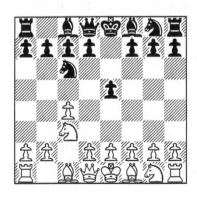

White will now choose from the following:

A: **3 g3** 121
B: **3 ♘f3** 123

A: 3 g3 f5!?

A reversed Grand Prix Attack, which is "not a good idea", according to Hikaru Nakamura. Nonetheless, it was most likely the great disparity in playing strength that was the difference in our encounter – upon examination, the positions are just fine so long as Black does not use the typical plan of trying to deliver checkmate right out of the opening. Come to think of it, he may have been saying that the opening was a bad choice against him in particular, which is no doubt true given that I had nothing prepared other than the usual recipe.

4 ♗g2 ♘f6 5 d3

After 5 e3, the gambit 5...d5!? has been very successful. The idea is to open up the game to reach the weak light squares on White's queenside, particularly the gaping hole on d3. If White tries to remain a pawn ahead,

Black obtains dangerous compensation; e.g. 6 cxd5 ♘b4 7 ♕b3?! ♘d3+ 8 ♔f1 e4 9 ♘h3 ♗d6 and White has great difficulties with both king safety and development. Instead, 7 d3 ♘fxd5 8 ♘xd5 ♘xd5 9 ♘f3 is the normal continuation, when Black's position is a bit loose but White needs to create some sort of off-board diversion to sneak his e-pawn back to e2. L.Gofshtein-N.Mitkov, Lisbon 1999, continued 9...♗d6 10 0-0 ♘f6 11 ♕b3 ♕e7 12 e4 fxe4 13 dxe4 and the game was equal after 13...♕f7 14 ♕c3 ♕h5 15 ♘d2 0-0, though White went on to win (see Game 88).

5...♗b4 6 ♗d2

Otherwise White's c-pawns will be doubled, providing long-term compensation for surrendering the bishop pair. A brutal example is J.Ramirez-J.Schuyler, Las Vegas 2007, which saw 6 a3? ♗xc3+ 7 bxc3 d6 8 ♖b1 0-0 9 e3? e4 10 d4 b6, followed by ...♗a6 (see Game 89).

6...0-0

7 ♘f3

Instead:

a) 7 e3 worked great for White in H.Nakamura-J.Schuyler, Las Vegas 2008: 7...♗xc3 8 ♗xc3 d6 9 ♘e2 ♕e8 10 h3, and since 10...♕h5?! would be met by 11 f4! I was already out of ideas and lost quickly. Meanwhile, Black is actually fine after 10...b6!? 11 0-0 ♗b7 to oppose White's strong bishop and work towards relieving him of the bishop pair. This is nearly equal according to *Houdini*, and can be used just as well against 10 ♕d2 (though 10 0-0 is a serious test).

Going back further, Black has 8...d5! which is three for three in my database, most significantly in O.Foisor-J.M.Degraeve, Le Touquet 1996 (see Game 90). And if that's not enough, in J.Iruzubieta-B.Gulko, San Sebastian 1996, Gulko casually played 7...♘e7!?, and after 8 ♘ge2, 8...c6! to guard the d5-square and preserve the dark-squared bishop. This too was nearly equal (see Game 91), although 8 a3 is more testing.

Last but not least, Black can try 7...f4!? which scored a full point in N.Spiridonov-K.Spraggett, Cannes 1992 (see Game 92). In case it's not obvious, my main recommendation is 7...♗xc3 8 ♗xc3 d5!.

b) 7 a3?! is very often played, and with very bad results. It is hard to justify spending a tempo to force an exchange which Black is interested in making anyway: 7...♗xc3 8 ♗xc3 d6 (again 8...d5!? 9 cxd5 ♘xd5 10 ♗d2 h6! 11 ♘f3 e4! or 11 ♕b3?! ♗e6 12 ♕xb7

♘d4 with excellent compensation) 9 ♘f3 ♕e8, and with White having squandered a tempo on a2-a3, Black's "typical plan" (described below) has done well, while if White delays castling, he runs other risks. F.Bruno-B.Kurajica, Lugano 1985, was a short lesson for White (see Game 93).

7...e4!

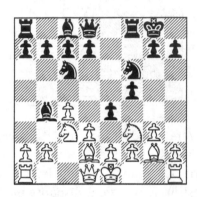

This rare line is best, taking advantage of White's previous move to establish a knight on the e4-square.

For the record, the "typical plan" is 7...d6 8 0-0 ♗xc3 9 ♗xc3 ♕e8, intending 10...♕h5, 11...f4, 12...♗h3, 13...♘g4, 14...fxg3 15 fxg3 ♗xg2 16 ♔xg2 ♖xf3 17 ♔xf3 ♖f8+ and wins! Some of the most astute readers may have noticed that five of White's moves were skipped – indeed that is a little snag. To see how Black's attack can work against an opponent with a pulse, check out M.Sher-K.Spraggett, Andorra 1993 (Game 94), though Spraggett did require a large assist from his GM opponent, and 7...d6 is not my recommendation.

8 dxe4 ♗xc3!

8...♘xe4 will normally transpose, but this new move order cuts down on White's options.

9 ♗xc3 ♘xe4 10 ♖c1

I expect White to try to preserve his pawn structure as he has in the analogous positions from the alternative move order. However, if 10 0-0!? ♘xc3?! 11 bxc3, White's open lines make it easy for him to pressure the queenside. So Black should retain the strong knight: 10...d6 11 ♕c2 a5 12 ♘d4 ♕e7 and 13...♗d7 with just a slight edge for White.

10...d6 11 0-0

The only time this position has been reached, Black started losing the thread with 11...♗e6?! 12 ♘d4 ♘xd4?! 13 ♕xd4 ♘xc3?! 14 ♖xc3 c5 15 ♕d2, when White had a pleasant long-term advantage and went on to win in the game Har.Becker-Joa.Franz, German League 1997.

Instead, after 11...♕e7 12 ♘d4 ♗d7 13 ♕b3 ♘c5 14 ♕c2 a5, White's edge is tiny.

B: 3 ♘f3 f5

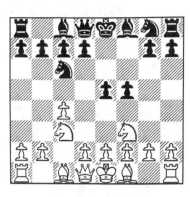

This move has a solid reputation and is a popular alternative to 3...♘f6.

4 d4 e4

And now mainly:

> **B1: 5 ♘g5** *124*
> **B2: 5 ♘d2** *125*

But also:

a) 5 ♘e5 – only Larry Christiansen (and *Houdini*) seems interested in playing this move, though he has an impressive 3-0 with it. After 5...♘f6 6 ♗f4, as in L.Christiansen-S.Conquest, Oviedo (rapid) 1992, the new move 6...♘h5!? 7 ♗d2 ♘f6 is fine for Black if he is content with a draw, because 8 e3 d6 9 ♘xc6 bxc6 10 ♗e2 ♗e7 11 0-0 0-0 is nothing for White. Otherwise Black can try 6...d6 7 ♘xc6 bxc6 8 e3 ♗e7 9 ♗e2 0-0 10 0-0 ♗e6, with a slight edge for White.

b) 5 ♗g5 ♗e7 6 ♗xe7 ♘gxe7 7 ♘d2 ♘xd4 8 ♘dxe4 ♘e6 9 ♘d2 b6! 10 e3 ♗b7 11 ♘f3 0-0 with easy equality and chances for more; e.g. 12 ♗e2 f4! is good for Black, as is 12 g3?! f4! 13 exf4 ♞xf4 14 gxf4 ♖xf4 15 ♗g2 (or 15 ♗e2) 15...♛f8!.

B1: 5 ♞g5 ♗b4

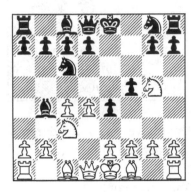

6 ♞h3

This retreat is necessary.

a) G.McKenna-J.Schuyler, Richmond 2008, instead continued 6 f3?! h6! 7 ♞h3 exf3, threatening 8...♛h4+ and 9...♛xd4. My opponent found 8 e3! which keeps White in the game, though 8...♛h4+ 9 g3 ♗xc3+ 10 bxc3 ♛h5 11 ♗g2 ♛f7 12 ♗xf3 ♛xc4 13 ♗h5+ ♚d8 would have allowed Black an edge. (A.Beliavsky-V.Bagirov, Minsk 1983, also saw White play 6 f3?!, but Black did not punish him and went on to lose.)

b) 6 g3?!, as in J.Timman-I.Sokolov, Dortmund 1999, is not a good idea either – the bishop should not be caught dead on the g2-square. After 6...♞f6 7 d5 ♞e5 8 ♛b3 ♛e7 9 ♗g2?! h6 10 ♞h3 ♛c5 11 ♗f4?! ♞xc4 White had little for the pawn.

After the text move, the position again resembles a reversed Grand Prix Attack. White's king's knight will soon reach the excellent f4-square, but the four moves it takes to get there is a high price, even in a blocked position.

6...♞f6 7 e3 ♗xc3+ 8 bxc3 d6 9 ♞f4 0-0

White's c4-pawn is weak and his bishops are not yet working, but he should be able to force through the c4-c5 break. If Black is not careful, this will bring White a significant advantage. However, White needs to be careful as well, because if the position opens up at the wrong time or in the wrong way, he will be punished for his slow development.

10 h4 b6 11 ♗a3 ♖f7!

This is a new move, and it makes us more comfortable by stepping out of the influence of White's a3-bishop and avoiding ♞e6 forks. It is also useful to guard the seventh rank and shield our king. The similar 11...♖e8 was tried successfully in R.Koch-M.Wiedenkeller, Reggio Emilia 1982/83, but it accomplishes a bit less and leaves Black vulnerable to the ♗b5 pin. It is worth noting that Black's results have been excellent in this variation even without the text move, though a few high-level players have successfully advocated White.

12 c5

If White does not play this now, 12...♗a6 is coming, and the c4-c5 break will be forever ineffective.

12...bxc5

12...d5!?.

13 ♗c4

Naturally, if 13 dxc5 then 13...d5! 14 c4? d4 and White's structure is awful.

13...d5 14 ♗b5 ♘b8 15 ♗xc5 c6 16 ♗e2 ♗a6

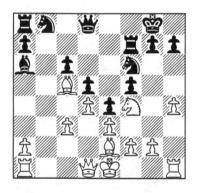

White has relieved himself of his pawn weakness, but the coming bishop exchange brings equality. Black's plans are to manoeuvre a knight to the lovely c4-square, trade off White's f4-knight, and fight for the b-file; e.g. 17 ♖b1 ♗xe2 18 ♕xe2 ♘bd7 19 ♘e6 ♕c8 20 ♗d6 ♘b6 21 ♘c5 ♘fd7 22 ♘xd7 ♖xd7 (or 22...♕xd7 23 ♗f4 ♖c8 and 24...c5) 23 ♗f4 ♘c4 24 0-0 ♖b7, which is still equal. Black has achieved his objec-

tives, but White's "bad" bishop is very strong. Black will not be better unless he can arrange to exchange the other pair of rooks.

B2: 5 ♘d2

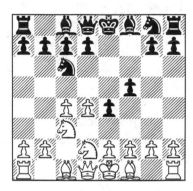

This move is not common here, but the position is important since it can be reached from a few different move orders.

5...♘f6 6 e3

6 ♘db1!? is a cute move, intending 7 ♗g5. *Houdini* likes 6...b6!? opening paths for the bishop and sketching out some territory on the queenside. Then 7 ♗g5 h6 8 ♗xf6 ♕xf6 9 e3 (or 9 ♘d5 ♗b4+ 10 ♘1c3 ♗xc3+ 11 bxc3 ♕d6 12 e3 ♘e7 13 ♘f4 g5 14 ♕h5+?! ♔f8 15 ♘e2 ♗a6 and Black is better) 9...♕f7 10 ♘b5 ♔d8 11 ♗e2 g5 leads to a murky position which Mr. H calls equal. Unfortunately, there are no games to draw on, and the computer convincingly shot down all my sensible ideas, so we are stuck with this nonsense. He continues 12 a3 h5 13 ♘d2 g4 14 ♕c2 h4 15 0-0-0 h3 16 g3, still equal.

6...♗e7!

6...g6 is just about always played, but the fianchetto is slow and somewhat accommodating, releasing the b4-square. Sokolov and Sigurjonsson both got squashed by White's huge queenside after ♖b1 and b2-b4. The text move keeps Black focused on where the play will actually take place.

7 ♗e2 0-0 8 0-0 d5!

Previously 8...♕e8 and 8...d6 have been tried. The text is an unplayed novelty that prevents Black from getting overrun on the queenside, reaching a satisfactory reversed Classical French.

9 cxd5

Or 9 a3 ♗e6 10 b4 a6!, strongly discouraging the further advance of White's queenside pawns.

9...♘b4 10 ♕b3 ♘bxd5 11 ♘c4 c6 12 ♗d2 ♕c7

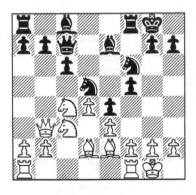

Intending 13...♗e6, 14...♖fd8, and Black is fine.

Chapter Eight
1 ♘f3 ♘c6

If you play 1...♘c6 against 1 e4 and 1 d4, you may as well play it against 1 ♘f3, since White will usually respond with 2 d4, 2 e4, or 2 c4, transposing to Chapters One, Five and Seven respectively. The only continuation with independent significance is:

2 g3 e5 3 d3 d5!

A reversed Pirc is quite safe for Black, as long as he is careful not to choose a sharp variation. I've played 3...f5 here in the past because it is extremely effective against the King's Indian Attack, but its value is questionable against other set-ups.

4 ♗g2 g6!

An excellent recipe. White's extra tempo amounts to little.

5 0-0 ♗g7 6 e4

White challenges the centre with 6 c4 less often. In Bu Xiangzhi-V.Ivanchuk, Khanty-Mansiysk 2011, Black played 6...dxc4 7 dxc4 ♕xd1 8 ♖xd1 e4 9 ♘fd2 f5, when White needed 10 f3 to equalize. Instead, after 10 ♘c3 ♗e6 11 ♘d5?! 0-0-0 Ivanchuk went on to win (see Game 95).

6...♘ge7 7 ♘bd2 0-0 8 c3 a5 9 a4 h6

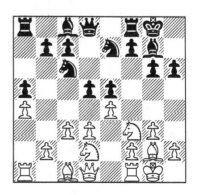

Black has outscored White here at all levels of play. K.Arakhamia Grant-

A.Raetsky, Bern 1995, showed Black expanding and using his space advantage after 10 ♖e1 ♗e6 11 exd5 ♗xd5! (see Game 96); while V.Frias Pablaza-A.Baburin, San Francisco 1997, saw Black's central control turning into a powerful tactical strike against White's king after 10 exd5 ♘xd5 (see Game 97).

Chapter Nine
Others

I used to "pre-move" 1...♞c6 in online blitz games – after all, it's playable against everything, right? Eventually I was embarrassed (several times!) by a player who sometimes opened 1 b4. After 2 b5, I did not feel like I had found the refutation to the Orang-utan! 2...♞e5 3 ♗b2?! ♞c4!? is not bad, but 3 e4 or 3 d4 leaves Black with no excuse for his knight placement.

In all seriousness, 1...♞c6 is just not the best way to start challenging White after 1 b3, 1 f4, 1 e3, 1 a3, or especially 1 b4. Play whatever you like, but in my opinion, 1...g6 – the "Dark Bishop"? – is simple and strong against all of these.

Against 1 b4 and 1 b3, 1...g6 may come as a surprise to the opponent, which is always nice. It also makes sense to oppose White's bishop on the long diagonal, especially since his will be loose, while ours (after we castle short) will be guarded – a tactical advantage.

Larsen's Attack
Based on the counter-fianchetto, *Hou-*dini and I have cooked up something new and fun against Larsen's Attack: 1 b3 g6 2 ♗b2 ♞f6 3 e4 ♗g7!? (3...d6 is much more common) 4 e5 ♞d5 5 c4 ♞f4!

This move is provocative and strong. White can keep advancing pawns, with tempo in some cases, but he will not be able to control the territory he imagines he is conquering, and he will become weak in an area of the board I like to call the "deep centre" – d3, e3, and the surrounding squares. After 6 g3 ♞e6 7 d4 d6 8 d5?! ♞c5 9 b4 (otherwise the knight is very powerful in conjunction with ...♗f5) 9...♘cd7 10 f4 0-0 11 ♘f3 c6! 12 ♕b3 cxd5 13 cxd5 dxe5 14 fxe5 a5 15 bxa5 ♘c5, White's position is approaching the later stages of a long and painful decline. It is easy to criticize White's play, but he was already worse very early; for instance, 8 ♘f3 0-0 9 ♘c3 dxe5 10 dxe5 ♘d7 11 ♘e4 b6 12 ♕d3 ♗b7 13 ♕e3 f5! 14 exf6 exf6 15 0-0-0 still leaves White struggling after 15...♖e8 or 15...f5.

Sokolsky's Opening (aka The Orang-utan, aka The Polish)

1 b4 g6 2 ♗b2 ♘f6 3 c4 ♗g7 4 ♘f3 0-0 5 e3 d6 6 d4 ♘bd7 7 ♗e2 e5 8 0-0 e4 9 ♘fd2 ♖e8

I know, there are other ways the game can go, but this is typical. Black has reached a King's Indian Attack in reverse, and in practice Black's attack has proven stronger (+12 -2 =4 is 77.7%). White's extra tempo, ♗b2, is just about useless because the bishop belongs on the a3-square.

In spite of his successes, Black has yet to produce a model for correct play.

In the games I can find, Black keeps allowing the enemy pawn to a6, which accelerates White's queenside initiative. The reader is better off studying the classic King's Indian Attacks by Fischer, Petrosian, Bronstein, Larsen, etc. They go (in reverse – I have translated here) ...♘f8, ...h7-h5, ...♗f5, ...a7-a6 (when White's pawn reaches a5), ...♘8h7, ...h5-h4 (and ...h4-h3 if possible), ...♘g5 with scary invasions coming on the light squares or (if White has played h2-h3) scary sacrifices on the h3-pawn.

Bird's Opening

Against 1 f4, I would warn against playing ...d7-d5, which gives White what he wants: the e5-square. Instead, after 1...g6 2 ♘f3 ♗g7 3 e3 d6 4 d4 ♘d7,

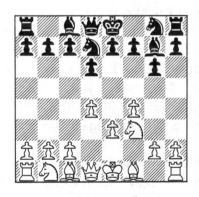

Black is +17 -1 =3 according to my database. Wow! Obviously White's position can't actually be that bad. What the statistics mean is that, for those interested in winning chess games, it is extremely important to combat the opponent's automatic plans. Then 5

♗d3 e5 6 c3 ♕e7 was no fun at all for White in A.Capaliku-J.Gombac, Nova Gorica 2010 (see Game 98); while 5 ♗c4 e6 has scored 100% for Black, most notably in A.Spichkin-D.Reinderman, Rijeka 2010 (see Game 99).

Of course, White does not have to play a Stonewall – just as popular is a reversed Leningrad Dutch with 3 g3, when one system has performed extremely well for Black: 3...b6!? 4 ♗g2 ♗b7 5 0-0 e6 6 d3 ♘e7 7 e4 d6

with 8...♘d7, 9...c5, 10...♕c7, and 11...0-0 to follow. Dzindzi pithily states that "any opening named after an animal is bad", but here the Hippopotamus is well-suited to combat both White's kingside expansion and his fianchettoed bishop. Black certainly made it look easy in P.Auchenberg-To.Christensen, Helsingor 1997 (see Game 100). An important idea is to play ...f7-f5 just when White is ready for his f4-f5 advance (though Christensen did not find this necessary).

Other others

As for 1 ♘c3 and 1 g3, 1...♘c6 should transpose to our repertoire at some point.

As I mentioned already, 1...g6 is a good answer to 1 e3, and also to 1 a3, when White is challenged to find any use for his opening move. If 1 h3, 1 h4, 1 ♘h3, 1 ♘a3, 1 a4, or 1 f3, you're on your own. 1 f3 is particularly troubling because it is not clear whether White is intending 2 ♘h3 and 3 ♘f2, or 2 g4!, or 2 ♔f2! and 3 ♔g3!!. May you be confronted with these problems frequently.

Chapter Ten
Miscellaneous Topics

Reducing the Workload – The Dark Knight for Dummies

Perhaps some readers have gotten the impression that the study material (which in my opinion is very small) can be substantially simplified. Indeed, it can. There is no sensible way to avoid Chapter One, but Chapter Two is, in some sense, unnecessary. After 1 d4 ♘c6 2 c4, Black can simply play 2...d6, which will almost certainly transpose to Chapter One. Likewise, Black need not learn Chapter Three. After 1 d4 ♘c6 2 d5, Black can just play 2...♘b8, with a likely transposition to Chapters One or Five. Chapter Four? Toss it. Just play 1 e4 ♘c6 2 d4 d6, probably transposing to Chapters One, Five, or Six.

In other words, don't play for an early ...e7-e5 and plan on fianchettoing the king's bishop whether it is necessary or not. The thing is, the positions from Chapters Two, Three and Four, are among my favourites in the Dark Knight System, so I would rather know them and play them than avoid them,

but anyone who prefers to fianchetto can study less and play his own favourite positions more.

Notice that when playing the System this way, White's f- and c-pawns are both free, so White could play a "Four Pawns Attack" if he so chooses. Without going into detail, I will point out that this is not a good way for White to fight for an advantage: 1 e4 ♘c6 2 d4 d6 3 d5 ♘b8 4 c4 g6 5 f4 ♗g7 6 ♘f3 ♘f6 7 ♘c3 0-0 8 ♗e2 e6!

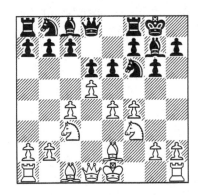

9 0-0 (9 e5!?) 9...exd5 10 cxd5 c6! 11 dxc6 ♘xc6 12 ♔h1 ♖e8 13 ♗d3 ♕b6, or 13...a6 and 14...b5, with equality.

The Light Knight Attack!?

If the Dark Knight System is so great, why not play it with an extra tempo? Well, the good news is that nobody can stop you; e.g. 1 ♘c3!? e5 2 d3 d5 3 g3 d4 4 ♘b1 ♘c6 5 ♗g2 with a reversed Dark Knight Pirc. Furthermore, there are many other possible move orders White can use. The bad news is that it will often be Black fighting for the advantage, not White. How can a system be good for Black and not for White? The answer is that Black and White have different opening objectives. In the DKS Black often loses some time with his knight, but this is mitigated by the fact that he has reached a position where tempi are relatively unimportant. Therefore, playing such a position a tempo up represents only a small gain, sometimes not enough even to equalize.

As for 1 ♘c3 d5 2 e4,

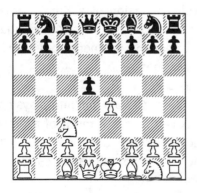

I believe White can fight for an advantage after 2...d4 (a practical one, if not a theoretical one), but in my ex-

perience Black usually plays 2...e6, 2...c6, or 2...♘f6 instead, transposing to his favourite defence (French, Caro-Kann, and Alekhine's, respectively), or just 2...dxe4 3 ♘xe4 and 3...♗f5, 3...♘f6, or 3...♘d7, with a good version of Black's favourite Caro-Kann variation. While these positions are all playable for White, there is little chance of getting Black out of his comfort zone.

Of course, real chess is not the same as theory, and for the right player and/or the right opponent, the "Light Knight Attack" could be the perfect weapon. The grandmaster Jörg Hickl has played 1 g3 e5 2 ♗g2 d5 3 d3 ♘f6 4 ♘f3 ♗d6 5 ♘c3 c6 6 e4 (or 6 0-0 0-0 7 e4) many times with good results.

Readers might choose to view the position as a Dark Knight Pirc reversed, and Hickl's move order is an excellent way to reach it since Black never had a good opportunity to play ...d5-d4. There is not much else to learn because Black's set-up is an extremely common one against 1 g3.

Illustrative Games

The games section serves several purposes:

- ♟ It shows typical middlegame and endgame ideas in the Dark Knight System – there is a whole game to be played, after all.
- ♟ It serves as a place to demonstrate some alternatives to the main recommendations.
- ♟ It shows by example why certain popular variations were rejected. Consider these games a warning.
- ♟ It shows how successful the Dark Knight System can be in practice.
- ♟ It shows how much fun it can be to play the Dark Knight System in your games!

A "good" King's Indian

Game 1
J.Paasikangas Tella-T.Lindqvist
Finnish Team Championship 1996

1 d4 d6 2 c4 e5 3 e3 ♘c6 4 d5 ♘ce7 5 ♘c3 f5 6 ♗d3 ♘f6 7 ♗c2 g6

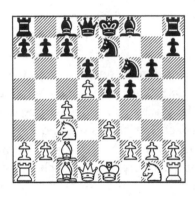

We would reach this position via the move order 1 d4 ♘c6 2 e3 e5 3 d5?! ♘ce7 4 c4 d6 etc. Black now plays an excellent version of a King's Indian – not an uncommon occurrence against an opponent inexperienced with the Dark Knight.

8 ♘f3 ♗h6!?

Why not? Now if White plays e3-e4, Black can relieve himself of a problem piece. If White does not play e3-e4, Black has the powerful e5/f5 pawn duo.

9 b4 0-0 10 ♗b3 a5 11 bxa5 ♖xa5 12 a4 ♔h8 13 ♘b5 ♘e4 14 0-0?! c6! 15 dxc6 bxc6 16 ♘a3 ♗e6

White has no compensation for Black's huge centre.

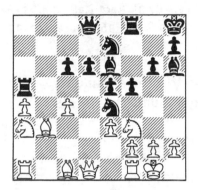

17 ♘d2 ♘c5 18 ♗c2 ♖a6 19 ♗b2 ♗g7 20 e4 f4?! 21 ♔h1 ♕d7 22 f3?!

White weakens his dark squares unnecessarily. Black should have to work for this.

22...♖fa8 23 ♘ab1 ♘c8 24 ♘c3 ♘b6 25 ♗b3 ♕f7 26 ♗c2 ♗f8 27 ♗a3 ♘cxa4 28 ♘xa4 ♘xa4 29 ♗xd6 ♗xd6 30 ♖xa4 ♖xa4 31 ♗xa4 ♕c7

Black has somehow managed to avoid winning any pawns, but his bishop pair provides a nearly decisive advantage.

32 h3?

32 ♕c2.

32...♗b4! 33 ♘b1 ♗xc4 34 ♖g1 ♗c5 35 ♖e1 ♗f2

Black soon won.

An anti-Stonewall – rare light-squared play

Game 2
J.Vialatte-F.Giroux
Paris 2006

1 d4 ♘c6 2 f4 d5

Black has not signed a contract to play on the dark squares, and White has already given himself a big hole on e4. Furthermore, with Black not having played ...♘f6, White is not guaranteed an outpost on e5.

3 ♘f3 ♗g4 4 e3 f6!?

Black may or may not get ...e7-e5 in, but he has certainly stopped ♘e5!

5 ♗b5 ♕d6 6 0-0 a6 7 ♗xc6+?!

This is not going to help the situation on the light squares.

7...♕xc6 8 c3?! ♘h6 9 ♘bd2

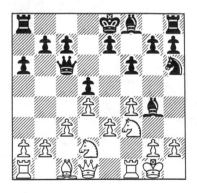

9...0-0-0?!

Black's knight needs to get to the

d6-square as soon as possible – 9...♘f5! 10 ♖e1 ♘d6! with a pleasant advantage. Black eventually gets the position he should have, but only with some co-operation from his opponent.

10 ♕e1 ♗f5 11 ♕e2 e6 12 ♖e1 ♗e4 13 c4 ♗b4!?

Black's plan, which he will soon execute, is to give up both bishops and play "good knight versus bad bishop". This fails to take into account White's development and queenside counterplay.

14 cxd5 exd5 15 a3 ♗xf3 16 ♕xf3 ♗xd2 17 ♗xd2 f5 18 ♖ac1 ♕e6 19 ♕e2 ♖d7 20 b4 ♔b8 21 b5 axb5 22 ♕xb5 ♘f7 23 ♗b4 ♘d6

24 ♕a4?

An incomprehensible positional mistake. The knight that lands on c4 is worth far more than the "tall pawn" on b4. However, in this roundabout way we see the proper fruition of Black's early advantage.

24...♘c4 25 ♗c5 b6 26 ♕a6 ♕c6 27 ♖b1 ♕a8 28 ♕b5? ♔c8! 29 a4

29 ♗b4 c6 traps the queen.

29...bxc5 30 ♕xc5 ♕a5 31 ♕c6 ♖d6 32 ♕b7+ ♔d7 33 ♖ec1 ♖a8 34 ♕b5+ ♕xb5 35 ♖xb5 ♖xa4 36 ♖b8 ♘xe3 37 ♖e1 ♖e6 38 ♖g8 ♖e7 0-1

Can White be made to pay for delaying d4-d5 - ?

Game 3
M.Tratar-M.Srebrnic
Slovenian Championship,
Ljubljana 2010

1 d4 d6 2 ♘f3 g6 3 c4 ♗g7 4 ♘c3 ♘c6

We would reach this by 1 d4 ♘c6 2 ♘f3 d6 3 c4 g6 4 ♘c3 ♗g7 – in this particular game White did not even have the option of playing 4 d5.

5 d5 ♘e5 6 ♘xe5 ♗xe5 7 e4 ♘f6

It seems odd to cut off the retreat for the dark-squared bishop, but the piece is very active where it is, and the danger is far less than it appears. White's lame attempt to trap the bishop on move nine goes nowhere. Such lovely dark square control!

8 ♗d3 0-0 9 ♘e2

In addition to the threat of f2-f4, White makes sure Black cannot damage his structure with ...♗xc3 – however, this retreat is still not the most accurate.

9...♘d7 10 h4 h5 11 ♘f4 ♘c5 12 ♗c2 e6!

White has forgotten about his development and now stands worse. White is a GM, by the way. The rest of the game is kind of brutal.

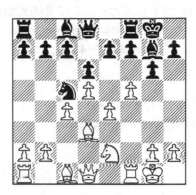

13 ♖b1 a5 14 f3?!

Be careful on the dark squares, White!

14...exd5 15 cxd5 c6 16 dxc6 bxc6 17 ♘e2 ♗a6 18 ♗g5 ♕c8?! [18...♕b6] **19 ♔f2 ♖b8 20 b3 ♖e8 21 ♖e1 ♘e6 22 ♗e3 d5! 23 exd5 cxd5 24 ♖c1 ♕d8 25 ♗d3 ♕xh4+ 26 ♔f1 ♗b7 27 ♕d2 d4 28 ♗g1 ♘f4 29 ♘xf4 ♗xf4 30 ♕xa5 ♗xf3 31 ♖c2 ♗g3 0-1**

Making White pay for delaying d4-d5

Game 4
A.Ipatov-R.Antoniewski
German League 2011

1 d4 d6 2 ♘f3 g6 3 c4 ♗g7 4 ♘c3 ♘c6 5 d5 ♘e5 6 ♘xe5 ♗xe5 7 e4 ♘f6 8 ♗d3 0-0 9 ♘e2 ♘d7 10 0-0 ♘c5 11 f4 ♗g7 12 f5?!

No sooner has White conquered the e5-square than he immediately relinquishes it. White (another grandmaster) receives the proper punishment – eventually.

12...e6 13 ♗c2 exf5 14 exf5 ♘d7?! 15 ♗f4? ♗xb2 16 ♗h6 ♕h4 17 ♗xf8 ♘xf8 18 ♘f4 ♗xa1 19 ♕xa1 ♗d7

White has sacrificed a pawn to trade off Black's powerful bishop, only to find that the exchange has not helped him. This is a typical result.

20 ♕c3 ♖e8 21 c5 ♗b5 22 g3 ♕e7 23 ♖b1 ♗a6 24 ♗a4 ♕e4 25 ♗c2 ♕e3+ 26 ♕xe3 ♖xe3 27 cxd6 cxd6 28 ♗a4 ♖a3 29 ♗b3 ♘d7 30 ♖e1 ♔f8

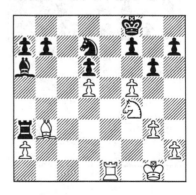

31 ♘e6+??

White's position was very unpleasant anyway, but he gets no compensation for the knight.

31...fxe6 32 dxe6 ♘e5 33 ♖c1 gxf5 34

♖c8+ ♔e7 35 ♖c7+ ♔f6 36 ♖xh7 ♗c4 37 e7 ♗b5 38 h4 d5 39 h5 ♘f3+ 40 ♔g2 ♘g5 41 ♖h6+ ♔xe7 42 ♖g6 ♘f7 43 h6 ♖a6 0-1

White plays an early e4-e5, accomplishing nothing

Game 5
Y.Balashov-G.Kuzmin
USSR Championship
Vilnius 1980

1 ♘f3 ♘f6 2 c4 g6 3 ♘c3 ♗g7 4 e4 d6 5 d4 0-0 6 ♗e2 ♘c6 7 d5 ♘b8

We would reach this by position with the move order 1 d4 ♘c6 2 ♘f3 d6 3 c4 g6 4 d5 ♘b8 5 ♘c3 ♗g7 6 e4 ♘f6 7 ♗e2 0-0.

8 h3 ♘a6 9 ♗e3 ♘c5 10 e5 ♘fd7 11 exd6 exd6 12 ♗d4

12...♘f6

A valid choice, though Black could just as comfortably have allowed the exchange with 12...a5 or 12...♖e8.

13 0-0 a5 14 ♖e1 ♖e8 15 ♗f1 ♗d7 16 ♖xe8+ ♕xe8 17 ♕d2 ♘fe4 18 ♘xe4 ♘xe4 19 ♕e3 ♗xd4 20 ♕xd4 ♘c5 21 ♖e1 ♕f8 ½-½

White avoids ♘xe5

Game 6
R.Fischer-J.Schuyler
Richmond 2008

1 ♘f3 ♘c6 2 e4 d6 3 d4 ♘f6 4 d5 ♘e5 5 ♘c3 ♘xf3+ 6 ♕xf3 g6 7 ♗g5 ♗g7 8 ♗b5+

White's bishop has no squares so he trades it, but I appreciate the extra breathing room.

8...♗d7 9 ♗xd7+ ♕xd7 [9...♘xd7!?] 10 ♕e2 0-0 11 0-0 e6

12 ♖ad1

On 12 ♕f3, I intend 12...♘e8 followed by 13...c6.

12...exd5 13 exd5?!

Instead 13 ♗xf6! ♗xf6 13 ♘xd5 is equal.

13...♖ae8 14 ♕f3 ♘g4 15 h3 ♘e5 16 ♕g3?!

16 ♕e2 is the lesser evil.

16...♕f5!

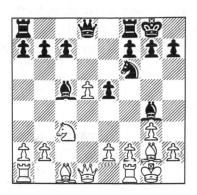

Black is better here, but there are many mistakes in the coming complications – White's next move really stirs things up.

17 ♘b5!? h6 18 ♗e3 ♕xc2 19 ♗d4?! [19 ♗xa7!?] **19...a6?** [19...♕c4! 20 ♘xa7 ♕xd5] **20 ♖c1? ♕e4 21 ♖fe1 ♕xd5 22 ♘xc7 ♕xd4 23 ♘xe8 ♖xe8 24 ♔h1 ♖d8 25 ♖c7 ♕b6 26 ♖e7? ♔f8 0-1**

White's alternate plan with g2-g3

Game 7
L.Altounian-J.Schuyler
Las Vegas 2008

1 ♘f3 ♘c6 2 d4 d6 3 d5 ♘e5 4 ♘xe5 dxe5 5 c4 e6 6 ♘c3 ♘f6 7 g3 exd5 8 cxd5 ♗c5 9 ♗g2 0-0 10 0-0 ♗g4

White has managed to keep his space plus without committing his e-pawn, which leaves me in some doubt as to the best squares for my pieces. My last is intended to provoke White to weaken his king position, a plan which I continue throughout the game.

11 ♕b3 ♗b6 12 h3 ♗f5 13 ♔h2 h6 14 ♕c4?!

This only helps me find the right plan. After this game, the knight transfer became the standard way for me to combat this whole variation with 3 d5. The alternative try 14 a4 would at least have given me a little problem to deal with.

14...♘e8! 15 ♘a4 ♘d6 16 ♕b3 ♗e4

White is intending to grab the bishop pair, so I already start working to relieve him of it. It is awkward for him to avoid the trade.

17 f3 ♗f5 18 ♗d2 ♗d7 19 ♘xb6 axb6 20 ♗b4 ♖e8 21 e4

Levon mentioned to me after the game that he played this to stop 21...♘f5, oddly overlooking the alternate route.

21...♘b5 22 ♗c3 c5 23 dxc6 bxc6 24 ♖fd1

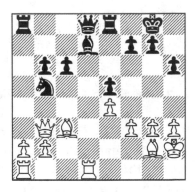

By now I am actually better if I just play the simple moves 24...c5 and 25...♘d4.

24...♕c7?! 25 ♗f1 ♗e6 26 ♗c4 ♗xc4 27 ♕xc4 ♘xc3 28 ♕xc3 ♖ed8 29 a3 ♖d6 30 ♖ac1 ♖ad8 31 ♖xd6 ♕xd6 32 ♖c2 ♕d1 33 ♖f2 ♖d3 34 ♕xc6 ♕e1 35 ♕c2 ♖d1 ½-½

After 36 ♕c8+ ♔h7 37 ♕f5+ g6 38 ♕xf7+ the result is a draw by perpetual check.

Don't play 5...e6??

Game 8
J.Bonin-J.Schuyler
New York 1988

1 d4 ♘c6 2 ♘f3 d6 3 d5 ♘e5 4 ♘xe5 dxe5 5 e4 e6?? [5...♘f6!] **6 ♗b5+ ♗d7 7 dxe6!!**

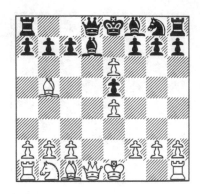

Whatever you do, don't let this happen to you!

7...♗xb5 8 ♕h5! ♗b4+!?

Following the disaster on move 5, this is the best chance in a terrible position.

9 ♘c3?! ♕d4?

Much better is 9...♗xc3+ 10 bxc3 ♕f6 when the continuation 11 exf7+ ♔f8 12 fxg8+ ♔xg8 is not so terrible for Black.

10 ♕xf7+ ♔d8 11 ♗d2 ♗xc3 12 0-0-0!

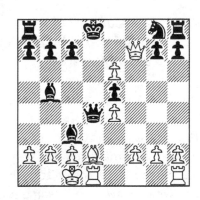

Ow!

12...♗xb2+ 13 ♔b1 ♘e7 14 ♗e3 ♗c3 15 ♕xg7 ♖g8 16 ♕xe5 1-0

The carnage is unspeakable.

Equal plus symmetrical equals win – fight the good fight

Game 9
H.Keskar-J.Schuyler
Hampton 2011

1 d4 ♘c6 2 ♘f3 d6 3 d5 ♘e5 4 ♘xe5 dxe5 5 e4 ♘f6 6 ♗d3 e6 7 dxe6?!

Obviously White can forget about an advantage after this – the question is, how do I beat my lower-rated opponent from this nearly symmetrical position? The fact is, if I play at all dynamically and keep my eyes open, there will be opportunities to create imbalances. One way to start is to delay castling.

7...♗xe6 8 0-0 ♗c5 9 ♗g5 h6 10 ♗h4 ♕e7 11 a3 ♖d8?! [11...0-0-0] **12 ♘d2 g5 13 ♗g3 ♗g4 14 ♕e1 ♘h5 15 ♗e2 ♘xg3 16 hxg3 ♗e6 17 ♘f3 f6 18 ♖d1 h5**

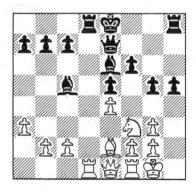

Black is nowhere near winning, but White certainly has a lot to worry about with ...h5-h4 and (after g3xh4) ...g5-g4-g3 coming.

19 ♖xd8+ ♕xd8?! [19...♔xd8!] **20 ♕c3**

♕e7 21 ♗c4 ♗c8 22 b4 ♗b6 23 a4 a6 24 a5 ♗a7 25 b5?! axb5 26 ♗xb5+ c6?! [26...♔f8!] **27 a6!**

I had overlooked this.

27...♕c5 28 ♕xc5?! [28 axb7! ♗xb7 29 ♗c4] **28...♗xc5 29 axb7 ♗xb7 30 ♗a4 ♔d7 31 ♖d1+ ♔c7 32 ♗b3 ♗c8**

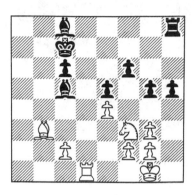

In spite of all the trades, this renews Black's kingside threats.

33 ♗f7?! h4 34 ♔f1 hxg3 35 fxg3 ♗g4 36 ♗b3 ♔b6 37 ♖d2 ♗b4?!

It is best for Black to cash out with 37...♖h1+ 38 ♔e2 ♖g1 39 ♔d3 ♗xf3 40 gxf3 ♖xg3. Instead, I kept trying to squeeze out a clear win with no risk, but I have underestimated White's ability to generate counterplay.

38 ♖d1 ♗c5 39 ♖d2 ♗e3? 40 ♖d6!

Somehow I overlooked this. Suddenly Black has no advantage at all.

40...f5! 41 exf5 e4 42 ♖xc6+! ♔xc6 43 ♘e5+ ♔c5 44 ♘xg4 ♗d4 45 f6

My opponent reasonably offered a draw here. I turned over my scoresheet and wrote the numbers 51 through 100 on the back.

45...♗xf6 46 ♘xf6 ♖f8 47 ♔e2 ♖xf6 48

♔e3 ♚d6 49 ♗xe4 ♖f2 50 ♔e3 ♖f1

If 50...♖xg2 51 ♔f3 ♖g1 52 ♔g4 and 53 ♔xg5 draws.

51 ♔e2 ♖f8 52 ♔e3 ♔e5 53 ♗c4 ♖d8

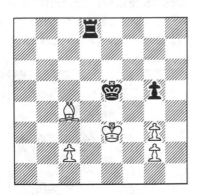

Somehow I will need to win one of the g-pawns and then generate zugzwang and/or mating threats. I wasn't sure how, but I kept on playing. To make the draw easier on himself, White needs to be alert for the chance to push the c-pawn, though he is understandably reluctant to loosen his bishop.

54 ♗d3 ♖d4 55 ♔f3 ♖a4 56 ♔e3 ♖d4 57 ♔f3 ♔d5 58 ♔e3 ♔c5 59 ♔f3 ♔b4 60 ♔e3 ♔c3 61 ♔e2 ♖a4 62 ♔e3 ♔b2 63 ♔f3 ♔c1 64 ♔e2 ♖b4 65 ♗f5 ♖a4 66 ♗d3 ♖d4 67 ♔e3 ♖d5 68 ♔f3 ♖d4 69 ♔e3 ♖b4 70 ♔e2 ♖a4 71 ♗f5 ♖a5 72 ♗d3 g4!?

It was important to try everything before playing this committal move, which presents slightly different challenges to White.

73 ♔e3 ♖a4 74 ♗e4 [74 c4!] **74...♔d1 75 ♔f4?! ♔e2 76 ♔f5 ♔f2 77 ♔f4 ♖c4 78 ♔e5 ♔e3 79 ♗d3 ♖a4 80 ♔f5 ♔f2 81**

♗e4 ♔xg3 82 ♔e5 ♔f2 83 ♗d5 ♔e3 84 c4 ♖a5 85 ♔f5 g3 86 ♔g4 ♔f2 87 ♔f4 ♖c5 88 ♔e5 ♔e3 89 ♔f5 ♖c8 90 ♔e5

Unfortunately, the time situation demanded that I stop notating here. In addition to zugzwang and mating threats, there is now a third winning possibility, which is somehow to drive the white king to d8 (or thereabouts), sacrifice the rook on d5, and win the resulting king and pawn endgame. This is, in fact, how I won, somewhere around move 120-130. Naturally, White could have held the position with correct play, but this is hardly relevant from a practical standpoint.

Winning the draw

Game 10
D.Haessel-J.Schuyler
Pawtucket 2008

1 d4 ♘c6 2 ♘f3 d6 3 d5 ♘e5 4 e4 ♘f6

I am planning 5...♘xf3+, but first I want White to figure out how to defend his e-pawn.

5 ♘xe5 dxe5 6 ♗b5+ ♗d7 7 ♕d3 a6 8 ♗xd7+ ♕xd7 9 ♘c3 e6 10 ♗g5 ♗b4 11 0-0-0 0-0-0 12 f3 ♕e7 13 ♕c4 h6 14 ♗xf6 gxf6 15 g4

The position has been equal since move 9, and now I am faced with the problem of generating some winning chances against my somewhat lower-rated opponent. Somewhere in my chess education I learned that Q+N work better together than Q+B, while R+B co-ordinate better than R+N. It is time to arrange the ideal exchange – which, fortunately, is not too difficult.

15...♕c5! 16 ♕xc5 ♗xc5 17 ♖d3 h5

My half-open files will not suffice for this position.

18 h3 ♖h7 19 ♖f1 ♖dh8 20 ♘d1 ♗d6

My idea is to block the d-file and cross my king over to the e7-square – a small improvement to my position. My opponent is sufficiently worried about this to weaken his dark squares in order to stop it.

21 c4?! ♗e7

I can't explain this move, but the tempo is not important.

22 ♔c2 hxg4 23 hxg4 ♖h2+ 24 ♖d2 ♗c5 25 ♘c3 ♗d4 26 ♖fd1 ♗e3

As the game develops, I am starting to understand better why the bishop and rooks work well together – one reason is that the bishop disrupts the co-ordination of the enemy rooks.

27 ♖e2 ♖8h3 28 ♖xh2 ♖xh2+ 29 ♔b3 ♖f2 30 ♖d3 ♗d4 31 a4 ♔d7 32 a5 ♔d6 33 ♘a4 ♔e7 34 ♔a3 ♖c2 35 ♔b3 ♖f2 36 ♔a3 f5!?

In spite of my hard work, Black is still nowhere close to winning. This is as good a try as any.

37 gxf5 exf5 38 ♖b3 fxe4 39 fxe4 f5 40 ♖xb7 fxe4 41 ♖xc7+ ♔e8

42 c5??

Oddly, White can hold with the "grovelling" manoeuvre 42 ♖h7! e3 43 ♖h1 ♖d2 (43...e2 44 ♖e1) 44 ♘c3. Fortunately for me, my opponent could not bring himself to consider this defence seriously.

42...e3 43 d6 e2 44 ♘b6 e1♕ 45 d7+ ♔e7 0-1

Mestrovic tries 7...g6!? and wins!

Game 11
D.Rasic-Z.Mestrovic
Croatian Team
Championship 2001

1 e4 ♘c6 2 d4 d6 3 ♘f3 ♘f6 4 d5 ♘e5 5 ♘xe5 dxe5 6 ♗b5+ ♗d7 7 ♕e2 g6 8 ♗xd7+ ♕xd7 9 ♘d2?!

9 c4 and 10 ♘c3 is simpler and stronger.

9...♗g7 10 ♘c4

10...♘h5

10...0-0!? 11 ♘xe5 ♕a4! and Black recovers the pawn one way or another.

11 g4?! ♘f4 12 ♗xf4 exf4

White has kindly released Black's fianchettoed bishop from its prison.

13 0-0-0 0-0 14 e5 e6 15 d6 cxd6?!

Too co-operative, allowing White to land his knight on the juicy d6-square. Instead, 15...♕a4 16 ♔b1 b5 17 ♘a3 cxd6 and Black is better.

16 ♘xd6 ♕a4 17 ♔b1 f3 18 ♕xf3 ♗xe5 19 ♖he1 ♗xd6 20 ♖xd6 ♖ac8 21 b3 ♕a5 22 ♖ed1 ♕c5 23 ♖1d2 b5 24 h4 a5 25 ♖6d3 ♕e5 26 ♖e2?! ♕h2! 27 h5 ♕g1+ 28 ♔b2 a4 29 a3 b4?! 30 axb4 ♖a8?! 31 ♖ed2 axb3 32 ♖d1

By now White has regained the advantage, but it is still not simple to play against heavy pieces with poor king protection.

32...♕h2 33 ♖xb3 ♕e5+ 34 ♕c3 ♕g5 35 f3 ♖fe8 36 ♕d4? [36 b5!] **36...♖ed8 37 ♖a3 ♖ab8 38 ♕e3 ♖xb4+ 39 ♔a2 ♕f6 40 ♖xd8+ ♕xd8 41 h6 ♕d5+ 42 ♖b3 ♖a4+ 43 ♔b2 ♖a8 44 ♕f4 e5 45 ♕b4 ♕d8 46 ♕c5 ♕d1 47 ♕a7 ♖c8 48 ♖c3 ♖f8 49 ♖d3 ♕e1 50 ♕e3 ♕a5 51 ♖a3 ♖b8+ 52 ♔c1 ♕c7 53 ♕c3 ♕e7 54 ♕e3 ♕h4 55 ♖b3 ♖c8 56 ♔b2 ♕f6 57 ♖b6 ♕e7 58 ♕b3 e4 59 f4?**

After a long defence, White cracks.
59...♕c7 60 ♖b7 ♕xf4 61 ♕d5? e3 62 ♖a7? ♕f6+ 0-1

Mestrovic wins again with 7...g6!?

Game 12
J.Barle-Z.Mestrovic
Slovenian Championship,
Krsko 1997

1 ♘f3 ♘c6 2 d4 d6 3 e4 ♘f6 4 d5 ♘e5 5 ♘xe5 dxe5 6 ♗b5+ ♗d7 7 ♕e2 g6 8 0-0 ♗g7 9 ♗xd7+ ♕xd7 10 c4 0-0 11 ♘c3 ♘h5 12 g3 c5 13 dxc6 ♕xc6 14 ♗e3 e6 15 b4 f5

White is still better. Black's kingside pawn majority is not as dangerous as it looks. Mestrovic soon drifts into a bad position without making any obvious mistakes, which is why I'm not crazy about this variation.

16 b5 ♕e8 17 ♗c5 ♖f7 18 f3 b6 19 ♗d6 ♖d7 20 ♖ad1 ♖c8 21 c5 bxc5 22 ♕c4 ♘f6 23 ♗xe5 ♖cd8 24 ♖xd7 ♘xd7 25 ♗xg7 ♔xg7 26 f4?!

26 ♘e2! is stronger, intending 27 ♘f4.

26...♕e7 27 exf5 exf5 28 ♘d5 ♕e6 29 ♕c3+ ♔h6 30 g4 fxg4 31 ♕d2 ♕e4 32 f5+ g5 33 ♖e1 ♕xf5 34 ♘e7 ♕f6 35 ♕d5 ♔h5 36 ♘f5 ♘f8 37 ♕xc5 ♕b6 38 ♕xb6 axb6 39 ♘g7+ ♔h6 40 ♘f5+ ♔g6 41 ♘e7+ ♔f6 42 ♘c6 ♖d2 43 ♖f1+ ♔g7 44 ♘e5 ♘g6 45 ♖f7+? ♔g8 46 ♖f5?? ♖d1+ 0-1

Not 46...♖d5?? 47 ♘xg6 ♖xf5 48 ♘e7+ and White wins, but after 46...♖d1+ 47 ♔f2 (or 47 ♔g2 ♘h4+) 47...♖d5 48 ♘xg6 ♖xf5 is check.

Beating the London System

Game 13
P.B.Pedersen-D.Bekker Jensen
Danish Team
Championship 2008

1 d4 ♘f6 2 ♘f3 g6 3 ♗f4 ♗g7 4 e3 0-0 5 ♗e2 d6 6 h3 ♘fd7 7 0-0 ♘c6 8 c3 e5

We would reach this by 1 d4 ♘c6 2 ♘f3 d6 3 ♗f4 ♘f6 4 e3 g6 5 ♗e2 ♗g7 6 h3 0-0 7 c3 ♘d7 8 0-0 e5.

9 ♗h2 f5 10 dxe5 dxe5 11 ♘a3 g5 12

♘c4 ♕f6 13 b4 f4

Houdini completely hates Black's position, but an aggressive stance on the kingside often reaps benefits. It is very difficult for White to solve the problem of liberating his entombed h2-bishop while at the same time keeping his king safe.

14 ♘fd2 ♘b6 15 ♘a5 ♕g6 16 e4 ♖d8

By now even Mr. H understands that White is not better.

17 ♕c2 ♘xa5 18 bxa5 ♘d7 19 ♖ad1 ♖e8 20 ♕a4 ♔h8 21 f3 h5 22 ♘b3 ♘f6 23 a6 g4 24 hxg4? hxg4 25 axb7? g3!!

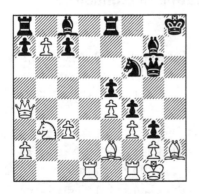

26 bxc8♕ ♖axc8 27 ♗xg3 fxg3 28 ♕xa7 ♕h6 29 ♖fe1 ♖a8 30 ♕c5 ♗f8 0-1

Beating the London System again

Game 14
R.Valenti-V.Tkachiev
Corsica (rapid) 1997

1 ♘f3 ♘f6 2 d4 g6 3 ♗f4 ♗g7 4 e3 d6 5 h3 0-0 6 ♗e2 ♘c6 7 0-0 ♘d7?! [7...e5!] 8 ♗h2 e5 9 c3 ♕e7 10 a4 f5 11 ♘a3 ♔h8 12 b4 e4

Black decides he will be able to get ...f5-f4 in later – this is slightly optimistic, but it pays off.

13 ♘d2 g5 14 ♕c2 ♘f6 15 b5 ♘d8 16 c4 ♘e6 [16...f4!?] 17 ♖fc1 f4 18 ♖ab1 ♕e8 19 ♘xe4?? fxe3 20 ♘xf6 exf2+ 21 ♔h1 ♗xf6 22 ♕e4 ♘xd4 0-1

Losing to the London System

Game 15
V.Golod-E.Sutovsky
Natanya (rapid) 2009

1 d4 ♘f6 2 ♘f3 g6 3 ♗f4 ♗g7 4 e3 d6 5 ♗e2 0-0 6 h3 ♘c6 7 0-0 ♘d7?! 8 c3 e5 9 ♗h2 f5 10 a4 ♕e7 11 b4 e4?!

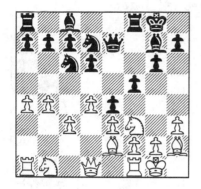

Opening up the game for White's dark-squared bishop. This is clearly bad since Black has little chance of achieving ...f5-f4 to close the diagonal again.

12 ♘fd2 ♘d8 13 a5 a6 14 c4! c5?

This stops White's planned 15 c5!, but it weakens too many squares, most especially d5 and d6.

15 ♘c3 cxd4 16 ♘d5 ♕f7 17 exd4 ♘e6 18 ♗xd6 ♘xd4 19 ♗xf8 ♘xf8 20 ♘b3!?

Giving back the exchange is not necessary, but it does help to clarify the position.

20...♘xb3 21 ♕xb3 ♗xa1 22 ♖xa1 ♗e6 23 ♖d1 ♖d8 24 ♕c3 ♗xd5 25 ♖xd5

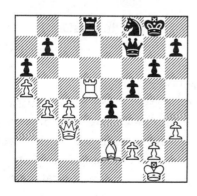

25...♖xd5?

This gives White's queen easy access, though Black's position was lousy anyway.

26 cxd5 ♕g7 27 ♕c5 ♕e5 28 ♗c4 ♕a1+ 29 ♔h2 ♕e5+ 30 g3 ♔g7 31 ♕b6 ♔h6 32 ♕d8? ♔g7??

My computer kindly tells me that Black can save the game with 32...♘d7!! 33 ♕xd7 ♕d4. The text move is hopeless.

33 d6 ♕b2 34 ♕e7+ ♔h6 35 ♕xf8+ ♔h5 36 ♗f1 e3 37 d7 e2 38 ♗g2 1-0

How to fight in the critical lines of the 1 d4 Dark Knight System

Game 16
H.Kmoch-F.Yates
Hastings 1927/28

1 d4 ♘f6 2 ♘f3 g6 3 c4 ♗g7 4 g3 0-0 5 ♗g2 d6 6 0-0 ♘c6 7 d5 ♘b8

Here 7...♘a5!? is recommended by theory, and is objectively best, though Yates makes a good case for the text move – and note that we would normally not have this option, reaching the game position by 1 d4 ♘c6 2 ♘f3 d6 3 g3 g6 4 d5 ♘b8 5 ♗g2 ♗g7 6 0-0 ♘f6 7 c4 0-0 or one of many similar move orders.

8 ♘c3 a5! 9 ♘d4 ♘a6 10 h3

White prevents 10...♘g4 but, as I am so fond of saying, a tempo is a tempo. This also necessitates a later ♔h2.

10...♘c5 11 ♗e3 ♗d7 12 ♕d2 ♕c8 13 ♔h2 e5

14 ⁇db5

White should have preferred 14 dxe6, though Black is fine after 14...⁇xe6, or even 14...⁇xe6 15 ⁇xe6 ⁇xe6 16 ⁇xc5 dxc5 17 ⁇xb7 ⁇ad8 18 ⁇f4 ⁇b6 19 ⁇f3 ⁇xb2, when Black's strong bishop and activity make up for the crippled queenside.

14...b6 15 ⁇ac1 ⁇h5 16 b3 f5

Yates's play has a very modern feel to it, but his next move is too optimistic.

17 f4 g5?! 18 ⁇xc5?!

After 18 fxg5 f4 19 ⁇f2 fxg3+ 20 ⁇xg3 ⁇xg3 21 ⁇xg3 White at least has a pawn for his trouble.

18...gxf4?

Yates bluffs again with this fake (and unnecessary) zwischenzug. However, the rest of the game he conducts masterfully.

19 gxf4? bxc5 20 e3 ⁇h8 21 ⁇f3 ⁇f6 22 ⁇g1 ⁇d8 23 ⁇g3 ⁇h6 24 ⁇f1 ⁇e8 25 ⁇e2 ⁇g6 26 ⁇gg1 ⁇e7 27 ⁇bc3 ⁇g8 28 ⁇g3 ⁇af8 29 ⁇d1 ⁇g7 30 ⁇g2 ⁇fg8 31 ⁇ff2 ⁇d7 32 ⁇ce2 ⁇h4 33 ⁇g1?! exf4 34 exf4 ⁇f6 35 ⁇h1 ⁇e7 36 ⁇f1 ⁇ge8 37 ⁇1e2?

The losing mistake, though White was about waist-deep in it anyway.

37...⁇g4 38 ⁇f3 ⁇xh3+ 39 ⁇g1 ⁇g7 40 ⁇d3 ⁇e3 41 ⁇xe3 ⁇xe3 42 ⁇c2 ⁇xg3! 43 ⁇xg3 ⁇d4+ 44 ⁇f1 ⁇e3+ 0-1

5...⁇a5!? – a strong alternative to 5...⁇b8

> ### Game 17
> **A.Galliamova-M.Krasenkow**
> Koszalin 1997

1 d4 d6 2 ⁇f3 g6 3 g3 ⁇g7 4 ⁇g2 ⁇c6 5 d5 ⁇a5

It is possible to consider this square any time White has fianchettoed, though it is more usual with a white pawn on c4 to harass. As it turns out, White does not enjoy the omission of c2-c4, as the d5-pawn becomes a target. In any case, Black must be active quickly on the queenside to justify the knight's position. The typical method is ...c7-c5 to gain space and make sure the knight doesn't get trapped – in this game Black has other ideas.

6 0-0 c6 7 e4 ♘f6 8 ♕e2 cxd5 9 exd5 ♗d7 10 ♘fd2 b5 11 b4 ♘c4 12 ♘xc4 bxc4 13 ♕xc4 ♖c8

14 ♕e2?!

It was already dangerous to win the pawn, and now White chooses the wrong retreat: 14 ♕h3 ♘xd5?! 15 ♗xd5 ♗xa1 16 ♗xf7+ ♔f8 17 c3 is good for White.

14...♘xd5 15 ♗xd5 ♗xa1 16 c3 0-0 17 ♗g5 ♗c6?! [17...♗f5!] **18 ♗xc6 ♖xc6 19 ♗xe7 ♖e8 20 ♕f3 ♕d7 21 ♗f6 ♖a6 22 ♘d2 ♖xa2 23 ♕f4 ♕f5 24 ♕xd6**

24...♗b2?!

Black should make space for his

king with 24...h6 or 24...h5. Against the text White is right back in the game after 25 ♗d4.

25 ♘b3? ♕e6 26 ♕xe6 ♖xe6 27 ♗d4 ♖a3

28 ♘a5?

28 ♘d2 was a better try, intending 28...♗xc3? 29 ♘b1.

28...♗xc3 29 ♘c4 ♖a1! 30 ♗xc3 ♖xf1+ 31 ♔xf1 ♖c6 32 ♗d4 ♖xc4 33 ♗xa7 ♖xb4 34 h4 ♔g7 35 ♔g2 ♔f6 36 ♗e3 ♔e5 37 ♔f3 h5 38 ♔g2 ♔e4 39 ♗c5 ♖b5 40 ♗e3 ♔d3 41 ♗f4 ♔e2 42 ♗e3 ♖b3 43 ♗c5 ♖f3 44 ♗d4 f5 45 ♔g1 ♖d3 0-1

Black, given plenty of rope, tries to hang himself but fails

Game 18
R.Aghasaryan-A.Chibukhchian
Kajaran 2011

1 d4 ♘c6 2 c4 e5 3 dxe5 ♘xe5 4 e3

White's unambitious play has already left him with no trace of an advantage. Frankly, the rest of the game sees Black try too hard to win, for which he was unjustly rewarded.

4...♘f6 5 ♘c3 ♗b4 6 ♗d2 0-0 7 ♗e2 c6 8 ♘f3 d6 9 0-0 ♖e8 10 ♕b3 ♗a5 11 ♖ad1 ♗c7 12 ♘d4 ♕e7 13 h3 ♘g6 14 ♖fe1 ♘h4 15 g3 ♘g6 16 ♗f1 h5 17 f4?!

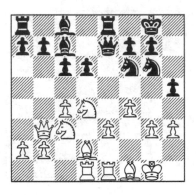

17...h4?! [17...♗b6 18 ♘a4 ♘e4!] 18 g4 ♗b6 19 ♘a4 ♗c7?! 20 e4 ♘xe4?! 21 ♗g2?!

21 ♘c3! was stronger, with the idea 21...♕f6 22 ♘xe4! ♕xd4 23 ♗e3! ♕xe4 24 ♗f2.

21...d5? [21...♕f6!] 22 cxd5 ♕f6 23 g5 ♕xd4+ 24 ♗e3 ♕xd1 25 ♕xd1 cxd5 26 f5? [26 ♕xd5] 26...♗xf5 27 ♕xd5 ♘d6

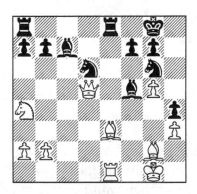

28 ♖c1? ♖xe3 29 ♖xc7 ♖d3 30 ♕c5?! ♘f4! 31 ♗f1? ♖d1 32 ♘c3 ♘xh3+ 33 ♔g2 ♖d2+ 34 ♔h1 ♘e4 0-1

Crushed on the d-file – don't let this happen to you!

1 d4 ♘c6 2 c4 e5 3 d5 ♗b4+ 4 ♗d2 ♗xd2+ 5 ♕xd2 ♘ce7 6 d6 ♘c6?

Circumstances may change, but right now the best square for this knight is e7, from which it controls d5 and has the option to attack d6 with ...♘f5. Black should only consider ...♘c6 after White has played e2-e4, clamping on d5 but opening a hole on the d4-square. Even after the correct 6...cxd6, Black can still be crushed in this fashion if he is not alert to all the methods of counterplay, so study **Position Two**. In this game, Black never got on the board.

7 ♘c3 cxd6 8 ♘b5 ♘f6 9 ♘xd6+ ♔f8 10 ♘f3 h6 11 e3 e4 12 ♘d4 ♕a5 13 ♕xa5 ♘xa5 14 ♘4b5 b6 15 ♗e2 ♔e7 16 0-0-0 ♗b7 17 ♖d4 ♘c5 18 ♘c3 ♘e6 19 ♖d1 a5 20 ♖hd1 ♘c5 21 ♘d5+ ♘xd5 22

置xd5 g6 23 ⌀xe4 ⌀xe4 24 罝e5+ ⌀d8
25 罝xe4 罝e8 26 罝ed4

26...罝e6 27 盦f3 罝a7 28 h4 h5 29 罝f4
⌀e7 30 盦d5 罝f6 31 罝xf6 ⌀xf6 32 罝d4
d6 33 ⌀d2 ⌀e7 34 ⌀c3 罝c7 35 a4 盦e6
36 罝d2 罝c5 37 b3 ⌀d7 38 f3 罝c7 39 e4
罝c8 40 e5 盦xd5 41 罝xd5 罝e8 42 罝xd6+
⌀c7 43 ⌀d4 罝g8 44 f4 罝e8 45 ⌀d5 罝e7
46 罝c6+ ⌀b7 47 e6 1-0

Middlegame and endgame ideas in the 3...盦b4+ structure

1 c4 ⌀c6 2 d4 e5 3 d5 盦b4+ 4 盦d2
盦xd2+ 5 豐xd2 ⌀ce7 6 ⌀c3 d6 7 e4 f5 8
exf5 盦xf5 9 盦d3 ⌀f6 10 ⌀ge2 0-0 11
0-0 盦xd3 12 豐xd3 ⌀h5 13 g3 豐d7 14
f3 a6 15 罝ad1 罝ae8 16 ⌀e4 h6 17 c5
⌀f6 18 ⌀2c3 ⌀f5 19 b4 ⌀xe4 20 ⌀xe4
g5 21 ⌀g2 ⌀d4

This is the position where we left off
when analysing in the theoretical section.

22 cxd6 cxd6 23 罝c1 罝f7 24 ⌀d2 ⌀g7
25 ⌀b3 ⌀xb3 26 axb3 豐f5 27 豐xf5
罝xf5 28 罝c7+ 罝f7 29 罝xf7+ ⌀xf7 30
罝c1 罝e7 31 ⌀f2 e4 32 f4 gxf4 33 gxf4
e3+ 34 ⌀e2 ⌀f6 35 罝c3 罝e4 36 罝xe3
⌀f5 37 ⌀d3 罝xb4 38 ⌀c3 罝xf4 39 罝e6
罝h4 40 罝xd6 ⌀e5 41 罝d7 b5 42 d6 b4+
43 ⌀d3 ⌀d5 44 罝a7 罝h3+ 45 ⌀c2
罝xh2+ 46 ⌀d3 罝h3+ 47 ⌀d2 ⌀xd6 48
罝xa6+ ⌀d5

49 罝b6? ⌀c5

49...罝xb3 (or on the next move) 50
罝xh6 罝c3 reaches the winning endgame rather sooner.

50 罝f6 罝h4? 51 ⌀e3 ⌀d5 52 罝f5+ ⌀e6
53 罝b5 ⌀d7 54 罝b6 h5 55 ⌀d3 罝g4 56

♖h6 h4 57 ♔e3 ♔e7 58 ♔f3 ♖g3+ 59 ♔f4 ♖xb3 60 ♖xh4 ♔d6 61 ♖h5 ♔c6 62 ♔e4 ♖c3 63 ♔d4 ♔b6 64 ♖g5 ♔a6 65 ♖h5 ♖c1 66 ♖h8 ♔b5 67 ♔d3 ♔a4 68 ♔d2 ♖c7 69 ♖h3 b3 70 ♖h6 ♔a3 71 ♖b6 ♔b2 72 ♔d3 ♖d7+ 73 ♔c4 ♔c2 74 ♔b4 b2 75 ♖c6+ ♔d2 0-1

A warning: beware the static king – a nice attack by White

1 d4 ♘c6 2 c4 e5 3 d5 ♗b4+ 4 ♘d2 ♘ce7 5 a3 ♗xd2+ 6 ♗xd2 d6 7 e4 f5 8 ♕h5+!?

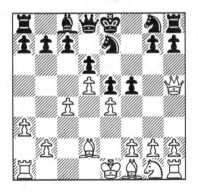

8...♔f8?!

8...g6 9 ♕h4 fxe4 is not the most fun ever, but it does leave Black with a pawn for his trouble. The text move is less accurate and demands more precision from Black in the coming moves in order to avoid a disaster like the one in the game.

9 f3 [9 exf5!] **9...♘f6 10 ♕h4 ♘g6 11**

♕f2 ♔f7?!

11...fxe4 12 fxe4 ♔f7 will allow Black to finish castling artificially with approximate equality.

12 exf5 ♗xf5 13 g4 ♗d7 14 h4 ♖e8 15 h5 ♘f4 16 0-0-0 ♗a4 17 ♖e1 b5 18 ♘h3 ♘xh3 19 ♖xh3 ♕d7 20 ♖h4 bxc4 21 g5 ♘xd5 22 ♗xc4 ♕c6 23 ♔b1 ♗b5 24 ♗a2 ♔f8 25 f4 e4?

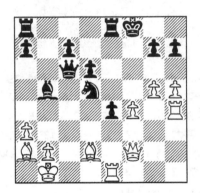

Black's position has been bad for a long time, but this ends the game.
26 ♕d4 ♗d3+ 27 ♔a1 e3 28 h6 ♖e5 29 hxg7+ ♔e7 30 fxe5 exd2 31 exd6+ ♔xd6 32 ♖h6+ ♗g6 33 ♕xd2 1-0

No problems for Black after 3...♗b4+ 4 ♗d2

1 d4 ♘c6 2 c4 e5 3 d5 ♗b4+ 4 ♘d2 ♘ce7 5 a3 ♗xd2+ 6 ♗xd2 d6 7 e4 f5 8 exf5 ♗xf5 9 ♘e2 ♘f6 10 ♘g3 ♗g6 11 ♗e2 0-0 12 0-0

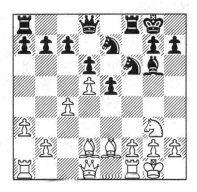

12...♘e4 [12...♘f5] **13 ♘xe4 ♗xe4 14 f3 ♗f5 15 ♗e3 b6 16 ♕d2 ♕d7 17 ♖ac1 ♔h8 18 ♖fd1 a5 19 b3 h6 20 ♕b2 ♗h7 21 ♔h1 ♘g6 22 ♗f1 ♘f4 23 g3 ♘h3 24 ♗g2 ♘g5 25 ♖f1 e4 26 ♗xg5 exf3 ½-½**

Fight for the e4-square or suffer the consequences!

Game 23
G.Grigore-P.Brochet
Creon 1999

1 d4 ♘c6 2 c4 e5 3 d5 ♗b4+ 4 ♘d2 ♘ce7 5 a3 ♗xd2+ 6 ♗xd2 d6 7 e4 f5 8 exf5 ♗xf5 9 ♘e2 ♘f6 10 ♘g3 0-0!?

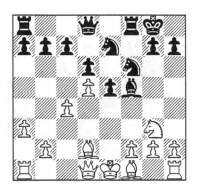

Black offers his other bishop, an invitation White is wise not to accept: 11 ♘xf5?! ♘xf5 12 ♗d3 e4 13 ♗c2 ♕e8 14 0-0 ♕g6 and 15...♖ae8 with a harmonious and menacing position. Who's afraid of the bishop pair?

11 ♗e2 ♕e8 [11...♕d7] **12 0-0 ♘e4** [12...♗g6] **13 ♗e3 ♘xg3** [13...♕g6] **14 hxg3 b6**

Although this was also played in Game 22, I don't think it helps Black. If he wants to, White can break through with b2-b4 and c4-c5 anyway, and now Black has to worry about penetration on both the c7- and c6-squares. Furthermore, it rules out the possibility of Black breaking with ...c7-c6. 14...♗d7 is more flexible.

15 g4 ♗d7 16 ♗d3

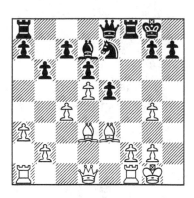

Taking advantage of tiny inaccuracies, White has built an advantage, taking over the b1-h7 diagonal, along with the critical e4-square. It's not so easy playing a Grandmaster. Remember to fight for e4! As it happens, Black still had plenty of chances.

16...♘g6 17 ♗e4 ♘f4 18 g3 ♕e7 19 f3?!

[19 ♕c2!] **19...♘h3+ 20 ♔g2 ♘g5 21 ♗xg5 ♕xg5 22 ♕d3 g6 23 ♖h1 a5 24 ♖h4 ♔g7?!** [24...♖f7] **25 ♖ah1 ♖h8 26 ♕c3 h6 27 b3?** [27 f4!] **27...♕f6 28 f4 g5?!**

28...exf4 29 ♕xf6+ ♔xf6 30 ♖xh6 ♖xh6 31 ♖xh6 ♖g8 holds the balance.

29 fxg5 ♕xg5 30 ♖h5! ♕xg4 31 ♕e3 ♔f7 32 ♖5h4 ♕g7 33 ♖xh6 ♖xh6 34 ♖xh6 ♖h8 35 ♖g6 ♕f8 36 ♕g5 ♔e8 37 ♖f6 ♕e7

38 ♕g6+?!

38 ♗f5 maintains more pressure. Presumably the mistakes here are due to a time scramble.

38...♔d8

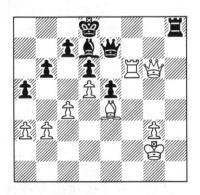

39 ♖f7 ♕e8??

39...♗e8! holds.

40 ♕f6+?

40 ♖xd7+! wins immediately.

40...♔c8 41 ♗h7 ♕d8 42 ♕g7 ♖e8 43 g4 ♗xg4 44 ♕xg4+ ♔b8 45 ♖g7 ♖f8 46 ♕d7 ♕xd7 47 ♖xd7 ♖f4 48 ♖d8+ ♔a7 49 a4 e4 50 ♖g8 ♖h4 51 ♗f5 ♖f4 52 ♗d7 e3 53 ♖e8 1-0

3...d6!? – an interesting alternative to 3...e6

Game 24
M.Drasko-Z.Mestrovic
Bosnian Team Championship 2003

1 d4 ♘c6 2 d5 ♘e5 3 e4 d6

Previously Mestrovic had successfully played 3...e6, but maybe he no longer believed in it? The text move winds up leading to a position considered in Chapter Six (see 6 ♘f3 in line B).

4 f4 ♘d7 5 ♘c3 c6 6 ♘f3 cxd5 7 exd5 ♘gf6 8 ♗e3 g6 9 ♗e2 ♗g7 10 0-0 0-0 11 ♕d2 a6 12 a4 ♕c7 13 ♗d4

13...♘b6?!

The position was equal, until this time-waster hands White an advantage. 13...♘c5 is better.

14 a5 ♘bd7 15 ♘a4 ♘e4 16 ♕e3 ♗xd4 17 ♘xd4 ♘ef6 18 ♘c3 ♕c5 19 ♖fd1 b5 20 axb6?! [20 b4] **20...♘xb6 21 b4 ½-½**

Perhaps nobody was in the mood for a fight – the position is equal again anyway.

GM uses Diebl's novelty 4...exd5!

Game 25
V.Erdos-R.Rapport
Hungarian Team
Championship 2012

1 d4 ♘c6 2 d5 ♘e5 3 e4 e6 4 f4 exd5 5 fxe5 ♕h4+ 6 ♔e2 ♕h5+ 7 ♔d2 ♕h6+ 8 ♔c3 ♕c6+ 9 ♔d2 ♕h6+ 10 ♔d3 ♕a6+ 11 ♔d2 ♕h6+ 12 ♔e1 ♕h4+ 13 ♔d2

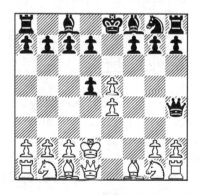

I can't help but get the feeling these guys are messing around. Black's next constitutes a risky attempt to play for the win.

13...♕f4+ 14 ♔c3 ♕xe5+ 15 ♕d4

15...♗b4+ [15...♕xe4!?] **16 ♔d3 dxe4+ 17 ♕xe4 ♕xe4+ 18 ♔xe4 ♘f6+ 19 ♔e3 ♗c5+ 20 ♔f3 b5 21 ♗d3?!**

According to *Houdini*, White is better after 21 ♗e3! ♗b7+ 22 ♔e2 ♗xe3 23 ♔xe3, though it hardly looks like a safe advantage. Then again, the text move doesn't look safe either, and White clearly has no advantage there.

23...♗b7+ 22 ♔g3 ♗d6+ 23 ♔f2 ♘g4+ 24 ♔f1 ♘xh2+ 25 ♔f2 ♘g4+ 26 ♔f1 ♘h2+ 27 ♔f2 ♘g4+ ½-½

An alternative to 4...fxe6!? – the "endgame" with 4...dxe6

Game 26
S.Gordon-N.Short
British Championship,
Sheffield 2011

1 d4 ♘c6

I must say, this warms my heart.

2 d5 ♘e5 3 e4 e6 4 dxe6 dxe6 5 ♕xd8+ ♔xd8 6 f4 ♘c6 7 c3 ♗c5 8 ♘f3 a5 9 a4 ♘h6

In this position, 9...♘f6 is also good.

However, it is nice for this knight to have a stable home, controlling important squares. Short's 10...f6 ensures that he will not be squeezed on the kingside, as does 14...h5.

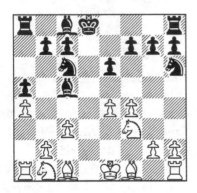

10 ♗d3 f6 11 ♔e2 ♔e7 12 ♘a3 ♗d7 13 ♘c4 ♘f7 14 h4 h5! 15 ♗e3 ♗xe3 16 ♘xe3 b6 17 ♖hg1 g5 18 g3 g4 19 ♘d4 ♘d6 20 ♖ac1 ♖hc8 21 b3 ♘e8 22 ♖gf1 ♘d8 23 e5 f5 24 ♖fd1 ♘b7 25 ♖d2 ♘c5 26 ♖cd1 ♘g7 27 ♘c4 ♘xd3 28 ♖xd3 ♖d8 29 ♘a3 ♘e8

30 ♔e3 ♖ac8 31 ♖3d2 ♖b8 32 ♖d3 ♖bc8 33 ♖1d2 ♖b8 34 ♔f2 ♖bc8 35 ♔e2 ♖a8 36 ♔e3 ♖ab8 37 ♔e2 ♖a8 38 ♔f2 ♖ac8 39 ♖d1 ♖b8 40 ♖3d2 ♖bc8 41 ♔e1 ♖a8

42 ♖d3 ♖ab8 43 ♖1d2 ♖a8 44 ♔d1 ♘g7 45 ♔c2 ♘e8 46 ♔b2 ♘g7 47 ♘c4 ♗e8 48 ♔a3 ♖dc8 49 ♘b5 ♗c6 50 ♖d4 ♘e8 51 ♘bd6 ♖d8 52 ♘xe8 ♖xd4 53 ♖xd4 ½-½

Wow, that was boring! Are you sold on 4...fxe6 yet?

A better advertisement for 4...dxe6

> *Game 27*
> **M.Gurevich-M.Rohde**
> Philadelphia (blitz) 1989

1 d4 ♘c6 2 d5 ♘e5 3 e4 e6 4 dxe6 dxe6 5 ♕xd8+ ♔xd8 6 ♗f4 ♘g6

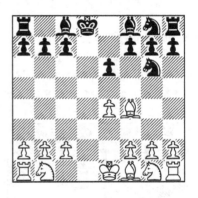

Although ...♘c6 is normally the best retreat for this piece, the difference is not so great that Black would decline the tempo gain. Here 6...♗d6! is also good, threatening 7...♘d3+ or 7...♘f3+.
7 ♗e3 ♘f6 8 ♘c3?!

This careless move allows Black to harass White's poor dark-squared bishop further, disrupting White's development. 8 f3 was called for.
8...♘g4 9 ♗d2 ♗c5 10 ♘h3 ♗d7 11

♗e2 ♘f6 12 0-0-0 ♚e7 13 f4?!

Again 13 f3.

13...♗c6

By now Black is a little better – White's position is too loose.

14 ♗d3 ♘h4 15 e5?

This is a terrible idea, releasing the strong c6 bishop. White needed to let go of the g-pawn and seek counterplay against Black's king with 15 f5!.

15...♘d5 16 ♘e4 ♗e3 17 c4 ♘xd2+ 18 ♖xd2 ♘b4 19 ♗b1 ♘xa2+ 20 ♚d1 ♖hd8 21 g3 ♘f3 22 ♖xd8 ♖xd8+ 23 ♚e2 ♘d4+ 24 ♚f2 ♘b4 25 ♖c1?! ♘b3 26 ♖c3 ♘d2 27 ♘xd2 ♖xd2+ 28 ♚e3 ♖xb2 29 ♗xh7 ♖xh2 30 ♘g5 ♖g2 31 ♘e4 a6 32 ♚d4 b6 33 ♘g5 ♘c2+ 34 ♚d3 ♘e1+ 35 ♚d4 a5 36 ♗g8 a4 37 ♗xf7 ♗d7 38 c5 0-1

Don't play 6...♗c5?!?!

1 d4 ♘c6 2 d5 ♘e5 3 f4 ♘g6 4 ♘f3 e6 5 dxe6 fxe6 6 e4 ♗c5?! [6...d5!] **7 ♗d3?! ♘h6 8 ♕e2 0-0 9 g3 a6?!** [9...d5!] **10 ♘c3 b5 11 e5 ♗b7 12 ♘e4 ♗b6 13 ♗d2 ♘f5 14 0-0-0 h6?! 15 ♖hf1 c5?!**

Black gets tired of sitting around waiting for the brutality, but this only makes things worse due to the new hole on d6.

16 ♘d6 ♗d5

17 c4?

White should play 17 ♗xf5!, maintaining the wonderful d6-knight.

17...bxc4 18 ♘xc4 ♘fe7?! [18...♖b8] **19 h4 ♘f5 20 ♖g1 ♘ge7 21 g4 ♘d4 22 ♘xd4 cxd4 23 ♖gf1 ♖b8 24 ♚b1 ♗c5 25 f5 ♘c6 26 g5 exf5 27 gxh6 ♕xh4 28**

hxg7 ♖f7 29 ♘d6 ♗xd6 30 exd6 ♗e4 31 ♖f4 ♗xd3+ 32 ♕xd3 ♕f6? 33 ♖h1 ♖xg7 34 ♖xf5 ♕e6 35 ♕h3 1-0

In spite of the inaccuracies, there is feeling of inevitability about the result of this game due to White's uncontested superiority in the centre and on the kingside.

4 ♗e3 f5!? – take one

Game 29
A.Beliavsky-A.Miles
European Championship
Saint Vincent 2000

1 d4 ♘c6 2 e4 e5 3 d5 ♘ce7 4 ♗e3 f5

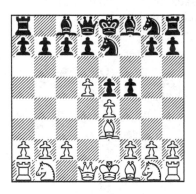

5 f3

White resigns himself to allowing Black a good King's Indian with an early and easy ...f7-f5. Instead, if 5 ♘c3 ♘f6 6 ♘f3 d6 7 exf5 c6 (7...a6!?), White's centre disintegrates. (In fact, White can still play for an advantage, but it is easy to see why this was not appealing.)

5...♘f6 6 ♘h3 d6 7 ♘f2

The great Beliavsky has not succeeded in casting any doubt on Black's idea. Now Miles should just get on with his comfortable King's Indian: 7...g6. The c-pawn can wait.

7...c6 8 c4 c5 9 g3 g6 10 ♘c3 ♗g7 11 g4 f4 12 ♗d2 g5 13 b4 b6 14 bxc5 bxc5 15 ♗d3?!

Doubtful. 15 h4 looks more to the point.

15...h5! 16 h3 ♔f7 17 ♗e2 ♘g6 18 ♕a4 ♗f8 19 ♖ab1 ♗e7 20 ♗c2

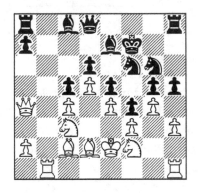

20...hxg4?!

I suppose it's a draw either way, but there is no disadvantage to maintaining the favourable tension. After this, I'm not sure who's playing for the win, or why.

21 hxg4 ♖xh1 22 ♖xh1 ♗d7 23 ♕a3 ♖b8 24 ♘b1 ♕b6 25 ♗c3 ♖h8 26 ♖g1 ♗c8 27 ♘d2 ♕a6 28 ♕xa6 ♗xa6 29 ♖b1 ♗d8 30 ♗a4 ♗c7 31 ♗b5 ♗c8 32 ♘f1 ♔e7 33 ♗c6 ♘h4 34 ♘d2 ♘g2 35 ♗b7 ♗d7 36 ♗a6 ♗b6 37 ♘f1 ♘h4 38 ♗e1 ♘g2 39 ♗d2 ♘h4 40 ♗b5 ♗c8 41 ♗e1 ♘g2 42 ♗d2 ♘h4 43 ♖b3 ♔d8 44 ♗c6 ½-½

4 ♗e3 f5!? – take two

1 e4 ♘c6 2 d4 e5 3 d5 ♘ce7 4 ♗e3 f5 5 f3 ♘f6 6 ♘c3 d6 7 ♕d2 g6 8 0-0-0 ♗g7 9 h3?! f4 10 ♗f2

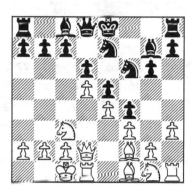

The pawn structure on the kingside makes it impossible for White to open lines there without creating a complex of weak squares and pawns. Black does have ways to create play on the queenside, as we will see.

10...0-0 11 ♔b1 a6 12 ♘ge2 ♗d7 13 ♘c1 b5 14 a3 ♕b8 15 ♘b3 ♖d8 16 ♘a5 c5 17 dxc6 ♘xc6 18 ♘xc6 ♗xc6 19 ♗h4 ♖d7 20 ♗xf6 ♗xf6 21 ♘d5 ♗h4 22 ♘b4 ♗b7 23 c4

White tries to free his terrible f1-bishop, but in the process opens lines against his own king.

23...♔g7 24 ♗d3?! a5 25 ♘a2?! [25 ♘d5] 25...b4! 26 axb4 axb4 27 ♕xb4?! ♗f2?!

Black's "bad" bishop turns into a

monster. Nevertheless, Black should insert 27...♕a7 28 ♘c3 ♗c6 29 ♕b3 and then 29...♗f2 perhaps, though Black has other good ways to continue the attack here.

28 ♘c3 ♗d4 29 ♔c2 ♕c8 30 ♘b5 ♗c5 31 ♕b3 ♗a6 32 ♖a1 ♗e3 33 ♖hd1

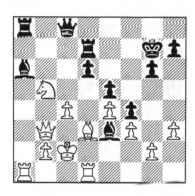

White has actually done an excellent job repairing his position and Black should no longer be able to break down the fortress.

33...♖b7 34 ♘xd6??

Oops!

34...♖xb3 0-1

White realizes too late that 35 ♘xc8 will be met by 35...♖ab8! intending 36 ♖xa6 ♖xb2+ 37 ♔c3 ♖8b3 mate. Of course White can defend the mate, but then he will remain a piece down.

Fighting the eternal ♘g5

1 e4 ♘c6 2 d4 e5 3 d5 ♘ce7 4 ♘f3 ♘f6?

Perhaps this is a database error? In any case, the reader should know that this is not an acceptable move order: 5 ♘xe5 ♘xe4 6 ♕e2 ♘d6 (not 6...♘f6? 7 d6! cxd6 8 ♘c4 ♕c7 9 ♗f4 and Black is busted) 7 ♘c3 already leaves Black with no good way to complete his development.

5 ♘c3? ♘g6 6 h4 h5 7 ♘g5!? ♗b4 8 ♗e2 d6 9 ♕d3 ♗d7 10 a3

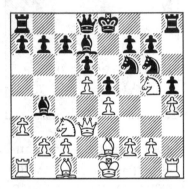

10...♗xc3+

As I mentioned in the theoretical section, it is better to retain this strong bishop with 10...♗c5. This is particularly true since Black will not inflict any structural damage with the exchange. White's queenside stays mobile and his bishops should come into their own sooner or later. Frankly, from this point on, I do not care for Black's position until the game is nearly over.

11 ♕xc3 c6 12 ♕b3?!

It makes more sense for White to open the game with 12 dxc6.

12...cxd5 13 exd5 0-0?! [13...♕c7] **14 ♘e6! fxe6 15 dxe6 ♗xe6 16 ♕xe6+ ♔h8 17 ♗g5 ♕b6 18 0-0-0 ♕xf2 19 ♗f3**

e4 **20 ♗xf6 ♖ae8**

21 ♕d7?! [21 ♗e7!] **21...gxf6 22 ♗xh5 ♖e7 23 ♕xd6 ♕f4+ 24 ♕d2 ♕xd2+ 25 ♖xd2 ♘f4 26 ♗d1 e3 27 ♖d4 ♘xg2 28 ♗e2 f5 29 ♔d1 ♖ee8 30 ♗f3 ♖d8 31 ♖xd8 ♖xd8+ 32 ♔c1 ♖d2 33 ♖g1 ♘xh4 34 ♗xb7 ♖d7?** [34...♖h2] **35 ♖h1?!** [35 ♗a6] **35...♖xb7 36 ♖xh4+ ♔g7 37 ♔d1 ♔f6 38 ♔e2 ♔g5 39 ♖d4 ♖e7 40 c4?? f4 41 ♖d1 ♖h7 42 ♔f3 ♖h3+ 43 ♔e4 e2 44 ♖e1 ♖e3+ 45 ♔d4 ♖e8 0-1**

Game 32
H.Meissner-A.Miles
European Cup, Slough 1997

---

1 e4 ♘c6 2 d4 e5 3 d5 ♘ce7 4 ♘f3 ♘g6 5 h4 h5 6 g3 ♗c5 7 ♗g5 f6 8 ♗d2 d6 9 ♘c3 ♗d7

Or 9...a6 – Black must play to preserve the dark-squared bishop.

10 ♗e2 ♘6e7

Miles prepares to defend the h-pawn, which was about to drop off.

11 ♘h2 g6 12 ♕c1 c6 13 ♗e3 ♗xe3 14 ♕xe3 ♕b6 15 ♕xb6 axb6 16 dxc6 bxc6

17 0-0 b5 18 a3 ♘c8 19 ♖fd1 ♘h6 20 ♘f1 ♔e7 21 ♘e3

21 a4.

21...♘b6 22 ♖ac1 ♘g4 23 ♗xg4 ♗xg4 24 ♖d3

Very slowly White is being out-played. Miles makes the most out of a small thing – his single, uncompromised pawn group. White needs to organize a pawn break, but he is showing no inclination to do so.

24...♘c4 25 ♘xc4?!

Now Black has b2 as a target. The immediate 25 ♖b1 was better.

25...bxc4 26 ♖e3 ♖hb8 27 ♖b1 ♖b7 28 f3 ♗e6 29 ♘d1 d5

Yikes! Black sure has a lot of centre pawns!

30 ♖a1 ♔d6 31 ♖e2 d4 32 ♔f2 c5 33 c3 ♗d7 34 ♖d2 ♔e6 35 ♔e2 ♖ab8 36 ♔e1 ♗a4

37 ♖a2?

White grows tired of the thankless defensive task.

37...♗b3 38 ♖a1 ♗xd1 39 ♔xd1 ♖xb2 40 ♖xb2 ♖xb2 41 a4 ♖g2 42 ♖a3 ♔d6 43 a5 ♔c7 44 a6 ♔b8 45 a7+ ♔a8 46 ♖a6 ♖xg3 47 ♖xf6 ♔xa7 0-1

Game 33
L.Christiansen-J.Benjamin
US Championship,
Seattle 2000

---

1 e4 ♘c6 2 d4 e5 3 d5 ♘ce7 4 ♘f3 ♘g6 5 h4 h5 6 ♗g5 ♘f6 7 ♘c3 ♗b4 8 a3

This seems odd. Doesn't White have anything better to do? Indeed 8 ♘d2 is better, but one way or another White does need to force our dark bishop off the board or we will be happy to preserve it with 8...a6.

8...♗xc3+ 9 bxc3 c6!

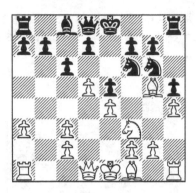

I am always reluctant to change the pawn structure on the queenside after saddling White with the doubled pawns – after all, the structure is already favourable, right? There is some logic there, but better players than me have demonstrated time and time again that Black should be willing to play on both sides of the board in this type of position, particularly since White has already made inroads on the kingside. Therefore 9...c6!, the only convenient pawn lever for either colour. Black targets the centre and prepares to break the annoying pin on f6.

10 c4 d6 11 ♘d2 ♛a5 12 ♗d3 ♘g4!

Benjamin reminds his opponent that 5 h4 cuts both ways – the g4-square is lovely this time of year. If 13 f3? f6 14 fxg4 ♗xg4 15 ♗e2 ♗xe2 16 ♛xe2 fxg5 17 hxg5 ♘f4 18 ♛f3 cxd5 19 exd5 0-0 with an obvious advantage for Black.

13 ♛e2 f6 14 ♗e3 ♘f4

Houdini doesn't like this, but Benjamin acquires the gorgeous e5-square

for his other knight.

15 ♗xf4 exf4 16 0-0 c5 17 ♘f3 ♘e5 18 ♖fb1 ♛c3 19 ♘xe5 ♛xe5 20 a4 g5

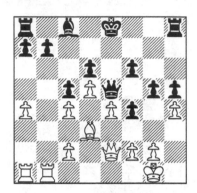

White is in trouble. Even the coming endgame gives little relief.

21 hxg5 fxg5 22 ♖a3 g4 23 ♛d2 ♖h7 24 ♛c3 ♛xc3 25 ♖xc3 ♗e7 26 g3 f3 27 a5 ♔f7 28 ♔f1 ♖b8 29 ♔e1?!

Crossing to the queenside with the king loses the e-pawn, though staying put is no bargain either. Black will bring his king to e5 and prepare to break with ...h5-h4.

29...♗f5 30 ♔d2 ♗xe4 31 ♗xe4 ♖xe4 32 ♖e3 ♖xe3 33 ♔xe3 ♔f6 34 ♔f4 ♔g6 35 a6 b6 36 c3 ♖f8+ 0-1

Game 34
W.Weisser-L.Trumpp
German League 2004

---

1 d4 ♘c6 2 d5 ♘e5 3 e4 ♘g6

I don't believe in this move order because of 4 h4!.

4 ♘f3 e5 5 c4 ♗c5

5...♘f6 is more accurate here, and if

6 ♘c3 then 6...♝b4. In addition to the structural damage we can inflict, it is not convenient for White to defend the e-pawn. On the other hand, White could force the game variation using the move order 4 c4 e5 5 ♘c3 ♝c5 6 ♘f3.

6 ♝e2 ♘f6 7 ♘c3 0-0 8 0-0 a5! 9 ♘e1 d6 10 ♘d3

This is an odd way to pursue the bishop – and quite unsuccessful, as White has released the d4-square.

10...♝d4 11 ♝f3 ♘h4?!

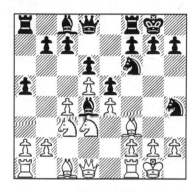

Setting a trap, which White falls right into, but it is best prepared by 11...h6 to prevent 12 ♝g5.

12 ♘b5? ♘xf3+! 13 ♕xf3?! ♝g4 14 ♕g3 ♝e2!

Suddenly Black's light-squared bishop is all in White's business.

15 ♖e1?!

15 ♘xd4 ♝xf1 16 ♘f5 ♘h5 17 ♕f3 ♝xd3 18 ♕xd3 is a better chance.

15...♘xe4 16 ♕h3 ♝xd3 17 ♘xd4 ♘c5

The smoke has cleared and Black has an extra centre pawn for no compensation. 17...♕f6! would have been even stronger.

18 ♘f5 ♕f6 19 ♘e3 ♕g6 20 b3 f5 21 ♝a3 ♘e4 22 ♘d1 ♝c2 23 ♝c1 f4 24 ♕e6+ ♕xe6 25 dxe6 ♘c5?! [25...♖fe8] **26 e7 ♖fe8 27 ♘c3 ♘d3?**

Black has let slip most of his advantage.

28 ♖e2 ♘xc1 29 ♖xc1 ♝f5

30 c5?! [30 ♘d5] **30...♖xe7 31 ♘d5 ♖f7 32 cxd6 cxd6 33 ♖d2 ♖d8 34 f3 ♝e6 35 ♘c7? ♖c8 36 ♖dc2 ♝f5 37 ♖c4 ♖ff8 38 ♔f2 ♔f7 39 ♘b5 ♔e7 40 ♖xc8?**

Equivalent to resignation, even if the game somehow lasted 27 more moves.

40...♖xc8 41 ♖xc8 ♝xc8 42 ♘c3 ♔e6 43 ♘e4 h6 44 ♔e2 d5 45 ♘c3 ♝d7 46 ♔d2

♔d6 47 ♔d3 ♗c5 48 ♔d2 ♗c6 49 ♔d3 ♗b5+ 50 ♔d2 ♗f1 51 g3 fxg3 52 hxg3 h5 53 ♘d1 g5 54 ♘e3 ♗b5 55 ♘f5 ♗d7 56 ♘e3 b5 57 ♔d3 h4 58 gxh4 gxh4 59 a3 h3 60 ♘f1 ♗f5+ 61 ♔c3 b4+ 62 axb4+ axb4+ 63 ♔d2 ♔d4 64 ♘g3 ♗d3 65 ♘h1 h2 66 ♘g3 ♗f1 67 ♘f5+ ♔c5 0-1

Game 35
B.Perrusset-I.Moullier
Paris 2005

1 d4 ♘f6 2 c4 ♘c6 3 ♘c3 e5 4 d5 ♘e7 5 e4 ♘g6 6 ♗e2 ♗c5 [6...♗b4!] 7 ♘f3 0-0 8 0-0 d6 9 a3 a5 10 ♗d2 ♕e7

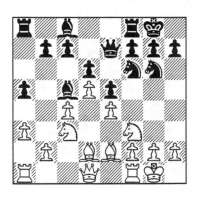

This generally useful move often makes ...♘h5 possible; e.g. 11 ♕c2 ♘h5!? 12 ♘xe5?? ♕xe5. In this game Black had other ideas.

11 ♖b1 ♗d7 12 b4?! axb4 13 axb4 ♗d4!

Once again the slippery dark bishop finds a home on the lovely d4-square.

14 ♗d3 ♖a3 15 ♖b3 ♖xb3 16 ♕xb3 ♖a8 17 ♕c2 ♗b6 18 ♕b2 h6 19 ♖a1 ♖xa1+ 20 ♕xa1

White has finally dealt with the can

of worms he opened up on the a-file, but his remaining pieces are not very well co-ordinated. Suddenly Black starts attacking. All the attacking moves are typical of the variation, and the rooks are not needed.

♘g4 21 ♗e1 ♘f4 22 ♗c2?

The only satisfactory defence is 22 ♗f1, though Black will still have some initiative.

22...♕f6!

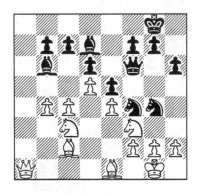

Black is threatening the crushing 23...♘h3+! 24 ♔f1 ♗xf2! 25 ♗xf2 ♘xh2+ 26 ♔e2 ♘f4+ 27 ♔d1 ♘xg2.

23 h3? ♕g6

23...♘xh3+! and 23...♘xf2! also win.

24 hxg4 ♕xg4 25 ♘h4 ♕xh4 26 ♗d1 ♘d3 27 ♗f3 ♗xf2+ 28 ♗xf2 ♕xf2+ 29 ♔h1 ♘f4 30 ♘d1 ♕h4+ 31 ♔g1 ♗g4 32 ♕a3 ♗xf3 33 ♕xf3 ♕e1+ 0-1

Game 36
D.Baramidze-E.Griezne
Baunatal 1999

1 e4 ♘c6 2 d4 e5 3 d5 ♘ce7 4 c4 ♘g6 5

♘c3 ♗c5 6 ♘f3 ♘f6 7 ♗e2 0-0 8 0-0 d6 9 ♕c2 a6

In the theoretical section I recommend 9...♗d7 and usually 10...a5, but the game move is quite reasonable. In either case, Black uses the same attacking ideas on the kingside.

10 a3 ♕e7

In addition to preparing ...♘h5, this holds up White's c4-c5 advance.

11 b4 ♗a7 12 ♘d1 ♘h5 [12...♘f4!?]

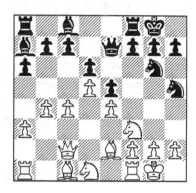

13 ♘e3?!

Here 13 g3 is best, which certainly makes it clear why White needs to omit h2-h3.

13...♘gf4 14 ♘f5?! ♕f6?!

At some cost, White has arranged not to be checkmated on the kingside. Black should slow down and play 14...♗xf5 15 exf5 e4 or 15...♖fe8 with positional advantages based on space, activity, and White's weak f5-pawn.

15 g3! ♗xf5 16 exf5 e4 17 ♗xf4 ♘xf4 18 gxf4 exf3 19 ♗xf3

You don't see this every day. Black is still slightly better, and his position is simpler to play, as we will see.

19...♕h6

20 ♖ae1?

White decides that with three f-pawns, he won't miss one. However, even tripled pawns control squares, and the f4-pawn is particularly important since it covers weak dark squares. Far better to give up the f5-pawn which is one more obstruction to White's sad bishop (though in fact White should not be eager to give up any of his pawns). After this his game slowly deteriorates.

20...♕xf4 21 ♕e4 ♕g5+ 22 ♕g4 ♕f6 23 ♖e4 ♖ae8 24 ♖fe1 ♖xe4 25 ♖xe4

Since the f4-pawn's disappearance White has had to be careful not to allow ...♗d4 and ...♗e5, but he can't defend everything.

25...♕b2 26 ♗e2?! ♕xa3 27 f6?

Time trouble?

27...♕a1+ 28 ♔g2 ♕xf6 29 f3 ♕d8 30 ♕f4 g6 31 ♗d3 ♔g7 32 h4 h5 33 ♕g5 ♖e8 34 ♕xd8 ♖xd8 35 ♖e7 ♗b8 36 b5 axb5 37 cxb5 ♔f6 38 ♖e4 ♗a7 39 ♖f4+ ♔g7 40 ♖e4 ♗b6 41 ♔g3 ♖a8 42 ♔f4 ♖a3 43 ♗e2 ♗f2 44 ♖e7 ♖a4+ 45 ♖e4

♖xe4+ 46 ♔xe4 ♗xh4 47 f4 ♔h6 48 ♗d1 ♗e1 49 ♗f3 ♗c3 50 ♗g2 ♗b2 51 ♗f1 f5+ 52 ♔f3 g5 0-1

Game 37
G.Kaidanov-A.Miles
Palma de Mallorca 1989

1 d4 ♘c6 2 e4 e5 3 d5 ♘ce7 4 c4 ♘g6 5 ♗e3 ♗b4+ [5...♘f6] 6 ♘d2 ♘f6 7 f3 ♕e7 8 g3 0-0 9 ♗h3 c6!

The strongest players are much more likely to do this than look to blockade the queenside.

10 a3 ♗c5 11 ♘f1?! b5!

White's slow manoeuvring does not take into account Black's option to open the position up. Black was better already, but now White is in serious trouble.

12 b4 ♗d4!

That square again! When will White learn not to play c2-c4 - ?

13 ♗xd4 exd4 14 ♕xd4 bxc4 15 d6 ♕e5

Understandably, White tries to close things again. Miles has correctly seen

that he will be winning the endgame if it comes to that.

16 ♘e2 a5 17 ♘e3?! [17 bxa5] 17...axb4 18 ♘xc4 ♕h5 19 ♗g2 c5 20 ♕e3 ♗a6 21 ♘b6 ♖ab8 22 axb4 ♖xb6 23 bxc5 ♖c6 24 ♖a5 ♘e5 25 ♘f4 ♕g5 26 ♕d4 ♖b8 27 ♖a1 h6 28 ♖xa6 ♖xa6 29 0-0 ♘c6 30 ♕c4 ♖a5 0-1

Brutality in the ♗e3 variation

Game 38
S.Brudno-J.Benjamin
Boston 2001

1 d4 ♘f6 2 c4 ♘c6 3 ♘c3 e5 4 d5 ♘e7 5 e4 ♘g6 6 ♗e3 ♗b4 7 f3 ♗xc3+ 8 bxc3 d6 9 c5 0-0 10 ♗d3 ♘d7! 11 cxd6 cxd6 12 ♘e2 ♕a5 13 0-0 ♘c5 14 ♗c4 ♗d7 15 ♗b3 ♖ac8 16 g3 f5

After constructing an ideal position on the queenside, Benjamin opens up the second front. The more I look at the Dark Knight System, the more I'm struck by how often it is Black who has the convenient pawn breaks, and how useful that is.

18...♕xe4+, winning the rook.

17...g5 18 ♕b3 ♗d7 19 ♘e2

19...♘eg6?

19...♗a4! 20 ♕e3 ♖fc8! and White cannot last long.

20 ♖g1 f6 21 ♘c3 ♖fc8 22 a4 ♔h8 23 ♔d2 b6 24 ♗a6 ♘h3 25 ♖gf1 ♘xf2 26 ♗xc8 ♖xc8 27 ♖xf2 ♕c5 28 ♖ff1 ♘f4 29 ♘e2 ♕a5+ 30 ♘c3 ♘e2 31 ♖fc1 ♘xc1 32 ♖xc1 ♔g8 33 f4?

White isn't having any fun at all, but this only makes things worse.

33...exf4 34 e5? fxe5 35 d6+ ♔f8 36 ♕b1 ♔g8 37 ♕b3+ ♔f8 38 ♕b1 ♕c5 0-1

Black loses because he's playing Karpov

Game 41
A.Karpov-D.Chevallier
France 1993

1 d4 ♘f6 2 c4 ♘c6 3 ♘c3 e5 4 d5 ♘e7 5 e4 ♘g6 6 ♗e3 ♗b4 7 f3 ♗xc3+ 8 bxc3 d6 9 ♕d2 ♘d7 10 h4 h6 11 g3 b6 12 ♘h3 ♘c5 13 ♘f2 ♕d7

There is nothing wrong with this move, but 13...f5 can be played, and so I believe it should be played.

14 ♖b1 a5 15 f4?!

In his annotations, Palliser gives this an '!' and indicates that it is the beginning of the end for Chevallier.

15...exf4 16 gxf4

16...♕e7?!

After this Black is a little worse. Meanwhile, should Black find 16...h5, he is a little better! In one stroke, Black stabilizes his knight, clamps down on White's weak g4-square, and immobilizes White's isolated h-pawn. Of course, with a small edge (or even a small disadvantage) Karpov will probably win – he does outrate Chevallier by 430 points.

17 ♗xc5! bxc5 18 h5 ♘f8 19 ♖g1 f6 20 ♗d3 ♘d7 21 ♕e2 ♗a6?

Black's situation will not improve with his king in the centre. For better or for worse, he must castle and try for ...f6-f5.

22 ♘g4 ♘b6 23 ♘e3 ♗c8 24 ♕g2 ♖g8 25 ♕g6+ ♔d8?! [25...♔f8] 26 ♔d2 ♗d7 27 ♕h7 ♕f8 28 ♖g2 ♔c8 29 ♖bg1 ♔b7

30 ☖xg7 ☖h8 31 ♕g6 ♗e8 32 ♕f5 ☖d8
33 ♕e6 ♗xh5 34 ♘f5 ♘c8 35 e5 fxe5 36
fxe5 ♕e8 37 ☖b1+ ♔a8 38 ☖xc7 ♕xe6
39 dxe6 dxe5 40 ☖xc5 e4 41 ♘d4 ☖xd4
42 cxd4 exd3 43 ☖xh5 1-0

Overall, an impressive game by Karpov, but not one that casts any doubt on Black's opening.

1 d4 ♘f6 2 c4 ♘c6 3 ♘c3 e5 4 d5 ♘e7 5
e4 ♘g6 6 ♘f3 ♗b4 7 ♗d3 ♗xc3+ 8 bxc3
d6 9 0-0 0-0 10 h3? ♘h5 11 ♔h2!?

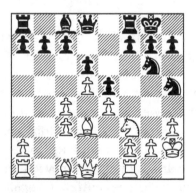

11...♘hf4

Because of 11 ♔h2, Black's normal attacking plan needs to be modified – 11...♘gf4?! 12 ♗c2 ♕f6?? 13 g4 traps a knight.

12 ♘g1?! ♘xd3!

They say bad bishops defend good pawns – but they don't if they're dead.

13 ♕xd3 f5 14 exf5?! [14 f3] **14...♗xf5
15 ♕g3?! ♕d7! 16 f4?! ♕a4**

This is why I like doubling White's pawns so much – it provides a ready-made target on the other front if the kingside play is running out of steam.

**17 fxe5 ♕xc4 18 ☖d1 ♘xe5 19 ☖d4 ♕c5
20 ♘e2 ☖ae8 21 ♘f4 ♘g6 22 ♘xg6
♗xg6 23 ♗g5 ☖e2 24 a4?! ☖ff2 25 ☖g1
♗e4 0-1**

1 d4 ♘c6 2 c4 e5 3 d5 ♘ce7 4 e4 ♘f6 5
♘c3 ♘g6 6 ♘f3 ♗c5

I prefer 6...♗b4 here, but we must know this position anyway via 4...♘g6 5 ♘c3 ♗c5 6 ♘f3 ♘f6.

**7 ♗d3 0-0 8 0-0 a5 9 a3 d6 10 ☖b1 ♘h5
11 b4 axb4 12 axb4 ♗b6 13 ♘a4 ♗a7
14 ♗c2 ♘hf4**

Here again, the h-knight goes first. This is to allow ...♗g4 and ...♘h4 – an effective plan with White's bishop already on c2. Black has a significant advantage and a powerful initiative.

15 c5 ♗g4 16 g3 ♕f6?

Black is almost winning at once with the alternative 16...♘h3+ 17 ♔g2 ♕d7 18 ♗e3 f5!, bringing a rook into the attack.

17 ♖b3 ♗xc5 18 ♘xc5 dxc5 19 bxc5 ♖a1 20 gxf4 ♘xf4 21 ♔h1 ♘h3 22 ♕e2 ♖fa8? [22...♖a2!]

23 ♖c3??

Instead, with 23 ♕e3! White has excellent chances to realize her extra material. After the text, she is completely busted.

23...♖8a2 24 ♔g2 ♖xc1 25 ♖xc1 ♘f4+ 26 ♔f1 ♘xe2 27 ♔xe2 ♕f4 28 ♖e3 ♗xf3+ 0-1

The catastrophe that is White's plan of g2-g3 and f2-f4

Game 44
**E.Schiendorfer-
D.Recuero Guerra**
European Junior Ch'ships,
Herceg Novi 2006

1 d4 ♘f6 2 c4 ♘c6 3 ♘c3 e5 4 d5 ♘e7 5 e4 ♘g6 6 g3 ♗b4 7 ♗g2 ♗xc3+ 8 bxc3 d6 9 ♘e2 0-0 10 0-0 ♕e7 11 ♕d3 ♗d7 12 ♗a3 ♖fe8 13 ♖ae1 b6 14 ♘c1 ♕d8

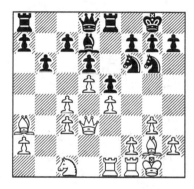

Not the most inspiring play so far. Now comes typical hara-kiri by White.

15 f4? exf4 16 gxf4 ♘h5 17 ♘e2 ♕h4 18 ♗c1 f5 19 ♔h1 ♖e7 20 exf5?? ♗xf5 21 ♕f3

21 ♕xf5 ♖xe2 22 ♖xe2 ♘g3+ 23 ♔g1 ♘xe2+ 24 ♔h1 ♘g3+ 25 ♔g1 ♘xf5 is hilariously brutal.

21...♗g4 22 ♕f2 ♖xe2 0-1

Game 45
C.Baluta-A.Cioara
Bucharest 1996

1 d4 ♘c6 2 c4 e5 3 d5 ♘ce7 4 e4 ♘g6 5

a3 ♘f6 6 ♘c3 ♗c5 7 h3 d6 8 ♘f3 a5 9 g3

This is amazing. I'm wondering when White will get around to moving his b- and f-pawns.

9...0-0 10 ♗g2 c6 11 0-0 cxd5 12 cxd5 ♗d7 13 ♖e1 ♕c8 14 h4? ♘g4 15 ♖e2 b5 16 ♗d2 b4 17 ♘a4

17...♗b5?!

Black has built his position admirably so far, but now he starts to lose the thread. 17...♗a7 18 axb4 ♗b5 was better.

18 ♘xc5 ♕xc5 19 h5 ♘e7?! [19...♗xe2]
20 ♗h3?! [20 ♗e3!] **20...♗d7?**

After this lemon, Black is actually worse for a moment.

21 ♗g2?

But only for a moment. 21 h6! g6 22 ♕b3 was correct.

21...bxa3 22 ♖xa3 f5?! [22...♗b5!] **23 ♗e3?! ♘xe3 24 ♖exe3 fxe4 25 ♖xe4 ♖ab8 26 ♕d2 a4 27 ♘h4 ♖b7 28 ♖ee3 ♖b4 29 ♖ac3?! ♕b6 30 ♖e2 h6 31 ♔h2? ♖d4?** [31...♗b5] **32 ♖d3?? ♖xd3 33 ♕xd3 ♗b5!**

Finally!

34 ♕e3 ♕xe3 35 ♖xe3 ♖xf2 36 ♔g1 ♖xb2 37 ♗h3 ♖b1+ 38 ♔f2 ♖b3 39 ♗e6+ ♔f8 40 ♖e1 a3 41 ♖c1 a2 42 ♘g6+ ♘xg6 0-1

A loss for Black – can this be right?

Game 46
Bu Xiangzhi-L.Christiansen
Deizisau 2000

1 d4 ♘f6 2 c4 ♘c6 3 ♘c3 e5 4 d5 ♘e7 5 e4 ♘g6 6 a3 ♗c5 7 ♗d3 a5 8 ♖b1 d6 9 h3 0-0 10 b4 axb4 11 axb4 ♗a7 12 g3?!

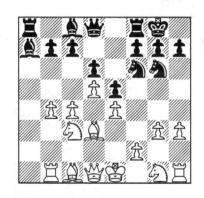

12...♘e8?!

This awkward move prepares the ...f7-f5 break, but Black never gets to execute this plan. Besides, 12...c6! is just sitting there waiting to be played. Yet again. One benefit to ...c7-c6 is that after ...c6xd5 c4xd5 White can no longer shut out the monster a7-bishop. Black would then be significantly better.

13 ♘f3 ♗d7

Black realizes that 13...f5?! hurts his

position, trading off White's lame light-squared bishop and allowing White to castle without dropping the h3-pawn. After the text move, White has equalized – though not for long.

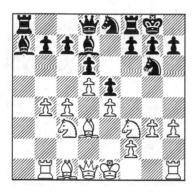

14 ♗g5?!

14 ♔f1! ♕c8 15 ♔g2 was correct.

14...♕c8 15 g4 c6 16 ♘e2 h6 17 ♗d2 cxd5 18 cxd5 ♕d8 19 ♘g3 ♗b6 20 0-0 ♘f4! 21 ♗xf4 exf4 22 ♘h5 ♘f6 23 ♘xf4 ♖e8

Black's pawn sacrifice has removed White's best minor piece from play and opened the gates for Black's pieces. This is a thematic idea in the Dark Knight System, and indeed in any posi-

tion where the opponent has put most of his pawns on one colour (especially in the vicinity of his king).

24 ♕c2 ♖c8

Houdini points out 24...g5! 25 ♘g2 (the knight's idiot square; but if 25 ♘e2 h5!) 25...♖c8 and 26...♘xe4. In the game White's knight becomes a real pain in the keister.

25 ♕b2 ♘xe4 26 ♘h5 ♘c3 27 ♖bc1 g6 28 ♕d2

Had White played 27 ♖fc1! he could have gone for 28 ♖xc3 ♖xc3 29 ♕xc3 gxh5 30 gxh5 with no fear of 30...♗xh3.

28...♘e2+ 29 ♔g2 ♖xc1 30 ♕xh6 ♘f4+ 31 ♕xf4 ♖xf1 32 ♔xf1 gxh5 33 ♕h6 f5 34 ♕g6+ ♔h8?!

Christiansen, who has been defending perfectly until now, slips. It is not good to allow ♕xh5 with check, and by winning the pawn White defends his own peon on h3.

35 gxf5 ♖f8 36 ♕xh5+ ♔g8 37 ♕g6+ ♔h8 38 ♕h6+ ♔g8 39 f6

39...♖f7??

39...♗xh3+ 40 ♕xh3 ♖f7 or 40...♖xf6 offers legitimate chances of survival.

40 ♘g5! ♗xh3+ 41 ♘xh3??

Suddenly Black is back in it. 41 ♔e1!! is completely winning; e.g. 41...♕d7 42 ♕g6+ ♔f8 43 ♗b5!.

41...♕xf6 42 ♗h7+ ♔h8 43 ♗g6+ ♔g8 44 ♗xf7+ ♔xf7 45 ♕h7+ ♔e8 46 ♕xb7 ♕d4? [46...♕f5!] 47 ♕c8+ ♗d8 48 ♕e6+ ♗e7 49 b5 ♕d3+ 50 ♔g2 ♕xb5

Black has recovered one pawn, but his queen is out of play and White takes the opportunity to enter a winning pawn endgame.

51 ♘f4 ♕b2 52 ♘g6 ♕f6 53 ♕xe7+ ♕xe7 54 ♘xe7 ♔xe7 55 ♔f3 ♔f6 56 ♔f4 ♔g6 57 ♔g4 ♔f6 58 f4 1-0

Hort plays the Kevitz, and lets Hübner off the hook

Game 47
R.Hübner-V.Hort
German League 1984

1 e4 ♘c6 2 d4 e5 3 dxe5 ♘xe5 4 f4 ♘c6 5 ♗e3 ♗b4+ [5...d5!] 6 c3 ♗a5 7 ♘f3 ♘f6 8 e5 [8 ♕a4!?] 8...♘g4 9 ♗c5? d6! 10 exd6 0-0

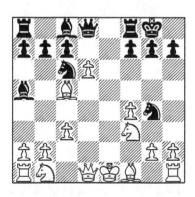

White is much worse here.

11 ♗e2 ♖e8 12 h3 cxd6 13 hxg4 dxc5 14 ♕xd8 ♖xd8?! [14...♗xd8] 15 ♘fd2 ♘e7 16 ♘a3 ♘d5 17 g3 ♗c7 18 ♗f3 ♘e3 19 g5

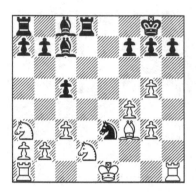

15...♗f5?!

19...♘f5! is better, forcing 20 ♘f1 (or 20 ♘e4, which is not very good either), because 20 ♖g1? loses to ♘xg3! 21 ♖xg3 ♖xd2! 22 ♔xd2 ♗xf4+ and 23...♗xg3.

20 ♘dc4 ♘xc4 21 ♘xc4 ♗d3

There is still some play, but Black has no real advantage.

22 b3 ♖ab8 23 ♔f2 b5 24 ♘e3 c4 25 ♘d5 ♗b6+ 26 ♔g2 ♔f8 27 ♖he1 ♖e8 28 b4 ♗f5 29 ♖xe8+ ♖xe8 30 a4 bxa4 31 ♖xa4 h6 32 gxh6 gxh6 33 ♘xb6 axb6 34 ♔f2 ♖d8

By now it is White who is trying for a win, though it is unlikely.

35 ♖a8 ♖xa8 36 ♗xa8 ♔e7 37 ♔e3 ♔d6 38 ♔d4 b5 39 ♗d5 f6 40 ♗f7 ♗d7 41 ♔e4 ♔e7 42 ♗g6 ♗c6+ 43 ♔d4 ♔d6 44 ♗h5 f5 45 ♗g6 ♗d7 46 ♗f7 ♗c8 47 ♗e8 ♗a6 48 ♔e3 ♔e7 49 ♗g6 ♗c8 50 ♔d4 ♔d6 51 ♗e8 ♗a6 ½-½

Game 48
M.Orso-G.Bordas
Budapest 2000

1 e4 ♘c6 2 d4 e5 3 dxe5 ♘xe5 4 f4 ♘c6 5 ♗c4 ♘f6 6 ♘c3 ♗b4 7 e5 d5 8 exf6 dxc4 9 ♕e2+ ♔f8!? [9...♗e6!] **10 ♗e3**

Had White been tempted by 10 fxg7+? ♔xg7, Black's last move would have been amply rewarded. The rook's rapid arrival on the e-file is a serious problem for White.

10...♕xf6 11 0-0-0 ♗e6

The inconvenience suffered by Black's king is not enough to make up for White's missing pawn and shortage of light-squared bishops.

12 ♘e4 ♕e7?! [12...♕f5] **13 ♘f3 c3 14 b3?!** [14 bxc3] **14...a5 15 ♔b1 a4 16 ♕b5??**

White is now lost. 16 ♗f2 is essential, though Black has a clear edge.

16...axb3 17 axb3

17...♗xb3 18 cxb3 ♕xe4+ 19 ♖d3 ♖a5 20 ♕c4 ♕xc4 21 bxc4 ♔e7 22 ♘d4 ♘xd4 23 ♗xd4 ♖ha8 24 ♖e3+ ♔d7? 25 ♖he1?

25 ♗xc3! ♗xc3 26 ♖d1+ and Black still has to show good technique.

25...♖a1+ 26 ♔c2 ♖1a2+ 27 ♔d3 ♖d2+ 28 ♔e4 f5+ 29 ♔xf5 ♖xd4 30 c5 ♗xc5 31 ♖xc3 ♖f8+ 32 ♔g5 ♗e7+ 0-1

Game 49
S.Fedorchuk-A.Miles
European Championship,
Ohrid 2001

1 e4 ♘c6 2 d4 e5 3 dxe5 ♘xe5 4 ♘c3 ♗c5 5 f4 ♘c6 6 ♘f3 d6 7 ♘a4 ♗b6 8 ♗d3 d5?!

An interesting attempt to take advantage of the decentralized knight, but Black is spending a tempo to open the position when he is behind in development and White will soon have the bishop pair.

9 ♘xb6 axb6 10 e5?!

Not terrible, but it makes no sense to close the position. The f5-square will be useful for all of Black's pieces.

10...♘ge7 11 0-0 ♗f5 12 ♘h4 ♗xd3 13

♕xd3 ♕d7

Black has equalized.

14 ♗d2 ♕g4 15 ♗e1 0-0 16 h3 ♕d7 17 ♗d2 ♖a4 18 ♗c3 ♘g6 19 ♘xg6 fxg6 20 g3 ♘e7 21 ♚h2 h5 22 b3 ♖e4 23 ♖ae1 ♕c6 24 ♗d2 ♘f5

25 ♕c3?!

The black knight becomes strong after this. 25 g4 was best.

25...h4 26 gxh4 ♘xh4?!

26...♕xc3 27 ♗xc3 ♚f7! was better.

27 ♕xc6 bxc6 28 ♚g3 ♘f5+ 29 ♚g4 ♚f7 30 ♖xe4 dxe4 31 ♖e1 ♖d8 32 ♗e3?! ♖d1! 33 ♖e2 ♚e6 34 ♗f2 ♖f1 35 a4 c5 36 a5?! bxa5 37 ♚g5? ♖h1 38 ♗xc5 ♖xh3 39 ♚xg6 ♖g3+ 40 ♚h7 e3 41 ♚g8 g5 42 fxg5 ♖xg5+ 43 ♚h7 ♖g7+ 44 ♚h8 ♖g3 45 ♖h2 ♚xe5 46 ♗a3 ♖g4 47 ♗b2+ ♚e4 48 ♗c3 ♖h4+ 49 ♖xh4+ ♘xh4 50 ♗xa5 e2 51 ♚g7 ♘f3 52 ♚f6 ♚e3 0-1

Game 50
Goh Wei Ming-F.Bellini
Turin Olympiad 2006

1 e4 e5 2 ♘f3 ♘c6 3 d4 exd4 4 ♘xd4

♗c5 5 ♘b3 ♗b6 6 ♘c3 d6

For our purposes, it is important to use the precise move order 6...♘ge7 7 ♕e2 d6.

7 ♕e2 ♘ge7 8 ♗e3 0-0 9 0-0-0 f5!

There's no time like the present.

10 g3 fxe4 11 ♘xe4 ♘f5 12 ♗f4 ♕e8

Mr. H says 12...♚h8 or 12...h6 with advantage to Black.

13 ♗g2 a5 14 ♖he1 ♕g6 15 c3?! h6 16 a4 ♗e6?! 17 ♕c2? [17 ♘ec5!] **17...♘h4 18 ♗h1 ♗g4 19 ♖d3 ♖ae8 20 f3? ♘xf3?** [20...♗e6] **21 ♗xf3 ♗xf3 22 ♖xf3 d5 23 ♘bd2 dxe4 24 ♖ff1 ♘e5 25 ♖xe4 ♘g4 26 ♖fe1 ♖d8 27 ♖e7?! ♕xc2+ 28 ♚xc2 g5 29 ♖1e6 ♖f7**

30 h3??

Instead of this blunder the simple 30 ♖g6+! ♔h7 31 ♖ee6 keeps White in the game.

30...♖xe7 31 ♖xe7 gxf4 32 hxg4 fxg3 0-1

Game 51
P.Bontempi-O.Jovanic
Nova Gorica 2008

1 e4 e5 2 ♘f3 ♘c6 3 d4 exd4 4 ♘xd4 ♗c5 5 ♗e3 ♕f6 6 ♘b5 ♗xe3 7 fxe3 ♕h4+ 8 g3 ♕d8 9 ♕g4 g5!

This Basmaniac-esque move is a bit funny-looking at first, but if we think about it, it is the dark squares that need coverage since we have a light-squared bishop and we are about to have a knight posted on the lovely e5-outpost. To be a little more concrete, it is beneficial to take the f4-square from White's queen.

10 ♘1c3 ♘e5 11 ♕e2 d6 12 h3 c6 13 ♘d4 ♘f6 14 0-0-0 ♕e7 15 ♕f2 ♗e6 16 ♗e2 0-0-0 17 ♘f5 ♗xf5 18 exf5

White's pawn structure has improved somewhat, but his bishop has not, nor has the gaping hole on e5. Furthermore, White no longer has the f5-hole to use.

18...♘ed7 19 ♗f3 ♘c5 [19...d5!?] 20 ♖he1 h5 21 ♖d4 ♕e5 22 h4 ♖hg8 23 ♖ed1 gxh4 24 gxh4 ♔c7 25 ♖f4?! ♖de8 26 ♔d2?

26...♘cd7?!

Black is reluctant to put any pawns on light squares for long-term positional reasons, but White won't reach the long term after 26...d5! 27 ♖e1 ♘ce4+ 28 ♗xe4 ♘xe4+ 29 ♘xe4 dxe4, which exposes the ludicrous placement of White's king; e.g. 30 ♔c1 ♕a5 31 ♔b1 ♖g2 32 ♕f1 ♕d2 33 ♖c1 ♕xe3 34 ♕xg2 ♕xf4 with a winning position. Instead, soon comes an avalanche of blunders that is presumably time-induced.

You know what? You don't want to see the rest of this. It's ridiculous and embarrassing.

Black eventually won the game on move 81.

[22...♘ed3!] **23 g3?** [23 ♕d2] **23...♘fd3
24 ♖d1 ♘xb2 25 ♖b1 ♘ed3 26 ♕b6
♘a4 27 ♕xb7 ♘xc3 28 ♖b6?!** [28 ♖b3]
**28...♘e5 29 ♖xa6 ♖xf3 30 ♖xf3 ♕e4 31
♘e1 ♘xf3 32 ♘1g2 ♘b5! 0-1**

Game 52
S.Vajda-S.Skembris
Naujac 1999

**1 e4 e5 2 ♘f3 ♘c6 3 d4 exd4 4 ♘xd4
♕f6!?**

Apparently this is a playable move
order, though it gives White the option
of 5 ♘b5!?, which is good enough for
some edge.

5 ♗e3 ♗c5 6 c3 ♕g6 7 f3 ♘ge7

In the theoretical section, I recommend the immediate 7...a6.

**8 ♕d2 a6 9 ♘c2 ♗xe3 10 ♘xe3 d6 11
♗e2 f5**

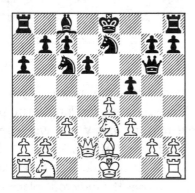

12 exf5 ♗xf5

12...♘xf5 is equally good.

13 0-0 0-0

13...0-0-0 is at least as good too.

14 ♘a3 ♖ae8 15 ♖ae1 ♔h8

It's time to take away White's option to snap off the bishop; i.e.
15...♗e6.

**16 ♘ac2 ♕h6 17 ♗d3 ♗xd3 18 ♕xd3
♘g6 19 ♘d5?! ♘ce5 20 ♕d4 c6 21
♘de3?!** [21 f4!] **21...♘f4 22 ♔h1 ♕g6?!**

Game 53
A.Motylev-S.Gligoric
Yugoslav Team
Championship 2000

**1 e4 e5 2 ♘f3 ♘c6 3 d4 exd4 4 ♘xd4
♗c5 5 ♗e3 ♕f6 6 c3 ♕g6 7 ♘d2 ♘f6 8
f4 ♘xd4 9 cxd4 ♗b4 10 f5 ♕g4 11
♕xg4 ♘xg4 12 ♗f4 d5 13 h3 ♘f6 14 e5
♘e4 15 g4 g6 16 fxg6 fxg6 17 a3
♗xd2+ 18 ♗xd2 h5 19 ♖g1 hxg4 20
hxg4 ♗e6 21 0-0-0 ♔d7 22 ♗g2**

22...♘f2?!

Black keeps an edge with 22...♘xd2
23 ♖xd2 ♖af8 or 23 ♔xd2 ♗xg4.

**23 ♖df1 ♖af8 24 ♗g5 ♘xg4 25 ♖xf8
♖xf8 26 ♗xd5 ♗xd5 27 ♖xg4 ♖f1+ 28
♔d2 ♖f2+ 29 ♔c3 a5 30 ♗h4 ♖f3+ 31
♔d2 ♗f7 32 d5 ♗xd5 33 ♖xg6 ♖b3**
½-½

Game 54
P.Hromada-L.Ostrowski
Moravian Team
Championship 2003

1 e4 e5 2 ♘f3 ♘c6 3 d4 exd4 4 ♘xd4 ♕f6 5 ♗e3 ♗c5 6 c3 ♕g6 7 ♘b5 ♗xe3 8 ♘xc7+ ♔d8 9 ♘xa8 ♗f4 10 ♕f3 ♗b8

I recommend 10...♗h6! in the theory section.

11 ♘d2 ♘f6 12 0-0-0 ♖e8

13 ♖e1?!

White should be willing to sacrifice the e-pawn, for which he will gain easy development; e.g. 13 g3 ♘xe4 14 ♘xe4 ♕xe4 15 ♕xe4 ♖xe4 16 ♗g2 ♖e7 17 f4 and, for one thing, it is no longer clear how Black will ever corral the wayward knight. The text move is far too passive, a recurring problem for White as the game goes on.

13...b6 14 ♗b5 ♗b7 15 ♘xb6 axb6 16 ♕e3 ♗c7 17 f3 ♘d5 [17...♔c8] 18 ♕f2 ♘f4 19 g3 ♘e6 20 ♗xc6?!

A bad idea, which weakens the light squares around White's king and sim-plifies Black's task of using his bishop pair.

20...♗xc6 21 ♘b3 ♗c5 [21...♔e7!] 22 ♘xc5 ♕g5+ 23 ♕e3 ♕xc5 24 ♕xc5 bxc5 25 b3 f5 26 exf5 ♖f8 27 ♖e3 ♖xf5 28 ♖he1 ♗d6

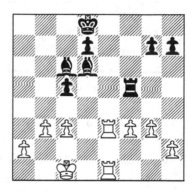

29 ♖f1? [29 f4] 29...g5 30 ♔b2 h5 31 ♖d1 ♔c7 32 ♖f1 ♔b7 33 a3 c4 34 b4 ♗c7? [34...h4!] 35 ♔c2?! [35 ♖c7!] 35...♗b6 36 ♖e7 ♔c8 37 f4 ♗g2 38 ♖d1 gxf4 39 ♖dxd7??

Here 39 gxf4 d5 is no bargain for White, but the text ends the game im-mediately.

39...f3 40 ♖b7 ♗d8 41 ♖f7 f2 0-1

Game 55
D.Campora-V.Tkachiev
Biel 1995

1 e4 e5 2 ♘f3 ♘c6 3 d4 exd4 4 ♘xd4 ♗c5 5 ♗e3 ♕f6 6 c3 ♕g6 7 ♘b5 ♗xe3 8 ♘xc7+ ♔d8 9 ♘xa8 ♗f4 10 ♕f3 ♗h6 11 ♕f5?! ♕xf5 12 exf5 b6 13 ♘a3 ♗b7 14 ♘xb6 axb6 15 ♘c4 ♔c7 16 ♖d1 d5!

A clever thrust.

17 ♘a3

If 17 ♖xd5?! ♘f6 18 ♖d1 ♖e8+ 19 ♗e2 ♗a6, White regrets his pawn grab.

17...♘f6 18 ♘b5+ ♔d7 19 ♗e2 ♖e8 20 ♔f1 ♖e5 21 h4 ♘e4 22 ♖h3 ♘d2+ 23 ♔e1 ♗a6 24 a4 ♘c4 25 b3 ♘d6 26 ♖hd3 d4! 27 cxd4?!

White's rooks will not enjoy languishing behind the isolated d-pawn. However, the position is not rich enough to offer Black good winning chances (in GM play).

27...♖e4 28 g4 ♗f4 29 ♔f1 ♘xb5 30 axb5 ♗xb5 31 ♖3d2!

Unlikely as it seems, this move saves the day, since 31...♗xd2 32 ♗xb5

(threatening both 33 ♖xd2 and 33 d5) 32...♖xd4 33 ♔e2 regains the piece.

31...♖xe2 32 ♖xe2 ♔d6 33 ♔e1 ♗xe2 34 ♔xe2 ♔d5 35 ♔d3 h6

Not 35...♘xd4?? 36 ♔c3 ♗e5 37 f4 ♗f6 38 g5.

36 ♖e1 ♗d6 37 ♖e8 ♗e7 38 h5 ♗f6 39 ♖c8 ♘xd4 40 ♖c7 ♘c6?!

40...♘xb3 is a better try.

41 f4 ♘e7 42 ♖a7 ♔c6 43 ♔e4 ½-½

1 e4 e5

Once, when GM Bisguier was analysing one of my games, he said he'd known all about ...♘c6 and ...e7-e5 since long before I'd been born. This makes sense because he was coached by Alexander Kevitz, by whose name this system is known.

2 ♘f3 ♘c6 3 d4 exd4 4 ♘xd4 ♗c5 5 ♘xc6 ♕f6 6 ♕f3 ♕xf3 7 gxf3 bxc6 8 ♗e3 ♗xe3 9 fxe3

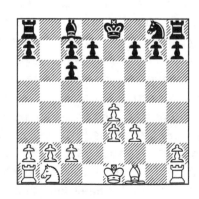

As I mentioned in the theoretical section, White has done pretty well here. Bisguier's plan takes care of any potential problems, though I think it's simpler to start with 9...d6.

9...♘f6 10 ♘c3

After 10 e5!? ♘g8 11 ♖g1 g6 12 ♘c3 f6 13 exf6 ♘xf6 14 0-0-0 0-0, White has little to nothing either, but I still see no reason to allow him this option.

10...0-0 11 0-0-0 [11 e5 ♘d5] **11...♖e8 12 ♗h3 d6**

Also possible is 12...g6 (a useful semi-waiting move), intending ...♖e5-h5. After the text, Black slips into a passive position.

13 ♗xc8 ♖axc8 14 ♖d4 a5?! [14...♘d7] **15 ♖c4 c5 16 ♖a4 ♖a8 17 ♘b5 ♖ec8 18 ♘a3?!** [18 e5!?] **18...♘d7 19 ♘c4 ♘b6 20 ♘xb6 cxb6**

Black has equalized (again). Nothing else happens.

21 c4 ♚f8 22 ♖a3 ♚e7 23 ♖b3 ♖ab8 24 a4 ♚e6 25 ♖d1 ♖c6 26 ♖g1 g6 27 ♚d2 ♖f8 28 ♖g3 f5 29 exf5+ ♖xf5 30 e4 ♖h5 31 h3 g5 32 ♚e3 h6 33 ♖d3 ♖h4 34 ♖b3 ♚e5 35 ♖d3 ♖c7 36 ♖b3 ♖b7 37 ♖d3

♚e6 38 ♖b3 ♚d7 39 ♖d3 ♚c6 40 ♚f2 ♖f7 41 ♚g2 ½-½

Game 57
J.Smeets-A.Beliavsky
Netherlands-Slovenia
rapid match, Maribor 2004

1 e4 e5 2 ♘f3 ♘c6 3 d4 exd4 4 ♘xd4 ♗c5 5 ♘xc6 ♕f6 6 ♕d2 dxc6 7 ♘c3 ♗d4 8 ♗d3 ♘e7 9 0-0 ♘g6 10 ♘e2 ♗xb2!

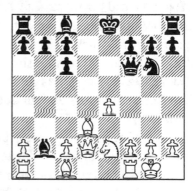

Beliavsky courageously grabs the pawn – the "principled" move (whatever that means).

11 ♗xb2 ♕xb2 12 f4 ♕a3 13 f5 ♘e5 14 ♕g5 ♗d7

I am recommending 14...♕f8!, when White has worries about proving full compensation, though Black had his chances in this game as well.

15 ♕xg7 ♕c5+ 16 ♚h1 0-0-0 17 ♕f6 h5 18 h3 ♚b8

18...♕d6!? with a structural advantage in the endgame.

19 ♖f4?! ♗c8 20 ♖h4?

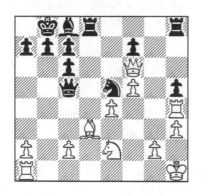

20...♖hg8?

Black is nearly winning with 20...♘xd3 21 cxd3 ♕f2 22 ♘f4 ♖hg8, because White's queen, knight, and king's rook are stuck in a very unhealthy co-dependent relationship.

21 ♖f1 ♖d6 22 ♕e7 ♕a5?! 23 ♖xh5 ♖d7 24 ♕f6 ♖d6 25 ♕e7 ♖d7 26 ♕f6 ♖d6 27 ♕e7 ♖d7 ½-½

Instead of repeating moves, Black was much better after 27...♘xd3 28 cxd3 (or 28 ♕xf7 ♘f2+!) 28...♕xa2 29 ♘f4 ♖xd3! (and not 30 ♘xd3?? ♕xg2 mate).

Game 58
B.Sultimov-N.Pokazanjev
Russia 2007

1 e4 e5 2 ♘f3 ♘c6 3 d4 exd4 4 ♘xd4 ♗c5 5 ♘xc6 ♕f6 6 ♕d2 dxc6 7 ♘c3 ♗d4 8 ♗d3 ♘e7 9 0-0 ♘g6 10 ♔h1 ♘e5 11 f4 ♘g4 12 ♕e1

White has certainly lost the theoretical battle since 12...♘xh2 13 ♔xh2 ♕h6+ is a draw by perpetual. But what if Black wants to win? Pokazanjev's move is very risky – in fact, it's objectively poor, but sometimes it's worth taking such risks. Perhaps Black should have deviated earlier: 10...0-0 is not a bad move, and avoids the present dilemma; 10...♕h4 is also reasonable according to *Houdini*.

12...♗d7?! 13 ♘a4?!

Out of book, White makes a poor choice. As we will see, Black does not even have to allow his bishop to be forced off the strong diagonal.

13...a6 14 c3 ♗a7 15 b4 ♕e7 16 ♖b1 0-0-0

Black is not fooled by White's

queenside demonstration, which is mainly bark and has little bite.

17 ♕g3 h5 18 h3? ♗f5!!

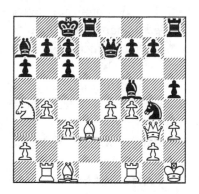

19 ♘c5

The bishop should not be taken: 19 exf5? ♘f2+! 20 ♖xf2 ♕e1+ 21 ♗f1 (or 21 ♔h2 ♗xf2 and 22...♕g1 mate) 21...♗xf2 22 ♗d2 ♕xb1 23 ♕xf2 ♖xd2 and wins – though White is just about lost anyway.

19...♗xc5 20 bxc5 ♗xe4 21 ♗xe4 ♕xe4 22 ♖b4 ♕e2 23 ♕f3

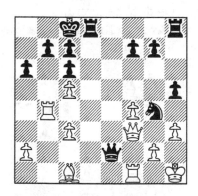

The endgame will bring White little relief – he cannot possibly hold onto his six isolated pawns.

23...♕xf3 24 gxf3 ♘f6 25 f5 ♖d5 26 ♗e3

♖xf5 27 ♗d4 ♘d5 28 ♖b2 ♖h6 29 c4 ♘f4 30 ♖fb1 ♘e6 31 ♗g1 ♖xf3 32 ♖xb7 ♖xh3+ 33 ♗h2 ♖d3 34 ♖a7 ♖f6 35 ♖xa6 ♖f2 36 a4 ♖h3 37 ♖a8+ ♔d7 38 ♔g1 ♖hxh2 39 ♖e1 ♖fg2+ 40 ♔f1 ♘f4 0-1

Dealing roughly with 7 ♗f4?!

Game 59
D.Von Wantoch
Rekowski-J.Peric
Yugoslav Junior Ch'ships,
Tivat 2001

1 e4 e5 2 ♘f3 ♘c6 3 d4 exd4 4 ♗c4 ♘f6 5 e5 ♘g4 6 0-0 ♗e7 7 ♗f4 g5! 8 ♗g3 h5! 9 h3 h4!

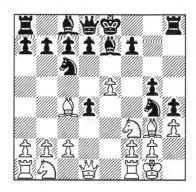

10 ♗h2?!

10 hxg4 hxg3 11 fxg3 d6 is relatively best, though still with advantage to Black.

10...♘xh2 11 ♔xh2 d6 12 ♗b5 dxe5 13 ♘xe5 ♕d6 14 f4 ♗e6 15 c4? gxf4 16 ♕f3 ♔d8?! [16...♔f8!] **17 ♘xc6+ bxc6 18 ♗xc6 ♖b8 19 b3 ♖g8 20 ♘d2 ♖g3 21 c5 ♕xc5 22 ♖fc1 ♖xf3 23 ♗xc5 ♖xh3+ 24 gxh3 ♗xc5 25 ♘e4 ♖b6 26 ♗a4 ♗d6 27**

♖d1 ♗e5 28 ♘g5 ♔e7 29 ♘f3 f6 30 ♘xd4 ♖d6 31 ♘c6+ ♔f8 32 ♖xd6 ♗xd6 33 ♘d4 f3+ 34 ♔h1 ♗d5 0-1

Black did not have a high rating, but she produced the model game.

Game 60
J.Becerra Rivero-A.Miles
Andorra 1995

1 e4 ♘c6 2 ♘f3

Like most high-rated players, White tries to narrow the knowledge gap with this second move. Instead, 2 d4 e5 (or in some cases 2...d5) fights in Black's home territory. Of course, there is nothing stopping Black from also knowing 2 ♘f3 d6 positions well.

2...d6 3 d4 ♘f6 4 c3 g6 5 ♗d3 ♗g7 6 ♘a3

Becerra Rivero is the only one to have tried this move here. Although decentralizing, it has the merit of not interfering with White's other pieces.

6...0-0 7 0-0 e5 8 dxe5?! ♘xe5 9 ♘xe5 dxe5

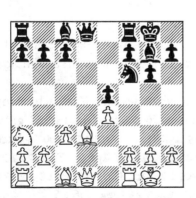

White's decision to exchange in the centre is not consistent with his previous play. The c3-pawn is intended to shorten the diagonal for Black's fianchettoed bishop and/or hold the d4-point, neither of which are meaningful anymore. White's d3-bishop is also misplaced, obstructing the open d-file. He no longer has any trace of an advantage. Perhaps White is trying to make a draw, in which case he has chosen the wrong opponent.

10 ♕e2 ♕e7 11 ♗g5 h6 12 ♗xf6?!

This small inaccuracy leads to White's future problems. We will witness dark-square torture yet again.

12...♕xf6 13 ♗c4 ♗d7 14 ♖ad1 ♖ad8 15 ♖d3 h5 16 ♕e3 a6 17 ♖fd1 ♗g4!? 18 f3 ♗c8

Miles's bishop manoeuvre softens up the dark squares for his unopposed dark bishop. There is certainly nothing concrete yet, but it is getting to where White needs to be careful.

19 ♗b3 ♖xd3 20 ♖xd3 h4 21 h3 ♕e7 22 ♘c4 ♔h7! 23 f4?!

This game reminds me of the old

story of the old lady who swallowed a fly, and a spider to catch the fly, and a bird to catch the spider, etc. White prevents ...♗h6 for now, but the new problems are bigger than the old ones.

23...exf4 24 ♕xf4 b5 25 ♘e3 ♗e5

26 ♕f3 [26 ♘d5!] **26...♕g5 27 ♖d1 ♔g7 28 ♖d5 ♕g3 29 ♘g4 ♕xf3 30 gxf3 ♗f4 31 ♔g2 ♖e8 32 ♖d1 f5 33 ♘f2 ♗g3 34 ♘h1 ♗d6 35 ♘f2 ♔f6 36 ♗d5 ♖h8 37 ♘d3 ♖h5 38 f4 fxe4 39 ♗xe4 ♖h8 40 ♗f3 ♖e8 41 ♗g4?**

In principle, this is a favourable trade for White, who relieves Black of the bishop pair, but the devil is in the details.

41...♗xg4 42 hxg4 ♖e3 43 ♔f1 ♗xf4 44 ♘b4 ♔g5 45 ♘d5 ♖f3+ 46 ♔e2 ♖g3 47 ♖d4 ♗d6 0-1

> ### Game 61
> **R.Zelcic-A.Miles**
> Pula 1994

1 e4 ♘c6 2 ♘f3 d6 3 d4 ♘f6 4 c3 g6 5 ♗b5 ♗d7

5...a6 is also fine, or even 5...♗g7 6 d5 a6 7 ♗a4 b5 8 dxc6 bxa4 9 ♕xa4 0-0 with compensation.

6 ♕e2 ♗g7 7 0-0 0-0 8 ♖d1 ♕e8 9 c4 e5 10 dxe5 ♘xe5 11 ♗xd7?! ♘xf3+ 12 ♕xf3 ♘xd7

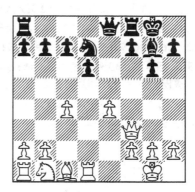

Black is already better.

13 ♕e2? f5 14 ♘d2 ♘c5 15 ♖e1 ♕f7 [15...♕a4!] **16 exf5 ♖ae8 17 fxg6?? hxg6?**

Overlooking 17...♕xg6 18 ♕f1 ♖xe1 19 ♕xe1 ♗d4, which wins immediately.

18 ♕f1 ♖xe1 19 ♕xe1 ♘d3 20 ♕f1 ♕xf2+ 21 ♕xf2 ♖xf2 22 ♘f3 ♖c2 23 ♗e3 ♘xb2 24 ♖b1 ♘xc4 25 ♗xa7 b6 26 ♗b8 ♘e3 27 ♘e1

27...♖e2?

Miles puts the game in jeopardy with this mistake. The c-pawn is Black's most valuable.

28 ♗xc7 ♗c3 29 ♘f3 ♖xg2+ 30 ♔h1 ♖f2 31 ♘g5 ♗e5 32 ♗xb6 ♖xh2+ 33 ♔g1 ♖e2 34 ♘f3 ♗f4 35 ♖e1 ♖xe1+ 36 ♘xe1 ♘c4 37 ♗d4 ♔f7 38 ♔f2 ♔e6 39 ♘g2 ♗d2 40 ♔f3 g5 41 ♔e4 d5+ 42 ♔d3 ♗a5 43 ♘e3 ♘xe3 44 ♗xe3 g4 45 ♗f4 ♗b6 46 ♗g3 ♔d7 47 ♗f4 ♔c6 48 ♗g3 ♗c5 49 a4 ♗d6 50 ♗e1? [50 ♗h4!] 50...g3 51 ♔e2 g2 0-1

Game 62
L.Rozman-J.Schuyler
Washington 2012

1 e4 ♘c6 2 ♘f3 d6 3 d4 ♘f6 4 c3 g6 5 ♗d3 ♗g7 6 0-0 0-0 7 h3 e5 8 ♘a3 d5!

White has the slow c2-c3 and h3-h3 under his belt, and the decentralizing ♘a3, so I felt it was time to hit back in the centre.

9 ♗g5?! dxe4 10 ♗xe4 exd4 11 ♗xc6?!

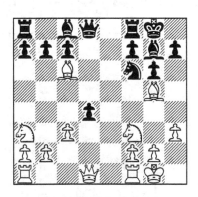

White was hoping to damage my structure instead of accepting the isolated d-pawn. This would have been fine for Black, but I saw something I liked better.

11...dxc3! 12 ♕a4?!

The critical tries involved saving the bishop, but since Black was getting three pawns for it, including the dangerous b2-pawn, I was willing to take my chances (and White was not).

12...bxc6 13 ♕xc6?

Either 13 bxc3 or 13 ♖ad1 was correct.

13...cxb2 14 ♖ad1 ♗d7 15 ♕c2 ♕c8?!

I was eager to break the pins, but analysis shows I could have safely made it harder for White to recover the b-pawn with 15...♖b8!.

16 ♕xb2 ♘e4 17 ♕b4 ♖e8

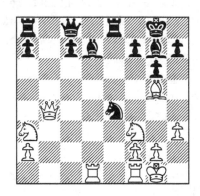

Incidentally threatening 18...♗xh3 19 gxh3 ♕xh3, which will win the piece back on the kingside.

18 ♔h2?

Not a working defence, though neither one of us noticed the obvious refutation: 18...♗xh3! 19 gxh3 ♕f5, again recovering the piece.

18...♗f8! 19 ♕a5 ♗d6+ 20 ♔g1 ♗xh3 21 gxh3 ♕xh3 22 ♖d3 ♘g3! 23 fxg3 ♕xg3+ 24 ♔h1 ♖e2 0-1

Do not try this at home, or even when away from home

Game 63
A.Zapata-A.Miles
Matanzas 1995

1 e4 ♘c6 2 ♘f3 d6 3 d4 ♘f6 4 ♘bd2 g6 5 c3 ♗g7 6 ♗b5 0-0 7 0-0 ♗d7

7...a6 is better, trying to pick up the bishop pair. Black's bishop may prefer to deploy on b7 or a6.

8 ♖e1 ♕e8 9 ♗f1 e5 10 h3 ♕d8 11 a4 ♖e8 12 a5 a6 13 d5 ♘e7 14 c4 ♖f8

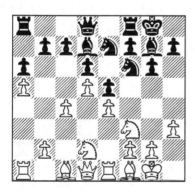

While each of Black's moves had its purpose, the overall impression is very poor. This is a bad King's Indian.

15 c5 ♘e8 16 ♘c4 ♘c8 17 ♕b3 ♗b5 18 ♗e3 ♖b8 19 ♖ac1 ♘f6 20 ♘fd2 ♘d7 21 cxd6 cxd6 22 ♕a3 ♘f6 23 ♘b6 ♗xf1 24 ♔xf1 ♘a7 25 ♕b4 ♘b5 26 ♘b1 ♘e8 27 ♘c3 ♘xc3 28 ♖xc3 ♘c7 29 ♘c4

Without making any obvious mis-

takes, most of White's pressure has dissipated.

29...♘b5 30 ♖cc1 f5 31 ♘a3 ♘xa3 32 ♕xa3 ♕d7 33 ♗b6 ♖bc8 34 ♕b3 ♗h6 35 ♖a1 ♗g5 36 ♖a4?!

By now, White is actually worse.

36...♗d8 37 ♖b4 fxe4 38 ♗xd8?! ♕xd8 39 ♖xb7 ♕xa5 40 ♕d1? [40 ♕b4] **40...♕c5 41 ♕d2 ♖f4?**

41...♖xf2+! 42 ♔xf2 ♖f8 wins.

42 ♔g1 ♕d4 43 ♖d1 ♕xd2 44 ♖xd2 a5 45 ♖b6 ♖c1+ 46 ♔h2 ♖f6 47 ♖b5 ♖f1 48 ♔g3 h5 49 ♖xa5 ♖f4 50 f3?? exf3?

Here 50...e3! 51 ♖c2 ♖h1 52 h4 g5.

51 gxf3 ♖1xf3+ 52 ♔g2 h4 53 ♖a6 ♖f6 54 ♖a4 ♖3f4 55 b4 ♔g7 56 ♖b2 ♔h6 57 ♖a7 ♖f3 58 b5? [58 ♔h2] **58...♖g3+ 59 ♔h2 ♖ff3 60 ♖a4 ♖xh3+ 61 ♔g1 ♖hg3+ 62 ♖g2 ♖xg2+ 63 ♔xg2 ♖b3 0-1**

Try this at home

Game 64
F.Nijboer-A.Miles
Linares 1995

1 e4 ♘c6 2 ♘f3 d6 3 d4 ♘f6 4 ♘bd2 g6

5 ♗b5 a6 6 ♗xc6+ bxc6

As we will see, this position is much easier to play than ...♗d7 of the previous game. Miles's methods of play are worth remembering and repeating.

7 0-0 ♗g7 8 e5 ♘d5 9 c4 ♘b6 10 ♕e2 0-0 11 ♖d1 a5 12 ♘f1 ♗a6 [12...f6!?] 13 b3 ♕d7 14 ♘g5 ♗c8 15 f4 a4 16 ♗e3 f6! 17 ♘f3 ♕e8 18 h3 fxe5 19 fxe5 h6 20 ♖ac1 axb3 21 axb3 g5

Black has been preparing ...♗f5, though after White's next the plan changes.

22 d5 cxd5 23 cxd5 ♗a6 24 ♕d2 ♗xf1 25 ♖xf1 ♕b5 26 ♖fd1?! ♕xb3 27 ♖xc7? ♘c4 28 ♕d3 ♕xd3 29 ♖xd3 ♖a1+ 30 ♔f2 ♘xe5 31 ♖d2 ♖f7 32 ♖a7? ♖b1? [32...♖h1] 33 ♖a4 ♔h7 34 ♔g3 ♖b3 35 ♖e4 ♖a3 36 h4?! ♘xf3 37 gxf3 gxh4+ 38 ♔g4 ♗f6 39 f4 ♖g7+ 40 ♔f5 h3 41 ♖h2 ♖g3 42 ♗c5? dxc5 0-1

1 e4 ♘c6 2 ♘f3 d6 3 d4 ♘f6 4 ♘c3 g6 5 ♗b5 a6 6 ♗xc6+ bxc6 7 0-0 ♗g7 8 ♕e2 0-0 9 ♖d1 ♗g4

This makes it easier to fight for the central dark squares and advances a clear plan. Nonetheless, I prefer 9...a5 and 10...♗a6.

10 h3 ♗xf3 11 ♕xf3 ♘d7 12 ♗e3 e5 13 ♕e2 ♖e8 14 ♕c4?!

White could have bottled up Black's bishop and rook with 14 d5!.

14...exd4 15 ♗xd4 ♗xd4 16 ♕xd4 ♕g5 17 ♕d2 ♕h4 18 ♖e1 ♘c5 19 f3 ♖e5 20 ♕f2 ♕e7 21 ♘e2 ♘e6 22 ♘d4 ♘xd4 23 ♕xd4 a5 24 ♕c3 ♖c5 25 ♕d2 ♖e8 26 a4 ♕f6 27 c3 ♖b8 28 ♖e2 ♖e5 29 ♖ae1 g5 30 ♕e3 c5 31 ♕d3 ♕e6 32 ♕a6 c4 33 ♕a7 ♖c8 34 ♕d4 ♖e8 35 ♔f1 f6 36 ♕d2 ♔f7 37 ♔g1 ♔e7 38 ♔h2 ♔d7 39 ♕d4 ♕f7 40 ♕f2 h5 41 ♔g1 c5 42 ♖d2 f5 43 ♖ed1 ♖8e6 44 ♕e2 fxe4 45 ♕xc4

Black has been pressing hard for the win, but without anything to work with. Now he is in danger.

45...♕f4?! 46 ♕a6?!

46 ♕b5+ ♔e7 47 ♕b7+ ♔f8 48 fxe4 is stronger.

46...exf3 47 ♖xd6+ ♔e7 48 ♕a7+ ♔f6 49 ♖xe6+ ♖xe6 50 ♕xc5 ♔g6 51 ♕d4 ♕f5 52 g4 hxg4 53 hxg4 ♕f7? 54 ♖f1?!

And here 54 b4!.

54...♖f6 55 ♔f2?! ♕b3 56 ♕d3+ ♔g7 57 ♖d1 ♕xb2+ 58 ♖d2 ♕b8 59 ♕d7+ ♔h6 60 ♔f1 ♕b1+ 61 ♖d1 ♕e4 62 ♕d2??

After this move White is losing. 62 ♖d2 held the balance.

62...f2 63 ♕d5 ♕xg4 64 ♕h1+ ♔g6 [64...♔g7!] 65 ♖d4

65...♕c8?

65...♕e6 (or 65...♕f5) 66 ♕e4+ (forced) 66...♕xe4 67 ♖xe4 ♔h5 wins, since if 68 ♖e2 then 68...♔g4 69 ♖xf2 ♖xf2+ 70 ♔xf2 ♔f4 etc.

66 ♕e4+ ♔h6 67 ♕e3 ♕f5 68 ♕d3? ♕xd3+ 69 ♖xd3 ♖g6??

69...♔h5 still wins.

70 c4 ½-½

♗c4 ♘c6 6 d5 ♘b8 7 h3 0-0 8 0-0 c6 [8...e5!] 9 a4! a5 10 ♖e1 ♘fd7!

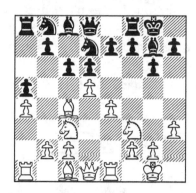

Black clamps down on the dark squares, incidentally stopping White from considering the e4-e5 break.

11 ♗e3 ♘a6 12 ♗d4 [12 ♗xa6!] **12...♘b4 13 ♗xg7 ♔xg7 14 ♘e2 ♕c7 15 c3 cxd5 16 ♗xd5 ♘c6 17 ♘ed4 ♘f6?!**

Weakening the dark square control. White now has 18 ♗xc6 bxc6 19 e5 with a pleasant advantage.

18 ♕b3?! ♘e5! 19 ♘xe5 dxe5 20 ♘f3 ♖a6 21 ♖ac1 ♘h5 22 ♗c4?! ♖f6 23 ♘d2?! ♕c5 24 ♖e3 ♖d8 25 ♘f1?! ♘f4 26 ♕b5 ♕c7 27 ♕b3 h5 28 ♕a2 ♖fd6 29 ♕b3 ♗d7 30 ♗b5 ♗e6 31 ♕c2 h4 32 ♖ee1 ♕c8 33 ♖e3 g5 34 f3?! ♘h5 [34...♕c5!] 35 ♖ce1 [35 ♖ee1] 35...♕c5 36 ♔h2 ♔f8 37 ♖d3?! ♖xd3 38 ♗xd3 ♗xh3! 0-1

Game 66
N.Praznik-A.Beliavsky
Bled 1999

1 e4 d6 2 d4 ♘f6 3 ♘c3 g6 4 ♘f3 ♗g7 5

Game 67
K.Nemcova-F.Olafsson
Marianske Lazne 2008

1 e4 d6 2 d4 g6 3 ♘c3 ♗g7 4 ♗e3 ♘c6 5

d5 ♘b8 6 ♕d2 c6 7 ♘f3 ♘f6 8 h3 b5?!

This is a great idea if it works out tactically, but it doesn't. 9 dxc6 b4 10 ♗b5 is a problem for Black. So let us imagine instead that the game went 8...0-0 9 ♗d3 b5 10 a3 a6 11 dxc6 etc.

9 a3 a6 10 dxc6 ♘xc6 11 ♗d3 0-0 12 0-0 ♗b7

Black's opening has been extremely successful – White's game has a cramped feel in spite of her central space advantage.

13 ♖fe1 d5?!

This "freeing" move is quite unnecessary. Black has many improvements he can make (such as ...♖c8, ...♘d7, ...♕a5, or even ...e7-e6) before he needs to consider taking action. It is White who will be left without anything constructive to do.

14 ♗h6?

I've never heard anyone say that it's a good idea to react to central action with play on the wings.

14...dxe4 15 ♗xg7 ♔xg7 16 ♘xe4 ♘d4 17 ♘xd4 ♕xd4 18 ♕c3 ♕xc3 19 ♘xc3 e6

White is slightly worse due to her very restricted bishop, though she solves this problem quickly.

20 ♘e4 ♖fd8 21 ♘c5 ♗c6 22 a4 bxa4 23 ♘xa4 ♗b5 24 ♘c5 ♖ac8 25 b4 ♖d4 26 ♗xb5 axb5 27 c3 ♖c4 28 ♖a7 ♔g8 29 ♖b7?! [29 ♖e3 ♘d5 30 ♖f3] **29...♖xc3 30 ♖xb5 ♘d5 31 ♖b7 ♘xb4 32 ♖xb4 ♖8xc5**

A theoretical draw, but Black has some practical chances.

33 ♖e2 ♖5c4 34 ♖bb2 g5!

This stops White from constructing the ideal defensive pawn formation for this endgame: f2/g3/h4. The point of the formation is that Black cannot create a passed pawn without trading off all the rest of the pawns.

35 ♔h2 ♔g7 36 ♖b5 ♔g6 37 ♖bb2 h5 38 ♖a2 h4 39 ♖e1 ♖c5 40 ♔g1 ♔f5 41 ♔f1 e5 42 f3 ♖3c4 43 ♖ee2 ♔f4 44 ♔f2 f5 45 ♖a3 ♖b5 46 ♖ae3?

The endgame has been getting harder to defend. Now, White is lost.

46...♖c1 47 ♖e1 ♖b2+ 48 ♖3e2 ♖cc2 49 ♖xc2 ♖xc2+ 50 ♔f1 ♖b2 51 ♔g1 ♔g3 0-1

Game 68
J.Hjartarson-F.Olafsson
Reykjavik 1995

1 e4 g6 2 d4 d6 3 ♘c3 ♗g7 4 ♗e3 ♘c6 5 d5 ♘b8 6 ♕d2 c6 7 ♘f3 ♘f6 8 h3 0-0 9 ♗e2 b5! 10 a3

White has nothing better than this lame try. Black has equalized already.

10...a6 11 0-0 ♗b7 12 ♖fe1 ♘bd7 13 dxc6 ♗xc6 14 ♗d3 ♗b7 15 ♗h6 ♖c8 16 ♖ad1 ♕b6 17 ♗xg7 ♔xg7 18 ♖e3 ♘e5 19 ♘xe5 dxe5 20 ♖e2 ♖fd8

By now Black is a little better, but the players soon decided to call it a day.

21 ♕e3 ♕d4 22 ♖de1 ♘h5 ½-½

Game 69
Y.Gruenfeld-I.Smirin
Israeli Team
Championship 1997

1 e4 d6 2 d4 ♘f6 3 ♘c3 g6 4 ♘f3 ♗g7 5 ♗e2 0-0 6 0-0 ♘c6 7 d5 ♘b8 8 h3 e5 9 dxe6 ♗xe6 10 ♗g5 h6 11 ♗e3 ♘c6 12

♕d2 ♔h7 13 ♖ad1 ♖e8 14 ♖fe1 ♗d7 15 ♗c4 ♗e6 16 ♗f1 a6

17 ♕c1

Very soon Black has all the play he needs. White can make him work harder with 17 a4.

17...♕c8 18 a3 b5 19 ♘d4 ♘xd4 20 ♗xd4 ♕b7 21 ♕f4 ♘d7 22 ♗xg7 ♔xg7 23 ♕d2 ♕b6 24 ♖e3 ♖ad8 25 g3 ♘f6 26 ♗g2 a5 27 b3 ♖b8 28 a4 bxa4?! [28...b4] 29 ♘xa4 ♕b4 30 ♘c3 ♘d7 31 ♔h2 ♘c5 32 f4 f6?! 33 ♕e2?! [33 f5!] 33...♗f7 34 ♘d5 ♗xd5 35 exd5 ♖xe3 36 ♕xe3 ♖f8 37 f5 g5 38 ♕e2 ♘d7 39 ♖a1 ♘e5 40 ♖a4 ♕c3 41 ♖e4 ♖b8 42 ♕h5 ♖b4 43 ♖e2 a4 44 ♕e8 axb3 ½-½

Game 70
B.Chatalbashev-M.Popchev
Cacak 1991

1 d4 d6 2 e4 ♘f6 3 ♘c3 g6 4 ♘f3 ♗g7 5 ♗e2 0-0 6 0-0 ♗g4 7 ♗e3 ♘c6 8 d5 ♘b8 9 ♘d4 ♗xe2 10 ♕xe2 c5 11 ♘f3 ♕b6 12 ♖ab1 ♕a6

Chernin points out that this queen

manoeuvre is both typical and strong.
13 ♕d2 ♘g4 14 ♗g5 ♖e8 15 ♕f4 ♘e5 16 ♘xe5 ♗xe5 17 ♕h4 ♕c4

18 ♖be1

White gains nothing by grabbing the pawn: 18 ♗xe7 ♘d7 19 f4 ♗d4+ 20 ♔h1 ♗xc3 21 bxc3 ♕xe4 is equal.
18...♗xc3 19 bxc3 f6 20 ♗h6 ♘d7 21 ♕g4 e6 22 f4 ♖ad8 23 dxe6 ♕xe6 24 ♕g3 ♕xa2 25 f5 ♕f7 26 fxg6 hxg6 27 ♕xd6 ♔h7 28 ♕f4?!

It is time to extricate the bishop.
28...♖e5 29 ♗g5 ♖f8 30 ♕h4+ ♔g8 31 ♗f4 ♖e6 32 ♖f3 g5 33 ♕g4 ♖fe8 34 ♗g3 ♘e5 35 ♗xe5 ♖xe5 36 h4?! ♕e6 37 ♕h5 ♔g7 38 ♖ef1??

Oops! Black had an advantage, but this throws the game.
38...♖h8 39 ♕xh8+ ♔xh8 40 ♖xf6 ♕c4 0-1

♘c3 0-0 6 0-0 ♗g4 7 ♗e3 ♘c6 8 d5 ♘b8 9 ♘g5 ♗xe2 10 ♕xe2 c6 11 ♖ad1 ♕a5 12 f4 ♕a6 13 ♕f3 ♘bd7 14 ♕h3 h6! 15 ♘f3 h5! 16 ♗d4?! c5 17 ♗xf6 ♘xf6 18 ♕h4?! b5

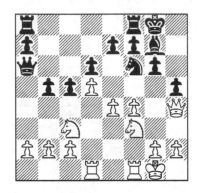

White hasn't gotten anything done on the kingside, but he has serious problems on the queen's wing.
19 ♘e2?! ♕a4 20 ♘g3 ♕xc2 21 e5 dxe5 22 fxe5 ♘g4 23 ♖d2 ♕c4 24 ♕xe7 ♖ae8 25 d6?!

A desperate try for complications which fails after Chernin's accurate treatment.
25...♗h6! 26 b3 ♕b4 27 e6 ♖xe7 28 dxe7 ♗xd2 29 exf7+ ♔xf7 30 exf8♕+ ♔xf8 31 ♘xd2+ ♔g7 32 ♘ge4 ♕d4+ 33 ♔h1 c4 34 bxc4 bxc4 35 h3 ♘e3 36 ♖f4 c3 37 ♘f3 ♕d1+ 38 ♔h2 ♘f1+ 39 ♔g1 ♘d2+ 40 ♔f2 ♘xe4+ 41 ♖xe4 c2 0-1

Game 71
R.Ziatdinov-A.Chernin
New York Open 1998

1 e4 g6 2 d4 ♗g7 3 ♘f3 d6 4 ♗e2 ♘f6 5

Game 72
So.Polgar-J.Fries Nielsen
Rimavska Sobota 1991

1 e4 g6 2 d4 ♗g7 3 ♘c3 ♘c6 4 ♘f3

If 4 ♗e3, Fries Nielsen intended 4...d5, an interesting and surprising move that I don't believe in.

4...d6 5 h3 ♘f6 6 ♗g5 0-0 7 ♕d2 d5

In the next game, Black tries the enterprising 7...a6.

8 exd5 ♘xd5 9 ♗h6 ♘xc3 10 ♗xg7 ♔xg7 11 ♕xc3 ♕d5 12 0-0-0!

12 ♗c4?! ♕a5 is ineffective.

12...♗e6 13 b3 ♗f5 14 ♘h4 ♗d7 15 ♖d2?! ♔g8 16 ♕e3 ♕d6 17 c3 a5 18 ♘f3 ♕a3+

19 ♔d1?!

Asking for trouble. 19 ♖b2 was correct.

19...a4 20 ♕h6 f6 21 ♗c4+ e6 22 d5 ♘e7?

Since White has counterplay in either case, it does not help to give up the pawn. Hence 22...♘d8!.

23 dxe6 ♗c6 24 ♘d4 axb3 25 ♘xc6 bxc6 26 ♗xb3 ♖ab8 27 ♖e1?!

The way to extricate the king is 27 ♔e2! ♖xb3 28 axb3 ♕xb3 29 ♖hd1.

27...♖xb3 28 axb3 ♕xb3+ 29 ♔e2 ♕c4+ 30 ♖d3?

Walking into a dangerous pin. 30

♔f3! is still approximately equal.

30...♘d5 31 g3?

My computer tells me that White is okay after 31 e7!! ♖e8 32 ♔d2 and that all other moves lose brutally. I won't try to explain, especially since I don't understand it myself.

31...♖a8 32 ♕d2 ♖a2 33 ♖b1 ♘xc3+ 34 ♔e1 ♕e4+ 0-1

35...♕h1 mate follows.

1 e4 ♘c6 2 ♘f3 d6 3 d4 ♘f6 4 ♘c3 g6 5 h3 ♗g7 6 ♗g5 0-0 7 ♕d2 a6 8 0-0-0 b5 9 a3 ♖b8 10 ♗h6 b4 11 axb4 ♘xb4 12 ♗xg7 ♔xg7 13 e5 ♘fd5 14 ♘xd5 ♘xd5 15 h4 h5 16 ♘g5?!

The knight can stay here as long as it wants, but it does not have important targets in Black's position.

16...c6 17 ♗c4 ♕b6 18 b3 ♗f5 19 exd6 exd6 20 g4 ♗xg4 21 ♖dg1?! ♗f5 22 ♘h3 ♕b4 23 ♕xb4 ♖xb4 24 ♖g3 a5 25

♗xd5 cxd5 26 ♖d1 ♖c8 27 ♖d2 a4 28 ♔b2 axb3 29 cxb3 ♖cc4 30 ♘f4 ♖xd4 31 ♖xd4 ♖xd4 32 ♘xh5+ ♔f8 33 ♘f6 ♖d1 34 h5 gxh5 35 ♘xh5 d4 36 ♖g5?! ♖d2+ 37 ♔c1 ♖xf2 38 ♘g3 ♗g6 39 ♖d5 ♖g2 40 ♘h5 ♖f2 41 ♘g3 ♖f3 42 ♘e2 d3 43 ♘c3 ♔e7 44 b4 ♔e6 45 ♖d4 ♖f2 46 ♘b5 ♖c2+ 47 ♔d1 ♗h5+ 48 ♔e1 ♖e2+ 49 ♔f1 d2 0-1

Game 74
N.Ryba-J.Schuyler
Washington 2012

1 e4 ♘c6 2 ♘f3 d6 3 d4 ♘f6 4 ♘c3 g6 5 ♗e2 ♗g7 6 0-0 0-0 7 h3 a6!?

Against a lower-rated opponent there is some concern that the natural move, 7...e5, will lead to a position with too few winning chances, in which case 7...a6 is often a good alternative.

8 a4 e5

It is nice for me to have the b5-square covered and his b4-square weak. Therefore, if 9 dxe5, Black will play 9...dxe5, keeping the extra pair of knights on the board.

9 ♗e3?!

It is almost always a bad idea for White to try to preserve the central tension in the Dark Knight Pirc. This is especially true when he has played h2-h3. Black is already at least equal.

9...exd4 10 ♘xd4 ♖e8

One Pirc author recommends 10...♗d7 first in this type of position, but I prefer to have my c-pawns dou-

bled! The half-open b-file co-ordinates well with the dark-squared bishop, and it is nice to have the d5-square securely guarded.

11 ♘xc6 bxc6 12 ♗f3 ♘d7 13 ♕d2 ♖b8 14 ♖ab1 ♕f6 15 ♗e2 ♕e5 16 ♖fd1 ♕a5

It is often deflating to computer-check your own games. This queen manoeuvre, which I was proud of during the game, accomplishes less than nothing after 17 b4! ♖xb4?! 18 ♘d5! ♖xa4 19 ♕xa5 ♖xa5 20 ♘xc7 ♖xe4 21 ♖xd6 with an edge for White.

17 ♗d4 ♗xd4 18 ♕xd4 ♖b4 19 ♕d2 ♘c5

This will not get anything done either. Black is not even threatening 20...♘xa4 because of 21 ♖a1 and 22 b3.

20 b3 ♘xe4 21 ♘xe4 ♖exe4 22 ♗f3 ♖e5 23 ♗xc6 ♗f5 24 ♗f3 ♕c5 25 c3 ♖b8 26 b4 ♕c4 27 ♖b2 ♖be8 28 ♕d4 ♕e6 29 ♔h2 ♗e4!

It isn't much, but I will have a little something to play for after stripping White's king of its best defender. Who knows? The e-file might even be worth something.

30 ♗xe4 ♖xe4 31 ♕d3 a5 32 ♕d5 ♕f6 33 ♕xa5 ♕xc3 34 ♖bb1 c5?!

This is another move that seemed very strong to me when I played it, but White can equalize starting with 35 ♕b6! (the text move is not bad, either). 34...♖e2 is a better try. But by now we were running low on time to reach move 40.

35 ♕b5 cxb4 36 ♖xd6 ♖8e5 37 ♕b8+ ♔g7 38 ♖d8 ♖f5 39 ♖g8+ ♔h6 40 ♕f8+ ♔g5 41 ♕d8+ f6 42 ♖e8 ♖d4 43 ♕e7?

Houdini finds 43 f4+! ♖fxf4 44 ♖e5+ with equality. White is lost after any other move.

43...♖xf2 44 ♖e1 ♖d3??

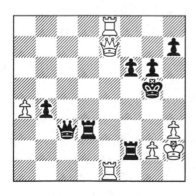

Threatening 45...♖xh3+ 46 ♔g1 ♖xg2+ and wins! Somehow I overlooked *both* of White's defences.

45 ♕xh7

Or 45 h4+! ♔xh4 46 ♕xh7+ ♔g5 47 ♖1e4, when Black has to find 47...♖xg2+! 48 ♔xg2 ♖d2+ 49 ♖e2 ♖d4! and draws (apparently).

45...♖dd2

This is the move that would have won last turn.

46 ♖g1??

Snatching defeat from the jaws of a draw. My opponent saw the correct continuation but misevaluated it: 46 h4+ ♔f5 47 ♖8e5+ ♕xe5 (47...fxe5 48 ♕f7+ ♔g4 49 ♖e4+ ♖f4 50 ♕xg6+ ♔xh4 51 ♕h6+ draws) 48 ♖xe5 fxe5 49 ♕f7+ ♔e4 50 ♕b7+ is no worse for White.

46...♕c6 47 h4+ ♔f5 0-1

Not the most beautiful game, but the opening was a success.

Game 75
N.Jhunjhnuwala-S.Gligoric
Lucerne Olympiad 1982

1 ♘f3 g6 2 e4 d6 3 d4 ♗g7 4 ♘c3 ♘f6 5 ♗e2 0-0 6 0-0 ♘c6 7 h3 e5 8 d5 ♘e7 9 ♗e3 c6!

White is unable to keep his centre intact, nor is he fast enough on the d-file to inconvenience Black.

10 dxc6 bxc6 11 ♕d2 ♕c7 12 ♖ad1 d5 13 exd5 ♘exd5 14 ♘xd5?!

Helpfully completing the opposing centre. Black starts building his edge.

14...cxd5 15 c3 ♗b7 16 ♗h6 ♘e4 17 ♕c1 ♖fe8 18 ♗xg7 ♔xg7 19 ♘d2 ♘c5 20 ♘b3 ♘e6 21 ♖fe1 a5

22 ♗b5 ♖e7?!

Black does not have a good reason to disconnect his rooks. However, White's next makes it easy to fix the problem.

23 ♗f1? [23 a4] **23...a4 24 ♘a1 ♖d8 25 ♘c2 f6 26 ♘b4 ♕b6 27 ♕c2 ♘c5 28 a3 ♖ed7 29 ♖e3 ♘b3 30 ♖ee1 ♖d6 31 ♕e2 d4 32 ♕b5 ♕xb5 33 ♗xb5 dxc3 34 ♖xd6 ♖xd6 35 bxc3 ♘c5 36 ♖e2 ♖d1+ 37 ♔h2 e4 38 ♔g3 f5 39 h4 ♔f6 40 ♗e8? h6?** [40...♖h1!] **41 ♗b5?** [41 ♔h2!] **41...♖h1 42 f4 g5 43 hxg5+ hxg5 44 fxg5+?! ♔xg5 45 ♔f2 f4 46 ♗c6? ♗xc6 0-1**

Since after 47 ♘xc6 the reply 47...♘d3 is mate.

Game 76
G.Bastrikov-E.Geller
Tashkent 1958

1 e4 e5 2 ♘f3 ♘c6 3 ♘c3 d6 4 h3 g6 5 d4 exd4 6 ♘xd4 ♗g7 7 ♗e3 ♘f6 8 ♕d2 0-0 9 0-0-0 ♖e8 10 f3 ♘xd4 11 ♗xd4 ♗e6 12 ♗f2 a6 13 ♔b1 b5 14 h4 c5 15 g4?

White can play the aggressive 15 h5!? or the defensive 15 a3 – the text move is too slow.

15...b4 16 ♘e2?!

16...♕a5?

Black gets a big advantage with 16...♘xe4! 17 fxe4 ♕f6, threatening mate and White's bishop.

17 ♘c1 ♗xg4?! 18 ♗g2?

Black's sacrifice is thematic, but not quite sound. 18 fxg4 ♘xe4 19 ♕f4 ♘c3+?! 20 bxc3 bxc3 21 ♗c4 is defence and counterattack.

18...♗e6 19 ♕xd6 ♖ac8 20 ♘b3 ♕a4 21 ♗h3? ♗f8?

Unnecessarily removing the bishop from the main diagonal and misevaluating the most direct continuation: 21...♗xh3 22 ♖xh3 c4 23 ♘c5 ♕b5 threatens 24...♖c6.

22 ♕h2?! ♗xh3 23 ♕xh3 c4 24 ♘c1 c3 25 ♗d4 cxb2 26 ♘b3 ♗g7 27 ♗xb2 ♕c6 28 ♖h2 ♖ed8 29 ♖hd2? ♖xd2 30 ♖xd2

30...♘xe4! 31 fxe4 ♗xb2 32 h5 [32 ♔xb2?! ♕c3+] **32...♕c3 33 ♕xc3 ♗xc3 34 ♖d1 ♔g7 35 ♖d6 ♗c4 0-1**

Game 77
D.Saduakassova-
Art.Minasian
Dubai 2011

1 e4 ♘c6 2 ♘f3 d6 3 ♘c3 ♘f6 4 d4 g6 5 h3 ♗g7 6 ♗e3 0-0 7 ♕d2 e5 8 d5 ♘e7 9 ♗h6

White trades her best minor piece for Black's obstructed bishop in the hope of weakening his king position.
9...♗d7!

Preparing ...c7-c6 and/or ...b7-b5.
10 ♗d3 c6

10...b5 11 a3 a5 and 12...b4 is also good.

11 dxc6 ♗xc6 12 ♗xg7 ♔xg7 13 0-0 ♕c7 [13...b5!?] **14 ♕e2 ♖fe8 15 ♗b5 a6** [15...d5!] **16 ♗xc6 ♕xc6 17 ♖ad1 ♖ac8 18 ♘d2?! d5 19 exd5 ♘exd5 20 ♘xd5 ♘xd5 21 c4 ♘f4 22 ♕e4 f5 23 ♕xc6 ♖xc6 24 b3 ♘e2+ 25 ♔h2 ♘c3 26 ♖a1 ♖d6 27 ♘b1 ♘xb1 28 ♖axb1 ♖d2**

Rook endgames are notoriously drawish, but according to Jesus de la Villa in *100 Endgames You Must Know*, this reputation is unearned. With his better rooks and king, Black has his winning chances.

29 a4 ♔f6 30 ♔g1 e4 31 ♖fe1 ♖ed8 32 ♔f1 ♔e5 33 c5 ♖c2 34 ♖ed1 ♖d3! 35 b4 ♖a3 36 ♖dc1 ♖xc1+ 37 ♖xc1 ♖xa4 38 c6 bxc6 39 ♖xc6 ♔d5 40 ♖c7 ♖xb4 41 ♖xh7 ♖b6 42 h4 ♔c4 43 g3 a5 44 ♖c7+ ♔b5 45 h5 gxh5 46 ♖f7 ♔c4 47 ♖xf5 ♖a6 48 ♖xh5 a4 49 ♖h8 a3 50 ♖c8+ ♔d4 51 ♖d8+ ♔e5 52 ♖d1 a2 53 ♖a1 ♔f5 54 ♔e2 ♖a3 55 ♔f1 ♔e5 56 ♔e2 ♔d4 57 g4 ♔e5 58 ♔d2 ♔f4 59 ♔c1

♔xg4 60 ♔b2 ♖a8 0-1

1 e4 d6 2 d4 ♘f6 3 ♘c3 g6 4 ♘f3 ♗g7 5
♗e2 0-0 6 0-0 ♘c6 7 ♗g5 h6 8 ♗f4 ♘g4
9 h3 e5 10 dxe5 ♘gxe5 11 ♘xe5 dxe5
12 ♗e3 ♘d4 13 ♗c4 ♕h4 14 ♘d5?!

Not appreciating the danger. By relinquishing control over e4, White sub-
jects himself to a powerful attack. 14 f3
or 14 ♗d3 is still approximately equal,
but nobody likes to play such moves.
14...c6! 15 ♘c7 ♗xh3!

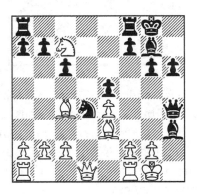

Now White must defend accurately
to survive, and even then he will be
worse – there is no good way for him to
retain a material advantage.
16 ♘xa8 ♕xe4

The queen's arrival on this square is
a nightmare for White, who has far too
many bishops lying around.
**17 gxh3 ♘f3+ 18 ♔h1 ♘h4+ 19 f3 ♕xe3
20 ♘c7 ♕f4 21 ♕d3 ♕g3 22 ♕e2 e4?!**

[22...♘f5!] 23 ♕h2 ♕xh2+ 24 ♔xh2
♘xf3+ 25 ♔h1 ♘d2 26 ♘e8?? [26 ♘e6!]
26...♘xc4 27 ♘xg7 ♔xg7 28 ♖fe1 f5 29
♖ad1 ♖f7 30 b3 ♘e5 31 ♖d6 ♘f3 32
♖ed1 ♖e7 33 ♖d7 ♔f7 34 ♔g2 f4 35
♖1d6 ♘h4+ 36 ♔f1 e3 37 c4 e2+ 0-1

1 e4 g6 2 d4 ♗g7 3 ♘f3 d6 4 ♘c3 ♘f6 5
♗e2 0-0 6 0-0 ♘c6 7 ♗e3 e5 8 dxe5
dxe5 9 ♕xd8 ♖xd8 10 ♗c4

One might think that White plays
for a win with little risk. However,
White (a GM) also lost in M.Hebden-
E.Sutovsky, Isle of Man 1999. Black's
next is to prevent the annoying 11
♘g5.
10...h6 [10...♘e8!?] **11 h3 b6 12 ♘d5**
♘a5! 13 ♘xf6+ ♗xf6 14 ♗e2 ♗b7 15 b4
♘c6 16 c3 a5 17 a3 ♘e7 18 ♘d2 ♗g5!

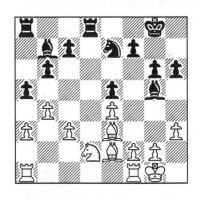

So far it's not much for Black, but
trading the worst minor for White's

best is the first step on the road to a win.

19 ♗xg5 hxg5 20 ♖ad1 axb4 21 axb4 ♔g7 22 f3 ♖a2 23 ♘c4 ♖xd1 24 ♗xd1 ♗a6 25 ♗b3 ♗xc4 26 ♗xa2 ♗xa2 27 ♖a1 ♗c4 28 ♖a7 b5 29 ♖xc7 ♔f6

Perhaps White should hold this, but he has a long and thankless defensive task ahead of him. Black's task is to penetrate with his king.

30 ♖a7 ♔e6 31 ♖a6+ ♔d7 32 ♖a7+ ♔d6 33 ♖a6+ ♘c6 34 ♔f2 ♔d7 35 ♔g3 ♘d8 36 h4 gxh4+ 37 ♔xh4 ♔e7 38 ♔g3 ♘e6 39 ♔f2 ♘f4 40 g3 ♘e2 41 ♖a3 ♔f6 42 ♔g2 ♔g5

And now White is lost. How did that happen?

43 ♔f2 f5 44 exf5 gxf5 45 ♔g2 f4 46 gxf4+ ♔xf4 47 ♔f2 ♘c1 48 ♖a8 ♘d3+ 49 ♔g2 ♔e3 50 ♔g3 ♔d2 51 ♖a3 ♔c2 52 ♔g4 ♔b2 53 ♖a7 ♔xc3 54 ♔f5 ♔xb4 0-1

Game 80
K.Wang-J.Schuyler
Washington 2012

1 e4 ♘c6 2 ♘f3 d6 3 d4 ♘f6 4 ♘c3 g6 5 ♗e3 ♗g7 6 ♕d2 0-0 7 ♗e2

White tries to play without h2-h3 – an uncommon plan. I was aware that 7...e5 was the main move, but as in Game 74, I wanted to spice things up. I couldn't remember for sure, but 7...a6 is usually a reasonable option.

7...a6?!

As it turns out, this is one position

where 7...e5! works a little better than usual and 7...a6 works a little worse than usual.

8 d5! ♘b8 9 a4!

Since a2-a4 is normally met by ...a7-a5, it stands to reason that Black's a-pawn is misplaced.

9...c6

I now believe that 9...b6 is the best move in the position, intending to follow with ...c7-c6, ...♗b7, ...♘bd7. At the time I was reluctant to try this since White had not spent a tempo on h2-h3 to prevent ...♗g4.

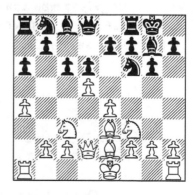

10 a5! ♘bd7 11 0-0 ♕c7 12 ♖fe1 ♘c5

This picks up the bishop pair, but I

will not be enjoying my pawn structure.

13 ♗xc5 dxc5 14 dxc6 bxc6

Ugly as this is, it is worse to allow White access to the d5-square.

15 ♗c4 ♖b8?!

Instead, 15...♘g4! frees the bishop and controls White's e-pawn.

16 e5 ♘g4 17 ♕e2 ♖xb2

Losing a bit of material, but it is no worse than anything else.

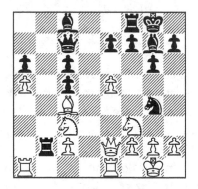

18 h3 ♘h6 19 ♗b3 c4?! [19...♘f5] **20 ♘a4 cxb3 21 ♘xb2 bxc2 22 ♕xc2 ♗e6 23 ♘d3 ♗d5 24 ♘d4 ♖d8?** [24...e6] **25 ♕c5 ♘f5 26 ♘xf5 gxf5 27 ♕b6 ♕xb6 28 axb6 ♖b8 29 ♖xa6 ♗c4 30 ♖a3?! e6? 31 ♘c5 ♗f8 32 ♘d7 ♗xa3 33 ♘xb8 ♗d5 34 b7 c5 35 ♘c6 1-0**

Game 81
R.Zelcic-M.Djurkovic
Pula 2001

1 e4 g6 2 d4 ♗g7 3 ♘c3 d6 4 ♗c4 ♘c6 5 ♘f3 ♘f6 6 ♕e2 ♗g4 7 e5 ♗xf3 8 gxf3 ♘xd4 9 exf6 ♘xe2 10 fxg7 ♖g8 11 ♔xe2 ♖xg7 12 ♗h6 ♖g8

"Everybody knows" three pieces are much better than a queen, but is this true regardless of how many pawns the queen has? Regardless of structural problems? Regardless of king position? As much fun as these positions can be to play, White is asking too much from his minors.

13 h4

This is played mainly to keep the bishop from getting cut off by an eventual ...g6-g5.

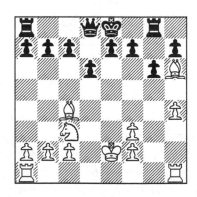

13...c6!

An important move to control White's minors, and uses those extra pawns well.

14 ℤhe1 ♕d7! 15 ℤad1 ♕f5

Activating the queen quickly is certainly the right idea, but 15...♕h3! (16 ℤh1 ♕f5) is more accurate.

16 ♗g5 0-0-0

17 ♔f1?

The queen is supposed to be harder to play, but not when the pieces have an exposed king. It is the GM who makes the first big mistake.

17...d5 18 ♗d3?! ♕h3+?!

This check would have been more useful to Black after grabbing the f-pawn.

19 ♔g1 f6 20 ♗f1 ♕xf3 21 ℤd3 ♕g4+ 22 ℤg3 ♕b4!

Black's queen is not done making trouble.

23 a3?! ♕a5?

White's bluff works. Every white pawn that disappears de-stabilizes White's pieces more. They are running short on support points, and they can't be left lying around loose. Hence 23...♕xb2!.

24 ♗d2 e5?! 25 ♘e4 ♕b6? [25...♕c7] 26

♘xf6 ℤgf8 27 ℤb3?

Just as White is getting back into the game, he plays this awful intermediate move, forcing Black to improve his queen position. White is not so badly off after 27 ℤf3, threatening 28 ♗h3+ and 29 ♘d7, while if 27...ℤf7 then 28 c4! ♔b8 (28...ℤdf8 29 ♗h3+ ♔c7 30 c5!) 29 ♘xd5 ℤxf3 30 ♘xb6 ℤxd2 31 ♘a4 ℤdxf2 and Black is "only" better.

27...♕c7 28 ℤf3?

White is in a bad way after 28 ♘g4 e4, but at least he doesn't lose more material.

28...ℤf7??

28...♕g7 29 ♗h3+ ♔c7 30 ♗g5 ℤd6 wins.

29 ♗h3+ ♔b8 30 ℤxc5 ♕xc5 31 ♗f4 ♕xf4 32 ℤxf4 ℤdf8 33 ♘d7+ ♔c7??

Yikes! When it rains, it pours. 33...♔a8! is still approximately even. The text walks into 34 ♘xf8 ℤxf4 35 ♘e6+.

34 ♘xf8 1-0

Game 82
H.Hughes-K.Richardson
British League 2004

1 e4 g6 2 d4 ♗g7 3 ♘c3 d6 4 ♗c4 ♘c6 5 ♘f3 ♘f6 6 0-0 0-0 7 ♗e3 ♘g4 8 ♗f4?! ♘xd4! 9 ♘xd4 e5 10 ♗e3 ♘xe3 11 fxe3 exd4 12 exd4 ♗e6 [12...c6!] 13 ♕d3 ♗xc4 [13...c5!] 14 ♕xc4 c6 15 ♔h1?! ♕b6 16 ℤad1 ℤad8?! [16...♕xb2] 17 b3 ♕a5 18 ℤf3 d5

19 exd5 cxd5 20 ♕c5 ♕xc5 21 dxc5 d4 22 ♘e2 ♖fe8 23 ♘c1 ♖c8 24 b4 b6 25 cxb6?!

It is no good to open the c-file for Black and allow him to press on the weak c2-pawn. 25 ♘b3 bxc5 26 bxc5 offers White better chances of a successful defence.

25...axb6 26 ♖f2 ♖c4 27 ♘d3 ♖ec8 28 ♔g1?! [28 a4] 28...♖xc2 29 ♖dd2? [29 a4] 29...♖xd2 30 ♖xd2 ♗h6 31 ♖b2 ♖c3 32 ♘e5 d3 33 ♘xd3 ♖xd3 34 ♔f1 ♖d2 0-1

1 e4 ♘c6 2 ♘f3 d6 3 d4 ♘f6 4 ♘c3 g6 5 ♗g5 ♗g7 6 ♕d2

Thanks to this move, and the fact that White is giving Black ...h7-h6 for free, the bishop no longer has enough squares to escape.

6...h6 7 ♗f4 g5 8 ♗g3 ♘h5 9 d5 ♘b8 10

♘d4 c5 11 ♗b5+ ♔f8!

The king is fine here. Black keeps the sensitive f5-square under control.

12 ♘f5 ♗xf5 13 exf5 ♕a5 14 ♗e2 ♘xg3 15 hxg3 ♘d7 16 0-0 c4 17 ♖fe1 ♖c8

Mohr has no shortage of ways to improve his position and has gained the advantage.

18 ♖ab1 ♖c7 19 ♕e3 ♗xc3 20 bxc3 ♘f6

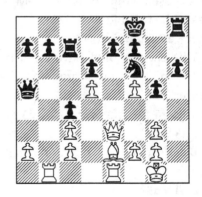

21 ♗xc4?

White is understandably unhappy with his position, but things are not yet as desperate as this. There will be no compensation for the piece.

21...♖xc4 22 ♕xe7+ ♔g7 23 ♕e3 ♔f8 24 ♕e7+ ♔g7 25 ♖xb7 ♖f8 26 ♕xd6

♕xd5 27 ♕a6 ♖xc3 28 g4 ♖xc2 29 ♖xa7 ♕d4 0-1

Game 84
D.Janowski-F.Yates
Marienbad 1925

1 d4 ♘f6 2 ♘f3 g6 3 ♘c3 ♗g7 4 e4 d6 5 ♗g5 ♘c6 6 ♕d2 h6 7 ♗e3 ♘g4 8 0-0-0

If the white bishop tries to slip away with 8 ♗f4, Black equalizes immediately with 8...♘xd4!.

8...♘xe3 9 ♕xe3 0-0 10 h3 a6

With the two players castled on opposite wings, the race is on.

11 g4 b5 12 ♖g1 ♘a5 13 ♗d3 c6 14 ♘e2?!

White is "racing" a little slowly. 14 e5 or 14 h4 is better.

14...♘c4 15 ♗xc4 bxc4 16 ♕c3 a5 17 e5 ♕b6 18 exd6 exd6 19 ♘g3

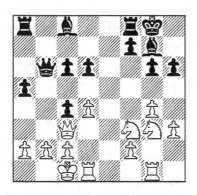

White is much worse, with no bishops and a weaker attack.

19...c5?! [19...♖b8] 20 ♘f5! cxd4 21 ♘3xd4 ♗xf5 22 gxf5 d5 23 ♖g2?! ♖ae8 24 f3 ♖e7?!

It is important to prevent 25 ♕d2, which allows White to escape the unpleasant pin and reorganize his defence. Hence 24...a4! 25 a3 ♖b8, threatening 26...♖fe8 and 27...♖e3.

25 ♕d2 a4 26 a3 ♖b8 27 c3 ♖eb7 28 fxg6 fxg6 29 ♕c2 g5 30 ♕xa4 ♕c5 31 ♖dd2 ♕f8 32 ♕a5 ♔h8 33 ♕xd5? ♕xa3! 34 ♕e4 ♕a1+ 35 ♕b1

What's the best move in this position?

35...♕a4?

Yates overlooks the problem-like 35...♕a8!!, which sets White the unenviable task of defending against ...♖a7-a1. (In fact Yates didn't play the second-best move either – 36...♕a5.)

36 ♖ge2 ♕a5 37 ♖e3 ♗f8 38 ♔d1 ♕c7 39 ♕f5 ♖a7 40 ♘b5 ♖a1+ 41 ♔c2 ♕h7 42 ♕xh7+ ♔xh7 43 ♘d6 ♗xd6 44 ♖xd6 ♖a2 45 ♖e7+ ♔g8 46 ♔d2 ♖axb2+ 47 ♔e3 ♖c2 48 ♖dd7 ♖xc3+ 49 ♔e4 ♔f8 50 ♖f7+ ♔g8 51 ♖g7+ ♔f8 52 f4 gxf4 53 ♖df7+ ♔e8 54 ♖c7 ♖g3 55 ♖h7 ♔f8 56 ♖h8+ ♖g8 57 ♖xh6 ♖e8+ 58 ♔f5 ♖g7 59 ♖h8+ ♖g8 60 ♖hh7 ♖g1 61 ♖h8+ ½-½

Game 85
A.Mista-M.Szelag
Koszalin 1999

1 e4 d6 2 d4 ♘f6 3 ♘c3 e5 4 ♘ge2 ♗e7 5 f3 0-0 6 ♗e3 exd4 7 ♘xd4 ♘c6 8 ♕d2 ♘xd4 9 ♗xd4 ♗e6 10 0-0-0 c6 11 g4 b5 12 b3 ♘d7 13 ♖g1 b4 14 ♘e2 c5 15 ♗b2

15...♘e5?!

Initiating complications that should not work out well for Black. 15...♖c8!? was better, with ideas of ...c5-c4.

16 ♕e3 ♕a5 17 f4 c4 18 fxe5 c3 19 ♘xc3 bxc3 20 ♗xc3 ♕xa2 21 exd6?!

21 ♔d2! ♕a3 (or 21...♗xb3 22 ♗d3 ♗xc2 23 ♖a1) 22 ♖a1 ♕c5 23 ♕xc5 dxc5 23 ♔e3 is good for White.

21...♗xd6 22 ♗xg7 ♗a3+

22...♖fc8! was stronger.

23 ♔d2 ♗b4+ 24 ♔c1??

Better is 24 ♗c3 ♖fd8+ 25 ♔e1 ♖xd1+ 26 ♔xd1 ♖d8+ 27 ♔e1 when White can still defend.

24...f6 25 ♗xf6 ♖xf6 26 ♕d4 ♖f2 27 ♕b2 ♗a3 0-1

Game 86
I.Jakic-Z.Mestrovic
Zadar 2001

1 e4 ♘c6 2 d4 d6 3 ♘c3 ♘f6 4 ♗g5 h6 5 ♗h4 g5 6 ♗g3 ♗g7 7 h4 g4 8 h5 e5 9 d5 ♘d4 10 f4?! exf4 11 ♗h4?! c5 12 ♕d2?!

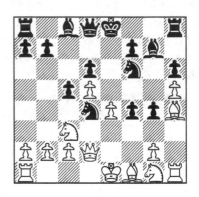

White's gambit was a poor choice, as in this position he has no real compensation for the pawn he has sacrificed.

12...♕b6 13 0-0-0 0-0 14 ♕xf4 ♘xh5 15 ♕d2 ♗d7?

15...f5! is just good for Black, whereas now White gains time for his attack.

16 ♗f2 ♘f6 17 ♗d3 ♖fe8 18 ♗e3 h5 19 ♗h6 ♖e5 20 ♖f1 ♖ae8 21 ♕f4 ♕d8 22 ♘ge2 ♘xe2+ 23 ♘xe2 c4 24 ♘g3 cxd3 25 ♗xg7 ♔xg7 26 ♘xh5+??

Missing the much stronger 26 ♖xh5! ♖xh5 27 ♕xf6+! ♕xf6 28 ♘xh5+ ♔g6 29 ♘xf6, when White comes out on top.

26...♖xh5 27 ♖xh5 ♘xh5 28 ♕xf7+ ♔h6 29 cxd3 ♕e7 30 ♕f2 ♗b5 0-1

R.Zelcic-Z.Mestrovic
Nova Gorica 2003

1 e4 ♘c6 2 d4 d6 3 ♘c3 ♘f6 4 ♗g5 h6 5 ♗h4 g5 6 ♗g3 ♗g7 7 f3 0-0 8 ♗f2 e5 9 d5 ♘d4

White has been getting very little done, so it is easy to justify Black's aggression.

10 ♘ge2 c5 11 dxc6 bxc6 12 ♘xd4 exd4 13 ♗xd4 c5?! [13...♖b8!] 14 ♗xf6?! ♕xf6

When will they ever learn? From now on White has a severe weak colour complex on the dark squares, and Mestrovic's play from this point on is impeccable.

15 ♖b1 ♗e6 16 ♗e2 ♖ab8 17 0-0 ♕f4 18 ♔h1 ♗xc3 19 bxc3 ♖xb1 20 ♕xb1 ♕e3 21 ♗d3 c4 22 ♖e1 ♕d2 23 ♗f1 ♕xc3 24 h3 ♖d8 25 ♕c1 ♖b8 26 ♖e3 ♕e5 27 ♖a3 ♖b2 28 ♕d1? a5 29 ♕c1 c3 30 ♖a4 ♕f4 31 ♕xf4 gxf4 32 ♗c4 ♖xc2 33 ♗d5 ♗xd5 34 exd5 ♖b2 35 ♖c4 c2 36 ♔h2 ♖xa2 0-1

L.Gofshtein-N.Mitkov
Lisbon 1999

1 c4 e5 2 ♘c3 ♘c6 3 g3 f5 4 ♗g2 ♘f6 5 e3 d5 6 ♘xd5 ♘xd5 7 cxd5 ♘b4 8 d3 ♘xd5 9 ♘f3 ♗d6 10 0-0 ♘f6 11 ♕b3 ♕e7 12 e4 fxe4 13 dxe4 ♕f7 14 ♕c3 ♕h5 15 ♘d2 0-0 16 f3 ♗h3 17 ♘b3 ♖f7 18 ♗e3 ♖af8 19 ♕c4

19...h6?!

After this, White has an edge. It is simpler and better to keep the knight out with 19...b6.

20 ♘a5 ♗xg2 21 ♔xg2 g5?! [21...b6] 22 h3 ♕g6? 23 ♘xb7 h5 24 ♖ad1 g4 25 ♘xd6 cxd6 26 ♖xd6 1-0

Black has no real counterplay.

Punishing the doubled c-pawns

J.Ramirez-J.Schuyler
Las Vegas 2007

1 c4 ♘c6 2 ♘c3 e5 3 g3 f5 4 ♗g2 ♘f6 5

d3 ♗b4 6 a3?

White greatly overestimates the value of the bishop pair and half-open b-file, spending a tempo to reach a position Black would happily play with a tempo less.

6...♗xc3+ 7 bxc3 d6 8 ♖b1 0-0 9 e3?

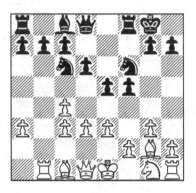

White's previous sins are minor relative to this positional catastrophe (which is nonetheless an extremely common mistake among amateurs). White's pawn structure will self-destruct in 5...4...3...2...1...

9...e4! 10 d4 b6! 11 ♘e2 ♗a6 12 ♘f4 ♗xc4

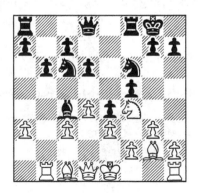

13 d5?

A hopeless try at complications.

13...♘e5 14 ♘e6 ♕e7 15 ♘xf8 ♘d3+ 16 ♔d2 ♕xf8 17 h3 ♘xf2 18 ♕a4 b5 19 ♕a5 ♘xh1 20 ♗xh1 ♕f7 21 ♖b2 ♕h5 0-1

White's play was poor, but not uncommon for a club player. That was how to win.

Game 90
O.Foisor-J.M.Degraeve
Le Touquet 1996

1 c4 e5 2 g3 ♘c6 3 ♗g2 f5 4 ♘c3 ♘f6 5 d3 ♗b4 6 ♗d2 0-0 7 e3 ♗xc3 8 ♗xc3 d5! 9 ♘e2 ♗e6 10 b3 ♕e7 11 a3 ♖ad8

Simple chess has brought Black a small advantage, but this will dissipate unless he takes action now.

12 ♕c2 ♗f7?!

12...dxc4 13 dxc4 ♘e4! was better.

13 0-0 ♗h5?!

This bishop transfer, typical of the Stonewall Dutch, makes far less sense without a closed centre.

14 ♖fe1 ♕f7 15 ♗b2 ♔h8 16 ♖ac1 ♖d6

17 b4 dxc4 18 dxc4 ♖fd8 19 ♗xc6?

Black's pieces are already poised to jump into White's holes after this ill-conceived trade.

19...♖xc6?

After 19...bxc6! White doesn't even get the e-pawn for his trouble (20 ♗xe5? ♖d2).

20 ♗xe5 ♘g4 21 ♖ed1 ♖e8 22 ♗f4 ♘xh2!? 23 ♔xh2 ♗f3 24 g4 fxg4 25 ♘g3 ♕f6

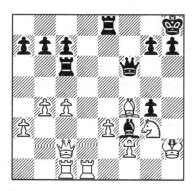

26 ♕d3??

26 ♔g1! ♕h4 27 ♔f1 holds on. The text just loses.

26...g5 27 ♕d4 gxf4 0-1

Game 91
J.Iruzubieta
Villaluenga-B.Gulko
San Sebastian 1996

1 c4 e5 2 ♘c3 ♘c6 3 g3 f5 4 ♗g2 ♘f6 5 d3 ♗b4 6 ♗d2 0-0 7 e3 ♘e7 8 ♘ge2?!

8 a3 or 8 ♘f3 is preferable.

8...c6 9 0-0 d6 10 d4 ♔h8 11 a3 ♗a5 12 b4 ♗c7 13 d5 ♗d7 14 a4 ♕e8

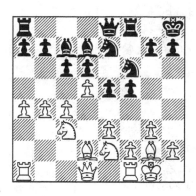

Black is already better.

15 dxc6 ♗xc6 16 e4 ♖c8 17 ♗e3 ♗xe4 18 ♗xe4?!

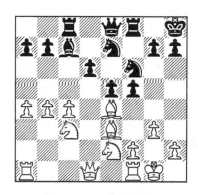

18...♘xe4?

After 18...fxe4, Black keeps his pawn, and with it a large advantage.

19 ♘xe4 fxe4 20 ♘c3 ♗b8 21 ♘xe4 ♕c6 22 ♘d2 ♘f5 23 ♕e2 ♗c7 24 b5 ♕d7 25 ♗xa7 b6? 26 a5 bxa5 27 b6 ♘d4 28 ♕e4 ♘c6 29 bxc7?! ♘xa7 30 ♖xa5 ♘c6 ½-½

Game 92
N.Spiridonov-K.Spraggett
Cannes 1992

1 c4 e5 2 g3 ♘c6 3 ♗g2 f5 4 d3 ♘f6 5

♘c3 ♗b4 6 ♗d2 0-0 7 e3 f4

This is not the best, but it is aggressive and sound. If 8 exf4 exf4 9 ♗xf4, Black gets good play with 9...d5!.

8 ♘f3 ♕e8 9 0-0 ♗xc3 10 ♗xc3 d6 11 exf4 exf4 12 d4 ♕h5 13 d5 ♘e7 14 ♘d4 ♗g4 15 f3 ♗d7 16 ♖e1 ♘g6 17 ♘e6 ♗xe6 18 ♖xe6 fxg3 19 hxg3 ♕g5 20 ♕e1 h5 21 ♔h2 h4 22 gxh4 ♘xh4 23 ♕g3 ♕h6 24 ♔g1 ♘f5 25 ♕h3 ♕g5 26 ♖ae1 ♖f7 27 ♖1e2 ♖af8 28 ♗d2 ♕g6 29 ♔h2?! [29 ♖2e4] 29...♘d4 30 ♗c3? [30 ♖2e4] 30...♘xe2 31 ♖xe2 ♕d3 32 ♖d2 ♕h7 33 ♗d4 b6 34 b4 ♖e7 35 c5? ♘h5 36 cxd6 cxd6 37 ♔g1 ♕b1+ 38 ♗f1 ♘f4 39 ♕h2 ♖f5 0-1

Game 93
F.Bruno-B.Kurajica
Lugano 1985

1 c4 e5 2 ♘c3 ♘c6 3 g3 f5 4 d3 ♘f6 5 ♗g2 ♗b4 6 ♗d2 0-0 7 ♘f3 d6 [7...e4!] 8 a3 ♗xc3 9 ♗xc3 ♕e8 10 0-0 ♕h5 11 ♕d2 f4 12 gxf4 h6

Otherwise White will play 13 fxe5

dxe5 14 ♕g5, and there is no attack.
13 fxe5 dxe5 14 d4 ♗h3

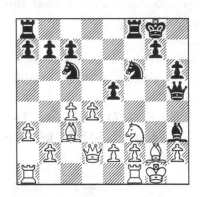

15 dxe5?!

Black's aggression usually pays dividends, but it is not without risk. Even at this late stage, White can escape to a good position with 15 ♗xh3 ♕xh3 16 ♘xe5 ♘xe5 17 dxe5 ♘g4 (or 17...♖ad8 18 ♕f4 and 19 ♕g3) 18 ♕d5+ ♖f7 19 ♕g2.

15...♖ad8 16 ♕f4 ♗xg2 17 ♔xg2?! [17 exf6!] **17...♘d5**

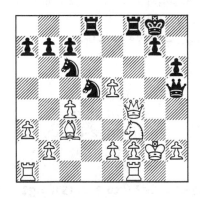

18 ♕c1??

White is worse now, but he survives after 18 ♕h4.

18...♘f4+ 0-1

Game 94
M.Sher-K.Spraggett
Andorra 1993

1 c4 e5 2 g3 ♘c6 3 ♗g2 f5 4 ♘c3 ♘f6 5 d3 ♗b4 6 ♗d2 0-0 7 ♘f3 d6 8 0-0 ♗xc3 9 ♗xc3 ♕e8 10 e3 ♗d7

Black, who is down a tempo on the previous game, is not ready for 10...f4?!. Instead, 10...e4 11 dxe4 ♘xe4 is fine for Black, but this is not why a player like Spraggett plays the reversed Grand Prix Attack.

11 ♖c1 ♔h8 12 b4 ♘d8 13 b5 ♖b8 14 a4 ♘e6 15 ♘d2 f4! 16 exf4 exf4 17 ♗xf6

Removing one of Black's most dangerous attacking pieces, but pulling his rook into the action. Besides, that was a very good bishop!

17...♖xf6 18 ♘e4 ♖h6 19 d4 ♕g6 20 ♖e1 ♖f8 21 ♖c3 b6 22 ♖d3 ♗c8 23 a5 ♖h5 24 ♗f3 ♖h6 25 axb6 axb6

According to *Houdini*, White has been at least a little better the whole time, but that doesn't take into consideration the difficulty and fatigue of defence. White makes a move he certainly wouldn't have made if he were fresh – but he isn't fresh, and that is no accident.

26 ♕e2?? fxg3 27 fxg3 ♘f4 28 ♕d2 ♘xd3 29 ♕xd3 ♗g4 30 ♗g2 ♕h5 31 h4 ♖e6 32 ♖f1 ♖xf1+ 33 ♕xf1 ♕f5 34 ♕a1 ♖e8 35 ♕a7 ♗f3 0-1

Game 95
Bu Xiangzhi-V.Ivanchuk
FIDE World Cup,
Khanty-Mansiysk 2011

1 ♘f3 d5 2 g3 g6 3 ♗g2 ♗g7 4 0-0 e5 5 d3 ♘c6 6 c4 dxc4 7 dxc4 ♕xd1 8 ♖xd1 e4 9 ♘fd2?! [9 ♘g5] 9...f5 10 ♘c3 ♗e6 11 ♘d5? 0-0-0

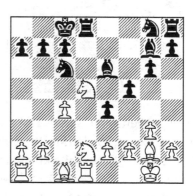

This is just awful for White, who can't activate any of his pieces. He soon pitches a pawn to free himself, but there is no compensation for this sacrifice.

12 ♘b3 ♘f6 13 ♗g5 ♗xd5 14 cxd5 ♖xd5 15 f3 exf3 16 ♖xd5 ♘xd5 17 ♗xf3 ♘db4 18 ♔f1 ♖e8 19 ♘c5 ♗d4 20 a3

♗xc5 21 axb4 ♘xb4 22 g4 ♘c2 23 ♖a5 ♗e3 24 gxf5 ♗xg5 25 fxg6 ♘e3+ 26 ♔g1 h6 27 ♖xa7 c6 28 g7 ♔c7 29 ♖a4 ♖g8 0-1

Game 96
K.Arakhamia Grant-
A.Raetsky
Bern 1995

1 ♘f3 d5 2 g3 g6 3 ♗g2 ♗g7 4 0-0 e5 5 d3 ♘c6 6 ♘bd2 ♘ge7 7 e4 0-0 8 c3 a5 9 a4 h6 10 ♖e1 ♗e6 11 exd5 ♗xd5!

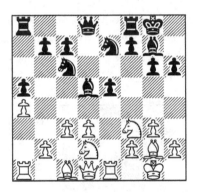

This prevents the active 12 ♘c4 because of 12...e4, exploiting the vulnerable situation of the white knight at c4. 12 ♕c2 f5 13 b3 ♕d7 14 ♗a3 ♖fe8 15 ♖ad1 g5 16 ♘c4 ♘g6 17 ♘e3 ♗f7 18 d4 e4 19 ♘d2 h5 20 f3 f4 21 ♘ec4 fxg3 22 hxg3 exf3 23 ♘xf3 ♕g4 24 ♘e3 ♖xe3 25 ♖xe3 ♕xg3 26 ♕f2 ♕xf2+ 27 ♔xf2 g4 28 ♘g5 ♗h6 29 ♘xf7 ♗xe3+ 30 ♔xe3 ♔xf7 31 ♖f1+ ♔g7 32 ♗d5 ♖e8+ 33 ♔d3 ♘d8 34 ♖f5 c6 35 ♗e4 ♘e6 36 c4?? ♘ef4+ 37 ♔e3 ♘g2+ 38 ♔d3 ♘e1+ 39 ♔e3 ♘c2+ 40 ♔d3 ♘xa3 0-1

Game 97
V.Frias Pablaza-A.Baburin
San Francisco 1997

1 ♘f3 d5 2 d3 g6 3 g3 ♗g7 4 ♗g2 e5 5 0-0 ♘e7 6 e4 0-0 7 ♘bd2 ♘bc6 8 c3 a5 9 a4 h6 10 exd5 ♘xd5 11 ♘c4 ♗f5 12 ♖e1 ♖e8 13 ♘h4 ♗e6 14 ♗d2 ♕d7 15 ♕b3 ♘de7 16 ♗f1 ♖ad8 17 ♖ad1 b6 18 ♗c1 g5 19 ♘g2 ♗g4 20 ♗e2 ♗xe2 21 ♖xe2 ♘f5 22 ♖ee1??

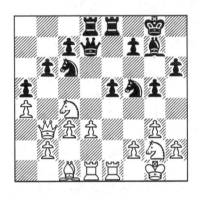

Black is already better, but this allows a winning shot as Black quickly exploits the weakened White kingside. **22...♘fd4! 23 cxd4 ♘xd4 24 ♕a2 ♘f3+ 25 ♔f1 [25 ♔h1? ♕h3] 25...♘xh2+ 26 ♔g1 ♘f3+ 27 ♔f1 ♕h3 28 ♘ce3 ♘d4 29 ♔g1 ♖e6 30 b3 ♖ed6 31 ♗b2 ♘f3+ 32 ♔f1 e4 33 dxe4 ♖d2 34 ♖xd2 ♖xd2 0-1**

Game 98
A.Capaliku-J.Gombac
Nova Gorica 2010

1 f4 g6 2 ♘f3 ♗g7 3 e3 d6 4 d4 ♘d7 5

♗d3 e5 6 c3 ♕e7 7 e4 ♘gf6 8 fxe5 dxe5
9 0-0 0-0 10 ♗g5 h6 11 ♗h4 c5 12
♘bd2?!

12 d5 c4 13 ♗c2 ♕d6 is best, though
this is not a problem for Black.

**12...cxd4 13 cxd4 exd4 14 ♘xd4?! ♘e5
15 ♗c2 ♖d8 16 ♘4b3?! [16 ♘2b3]
16...♗e6?!**

White is in trouble, but 16...a5! is
stronger; e.g. 17 a4 b6 and 18...♗a6.

**17 ♕e2 ♖ac8 18 ♖ac1 ♗g4 19 ♕f2 g5
20 ♗g3 ♘h5**

I sense a dark-square catastrophe
on the horizon for White.

**21 ♔h1 ♘xg3+ 22 ♕xg3 a5! 23 ♘f3 ♗xf3
24 gxf3 ♘g6 25 ♘xa5 ♖d2 26 ♗b3 ♖xc1
27 ♖xc1 ♗e5 28 ♕e1 ♖xh2+ 29 ♔g1 ♘h4
30 ♕e3 ♗d4 31 ♖c8+ ♔h7 32 ♖h8+ ♔g6
33 ♖g8+ ♔h5 34 ♕xd4 ♘xf3+ 0-1**

Game 99
A.Spichkin-D.Reinderman
European Championship,
Rijeka 2010

1 f4 g6 2 ♘f3 ♗g7 3 e3 d6 4 d4 ♘d7 5

♗c4 e6

It is most important to blunt the
bishop.

6 0-0 ♘e7 7 ♘c3 0-0 8 ♗b3 c5 9 ♕e2 d5

White's light-squared bishop is now
both passive and in danger.

**10 a4 b6 11 ♖d1 ♗b7 12 ♗d2 a6 13
♗e1 ♘f5 14 ♗f2 ♕c7**

**15 g3?! ♘d6 16 h4 c4 17 ♗a2 b5 18 h5
b4 19 ♘b1 ♘b6?! [19...a5!] 20 hxg6
fxg6 21 a5 ♘a4 22 c3 bxc3?! 23 ♘xc3
♘xc3 24 bxc3 ♖ab8 25 ♗b1**

White, who was practically lost, is
now back in the game.

**25...♗c8 26 ♘g5?! ♗f6 27 ♘f3 ♖b5 28
♕a2 ♗d8 29 ♗c2 ♖xa5 30 ♕b1 ♖xa1 31**

♕xa1 ♘b5 32 ♗a4 ♗e7 33 ♗e1 ♗d7 34 ♘e5 ♗e8 35 ♖c1 ♗d6 36 ♘f3 h6 37 ♗c2 ♘a3 0-1

Did White's flag fall? Black hasn't made any progress on the board since winning the a-pawn.

Game 100
**P.Auchenberg-
To.Christensen**
Helsingor 1997

1 f4 g6 2 ♘f3 ♗g7 3 g3 b6 4 ♗g2 ♗b7 5 0-0 e6 6 d3 d6 7 e4 ♘e7 8 ♕e2 ♘d7 9 ♘bd2 0-0 10 g4 c5

Black has actually gained the advantage with his simple development scheme. White's plan to attack on the kingside is slow.

11 ♖f2 ♕c7 12 ♘f1 c4 13 ♘g3 cxd3 14 cxd3

Black needs to start using the c-file as soon as possible. His next few moves do not work towards that, and he starts drifting.

14...♗a6?! 15 ♗e3 ♘c5 16 ♖c1 ♕d7 17 ♘e1 ♘c6 18 ♕d2 ♗d4?! 19 ♗xd4 ♘xd4

20 ♕b4? [20 f5!] 20...e5 21 ♗f1? ♕xg4 22 fxe5 dxe5 23 ♖g2 ♕f4 24 ♕d2 ♕xd2 25 ♖xd2 ♖ac8 26 ♖cd1 ♘ce6 27 ♗h3 f5 28 exf5 gxf5 29 ♔f2 ♘f4 30 ♗f1 h5 31 h4 ♔h8 32 ♘g2? ♘de6? [32...♘h3+!] 33 ♘e3 ♘g7 34 ♗e2 ♖cd8 35 ♗f1 ♖d4 36 ♘c2 ♖d6 37 ♘b4 ♗b7 38 ♘c2 ♖fd8 39 ♘b4 ♖d4 40 ♘c2 ♖4d6 41 ♘b4 a5 42 ♘c2 ♘g6 0-1

Adieu

With this, I bid my readers adieu. I hope this book was more fun for you to read than it was for me to write. Har! I wish you many successes with 1...♘c6 and the Dark Knight System.

Index of Variations

Chapter One

1 d4 ♘c6 2 ♘f3 (others – 15) 2...d6

A: 3 c4 g6 4 d5 ♘b8 5 ♘c3 ♗g7 6 e4 ♘f6 7 ♗e2 0-0 – 19

C1: 6 0-0 – 27
C2: 6 h3 – 28

D: 3 g3 g6

D1: 4 d5 – 30
D2: 4 ♗g2 – 31

E: 3 ♗g5 – 33

Chapter Two

1 d4 ♘c6 2 c4 e5 3 d5 ♗b4+

Chapter Three
1 d4 ♘c6 2 d5 ♘e5

Chapter Four

1 e4 ♘c6 2 d4 (others – 55) 2...e5

A: 3 d5 ♘ce7 – 57
   A1: 4 ♘f3 ♘g6 – 58

     A11: 5 h4! – 59
     A12: 5 ♗e3 – 61
  A2: 4 c4?! ♘g6 – 62

     A21: 5 ♘c3 – 62

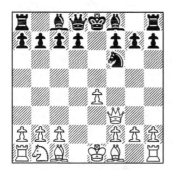

C: 3 ♘f3 exd4 – 79

C1: 4 ♘xd4 ♗c5 – 80

C11: 5 ♗e3 ♛f6 6 c3 ♛g6 – 81
C111: 7 ♘d2 – 82
C112: 7 ♘b5 – 84
C12: 5 ♘xc6 – 85
C2: 4 ♗c4 ♘f6 – 88

C21: 5 0-0 – 88

Chapter Five

1 e4 ♘c6 2 ♘f3 d6 3 d4 ♘f6 4 ♘c3 g6

Chapter Six

1 e4 ♘c6 2 ♘c3 ♘f6 3 d4 d6

Chapter Seven

1 c4 ♘c6 2 ♘c3 e5

Chapter Eight

1 ♘f3 ♘c6 – 127

Chapter Nine

Index of Games